VICO
Genealogist
of Modernity

VICO

Genealogist
of Modernity

ROBERT C. MINER

University of Notre Dame Press
Notre Dame, Indiana

Manufactured in the United States of America

A record of the Library of Congress Cataloging-in-Publication Data is
available upon request from the Library of Congress.

ISBN 0-268-03468-0 (cloth : alk. paper)

∞ *This book was printed on acid-free paper.*

For

HEATHER

They don't recognize that humanity, developing by a historical living process, will become at last a normal society, but they believe that a social system that has come out of some mathematical brain is going to organize all humanity at once and make it just and sinless in an instant, quicker than any living process! That's why they instinctively dislike history, "nothing but ugliness and stupidity in it," and they explain it all as stupidity!
                              — Dostoyevsky, *Crime and Punishment*

C O N T E N T S

Citations to Vico in the notes furnish a short title, chapter or paragraph number, name of editor, volume number or abbreviated edition title, and page number. In citations to the various works of the *Diritto universale,* a paragraph number immediately follows the page number, if the chapter cited has more than one paragraph.

Full information about the editions I have used may be found in the bibliography. Since the newer editions of Vico are generally more accessible and better organized, I have not cited the Laterza edition of Croce, Gentile, and Nicolini—once regarded as standard—except when referring to correspondence, occasional pieces, or suppressed parts of the *Scienza nuova* not printed in the editions of Cristofolini or Battistini. Additionally, comparisons of the present work with recent Italian scholarship will be facilitated, since the latter increasingly prefers the newer editions to that of Laterza.

Except where indicated, I have made my own translations. Although I have often departed from their renderings, I have found the Bergin and Fisch translations very helpful. The short titles below refer to the corresponding texts:

Orazioni	*Le orazioni inaugurali* (1699–1707)
De ratione	*De nostri temporis studiorum ratione* (1709)
De antiquissima	*De antiquissima Italorum sapientia ex linguae latinae originibus eruenda. Liber primus sive Metaphysicus* (1710)
Prima risposta	*Risposta del signor Giambattista Vico nella quale si sciolgono tre opposizioni fatte da dotto signore contro il primo libro "De antiquissima Italorum sapientia"* (1711)

Seconda risposta	*Riposta di Giambattista Vico all'articolo X del tomo VIII del "Giornale de' letterati d'Italia"* (1712)
Sinopsi	*Sinopsi del diritto universale* (1720)
De uno	*Liber unus: De uno universi iuris principio et fine uno* (1720)
De constantia	*Liber alter: De constantia iurisprudentis* (1721)
Notae	*Notae in duos libros* (1722)
Scienza nuova prima	*Principi di una scienza nuova intorno alla natura delle nazioni per la quale si ritrouvano i principi di altro sistema del diritto naturale delle genti* (1725)
Vita	*Vita di Giambattista Vico scritta da se medesimo* (1725–28, 1731)
Vici vindiciae	*Vici vindiciae. Notae in acta erudiotrum lipsienza . . .* (1729)
Scienza nuova seconda	*Principi di scienza nuova d'intorno alla comune natura delle nazione* (1730)
De mente heroica	*De mente heroica* (1732)
Scienza nuova	*Princìpi di scienza nuova d'intorno alla comune natura delle nazioni, in questa terza impressione dal medesimo autore in un gran numero di luoghi corretta, schiarita, e notabilmente accresciuta* (1744)

P R E F A C E

This is a book about genealogy. It is also a book about Vico, or more precisely, Vico as a practitioner of genealogy. But what is genealogy? Rather than attempt a preliminary definition of genealogy at the outset, it seems more advisable to proceed in operationalist fashion. If physics is whatever physicists do, and life science whatever life-scientists do, then genealogy is whatever genealogists do. If anyone is a genealogist, the author of *On the Genealogy of Morals* is. Hence we may begin with Nietzsche.

Whom does Nietzsche recognize as a genealogist? First, himself. Nietzsche regards his own historical practice as exemplary, as a model for other genealogists to follow. Nietzsche acknowledges, however, that he did not invent genealogy. In the preface of *On the Genealogy of Morals*, Nietzsche speaks of the "English genealogists" that precede him. Nietzsche identifies the English genealogists as authors of books about morality that have historical pretensions. Their books attempt to illuminate the content of concepts like "good" and "evil" by tracing the meanings of these words to their origins. The single example Nietzsche gives of such a book is Paul Rée's *The Origin of Moral Sensations* (1877).[1] If some initial approximation of genealogy is required, one might say the following: genealogy is a species of historical explanation that privileges linguistic and etymological evidence.

Although Rée and the English historians whom he follows are genealogists, they are not its most adept practitioners. They put forward "an upside-down and perverse species of genealogical hypothesis."[2] It is not that they are wrong to seek insight through historical inquiry. It is rather that their actual procedure is radically unhistorical, to such a degree that "the historical spirit itself is lacking in them."[3] In holding, for example, that the term "good" was originally used to indicate the approval of unselfish actions by their recipients, the English genealogists impose their own prejudices about the value of utility and benevolence onto the origins they claim to investigate. Nietzsche regards this anachronistic projection of contemporary values as not only an intellectual error, but also a sign of conceit. "This pride has to be humbled," he declares.[4]

Is Vico a genealogist in Nietzsche's sense of the term? If what defines a genealogist is simply a commitment to explaining cultural phenomena by adverting to their genesis, then it is obviously the case that Vico is a genealogist. What else would one say about a writer who takes it as a methodological principle that "doctrines must begin from where the matters they treat begin," on the ground that "the nature of things is nothing but their coming into being at certain times and in certain guises"?[5] If Rée and the English historians of morality, as upside-down and perverse as they might be, count as genealogists, then Vico would also qualify. In the minimal sense of the concept, as understood by Nietzsche, Vico is a genealogist.

Nietzsche rightly views his own history of morality as superior to that of the unnamed English genealogists. Their lack of an authentic historical sense, due in part to their lack of philological acumen, ensures their inability to be equal rivals to Nietzsche. Should Vico—who, like Nietzsche, comes from philology—be regarded as a genealogist in a more exalted sense of the term? The thesis of the following pages is that Vico's texts exemplify a genealogical approach to modernity. Far from resembling the upside-down, backwards genealogy of "the English," Vico's genealogy is comparable to Nietzsche's. That Vico cannot be conflated with the historians mocked by Nietzsche is suggested by the fact that Vico already exposes the very error that Nietzsche ascribes to the English genealogists. Far from being used to describe altruistic, unselfish action, the term "good" originally meant the same as "strong," and was used by aristocracy in reference to itself. More than a century and a half before Nietzsche, Vico makes this claim in the *Scienza nuova*.[6] Like Nietzsche, Vico condemns academic perspectives that project current prejudices onto past origins. They are infected by the pride that he calls the "conceit of scholars." Possessing the historical spirit in abundant degree, Vico does not hesitate to use it polemically against philosophers and philologists who lack it. The question that Nietzsche poses to some future academy—"What light does linguistics, and especially the study of etymology, throw on the history of the evolution of moral concepts?"[7]—is a question that Vico has already asked. It is a question that drives the *Scienza nuova*, a text whose approach to the history of ideas and institutions is informed by the presupposition that "ideas and languages accelerated at the same rate."[8]

An intellectually honest Nietzschean cannot write Vico off as an historian in the "English" mode, a bungler who would utterly fail to qualify as a serious rival. Such a Nietzschean might instead dismiss Vico on the slightly more charitable ground that what he offers is an anticipation—brilliant in some respects and defective in others—of the genealogy that Nietzsche develops more fully and rigorously. If this were the case, then Vico's perspective would not constitute a genuine rival to that of Nietzsche, since rivalry requires both common ground and clear opposition. Vico is not, however, a mere precursor to Nietzsche. Where Nietzsche tends to see the path to cultural renewal as consisting in a rejection of otherworldly religion, accompanied by a complex reappropriation of pagan culture, Vico's historicism ultimately affirms the value of Platonism and Christianity, the two things Nietzsche despises most. What Bernard Williams attributes to Nietzsche's genealogy is also true of Vico's: it "typically combines, in a way that analytical philosophy finds embarrassing, history, phenomenology, 'realistic' psychology, and conceptual interpretation."[9] The conclusions of the two genealogies, however, could not be more starkly opposed. Nietzsche and Williams curse the "metaphysically higher." Against anti-metaphysical attitudes, with the aid of St. Augustine as his "particular protector," Vico attempts to integrate the higher and the lower, fusing them within a perspective that his *Autobiography* describes as a synthesis of Tacitus and Plato.

Several contemporary writers have perceived the desirability of an "alternative genealogy" that takes history seriously while drawing non-Nietzschean conclusions. Alasdair MacIntyre, for example, characterizes "genealogical narrative" as having "the function of not arguing with, but of disclosing something about the beliefs, presuppositions and activities of some class of persons. Characteristically it explains how they have come to be in some impasse and why they cannot recognize or diagnose adequately out of their own conceptual and argumentative resources the nature of their predicament."[10] MacIntyre calls for the construction of a "subversive history" that would undermine the claims of liberal secular modernity. The argument of this book is that what Vico provides is precisely such a subversive history. In the pivotal chapter of *After Virtue*, MacIntyre poses the question "Nietzsche or Aristotle?" By

"Aristotle" he intends something like the author of the *Nicomachean Ethics,* but shorn of "metaphysical biology" and capable of thinking genealogically—in short, an Aristotle much like Vico. MacIntyre himself points to Vico, whom he rightly describes as an Aristotelian "to a greater or lesser degree," as evidence for the possibility of "an historicist defense of Aristotle" that would provide an alternative to both modern liberalism and Nietzschean genealogy. Hence one could rephrase *After Virtue*'s question as "Nietzsche or Vico?" It is fair to say that in his subsequent work, MacIntyre chose not to take the Viconian path, devoting his attention instead to Aquinas. The premise of this book is that the genealogical option toward which MacIntyre gestured but did not explore ought to be pursued.

Some may object that interpreting Vico with the theme of genealogy in mind is hermeneutically irresponsible, because it approaches the texts with questions that were not Vico's own. Our response to this charge is that reading Vico with the intention of understanding his critique of secular modernity is the key to discovering the author who concludes his masterpiece with the declaration that "if one does not have piety, one cannot be wise."[11] Under the influence of Croce and Berlin, secular interpreters have not hesitated to impose their own tendencies on Vico, often neglecting both particular loci in the *Scienza nuova* and entire texts (especially the rarely studied *Diritto universale*) that conflict with their image of Vico as a cosmopolitan relativist or secular romantic. The interpretation offered in these pages is not exhaustive, but it seeks to improve upon previous accounts by considering the full range of his texts, including theological writings that are often neglected. It is not the case, moreover, that one necessarily falsifies Vico by approaching him with contemporary questions. With Gadamer, who noted the exemplary significance of Vico for his own project,[12] we deny that the history of philosophy can be well understood by an interpretive stance that aims to be "purely historical," operating with no presuppositions except for those of common sense.[13] On the contrary, the most penetrating expositions of a past thinker seek to bring his thought into a dialogue with the present. We see no reason to assume that thought is forever trapped within its immediate historical framework. This assumption is not only arbitrary and unjustified, it also serves the ideological function of "keeping the past past" and thereby insulating the present from historically informed critique.

This study is divided into three parts. Part 1 exhibits Vico's early thought as a critique of the discourse of modern rationalism. Vico's critique is "genealogical" to the extent that its primary goal is *not* to provide demonstrative refutations of Descartes, Spinoza, and other canonically modern thinkers. Its aim, rather, is to question their motives and method. Part 2 exhibits the *Diritto universale* as the study in which Vico discovers history and articulates something like a historicist view of human culture. My argument is that, while the *Diritto universale* is not itself a genealogy, it contains the essential ingredients of a genealogy and thereby paves the way for the *Scienza nuova*. In Part 3, we undertake a reading of the *Scienza nuova*. This is the work that most fully articulates Vico's genealogy of modernity, although in order to be well read, an interpretation of the prior works is absolutely required. (This view is maintained against those who falsely infer the hermeneutic irrelevance of the earlier works from Vico's preference that the *Scienza nuova* alone survive him.) In the *Scienza nuova,* Vico provides "new principles by which to demonstrate the argument of St. Augustine's discussion of the virtue of the Romans."[14] The vices of his opponents are exposed not as intellectual errors, but as conceits, *borie,* that are rooted in self-love and a lack of self-knowledge, in contrast with the "humility" of Vico's own perspective. The result is an overall reading of Vico that exhibits his thought as a counterexample to Foucault's claim that genealogy is necessarily impious.

I would like to acknowledge the many friends and colleagues who have stimulated and enlarged my thinking about Vico, genealogy, and modernity. At the University of Notre Dame, an early ancestor of this book was produced in the form of a Ph.D. thesis. I wish to express my gratitude to Mark Jordan for his careful direction and continued friendship. David Burrell, C.S.C., not only co-directed the dissertation, but also provided invaluable paternal and pastoral care to my family. I have benefited greatly from the sharp wit and sound judgment of David Solomon, who supported the project from the beginning, as did Stephen Watson and Ralph McInerny. A special debt of gratitude is due to Christian Moevs, who not only resists dualisms in general, but specifically embodies the Viconian ideal of uniting philosophy and philology.

An initial version of this project was conceived at Cambridge under the tutelage of John Milbank, whose own work on Vico I have found immensely suggestive. Thanks are also due to Francis McHugh of St. Edmund's College. I am grateful to Donald and Molly Verene of the Vico Institute at Emory University for allowing me to consult the holdings of its library on short notice. Thanks to Giorgio Pinton for showing me his work on the translation of the *Diritto universale*. The support of my colleagues in the Department of Philosophy at Boston College during preparation of the final manuscript is much appreciated.

Finally, I wish to express gratitude to my parents Mary and Robert Miner, my in-laws Peggy and Ronny Fritz, and my grandmother Jeanette Moseley. The *sine qua non* in this, as in everything, is Heather. This book is dedicated to her.

PART 1

Humbling Modern Pride:
Genealogy in the Early Vico

Ancients and Moderns

Modern thinkers, despite their considerable achievements, are full of pride. In love with their own accomplishments, they fail to acknowledge the possibility that, in some respects, their knowledge is inferior to that of the ancients. This theme runs throughout Vico's oeuvre, culminating in the *Scienza Nuova*'s analysis of the "conceit of nations" and the "conceit of scholars." It also lies at the center of the first book that Vico deemed worthy of publication, *De nostri temporis studiorum ratione*.

De ratione is not a crude antimodern polemic. It presents itself as a balance sheet designed to compare the advantages and disadvantages of modern method with those of antiquity. Vico's professed aim in lining up the costs and benefits of modernity is "not to condemn the disadvantages of our age or those of antiquity, but to bring together the advantages of both."[1] With respect to technical advances in the natural sciences, Vico does not hesitate to admit the superiority of the moderns. Gadamer rightly contrasts Vico's positive valuation of rhetoric with "the anti-rhetorical methodology of modern times," but errs in making him speak from a "position of opposition to modern science."[2] The road taken by *De ratione* is more complex than that. Vico begins by acknowledging the considerable gains of modern natural science. He proceeds, however, to question the understanding of natural science adopted by proponents of the geometrical method and to raise the suspicion that the project of mastering nature is grounded in self-love. *De ratione* applies a similar mode of suspicion to versions of modern ethics that seek to minimize or eliminate the need for the virtues, especially practical wisdom (*phronesis, prudentia*).

That Vico admires the accomplishments of the new science is clear. Along with the modern inventions of the cannon, the sailing ship, the clock, and the suspended church-dome (to reproduce one of Vico's many lists in *De ratione*), he admires the astronomy and physics of Galileo. He does not, however, find plausible the distinctively Cartesian reading of modern science. Its overvaluation of geometrical method leads to the boat constructed by Perot, whose proportions had been "carefully calculated beforehand according to the rules of analytical geometry" but which sank to the bottom of the sea as soon as it hit the water.[3] Vico does not mention Descartes by name in *De ratione*. Instead, he speaks of those who strive to make exclusive use of the "critical art" (*ars critica*), seeking to deny all cognitive value to the "topical art" (*ars topica*)—the skill of reasoning from received commonplaces (*topoi* or *loci communes*) to a conclusion that best fits the situation at hand. Those who one-sidedly elevate the *ars critica* do so not because they possess a clear argument against the uselessness of rhetorical commonplaces, or because they understand the authentic method of modern science. What actually motivates the purveyors of the *ars critica,* Vico holds, is not the disinterested pursuit of truth, but the particular desire to rewrite the curriculum from the anti-rhetorical perspective that reduces eloquence to sophistry. By including only the texts and topics they favor, and thereby eliminating humanistic disciplines that train the mind in ways that cannot be quantified, Cartesian pedagogies may be unmasked as ideologies that seek to promote and perpetuate their own power.

It is important to distinguish Vico's hostility to the *ars critica,* as promoted by Descartes and Arnauld, from opposition to critical thinking as such. In *De ratione,* Vico's argument for the *ars topica* is primarily pedagogical. Only after immersion in the arts of painting, poetry, and rhetoric, arts that develop the memory and imagination, should one study logic, algebra, and geometry (though synthetic rather than analytic, as we will see). Learners who acquire the critical aptitude after education in the *ars topica* will be in a better position "to judge anew, using their own judgment on what they have been taught."[4] Those impressed with Vico's defense of topics and his polemic against the approach embodied by the Port-Royal logic often tend to neglect the fact that he also maintains a large role for the *ars critica* in the attainment of truth.[5] Minds that are fluent in topics but neglect criticism fall short because they "often latch on to falsehoods"; the reverse error is committed by those who "do not also consort with probabilities."[6] In *De ratione* and throughout his writings, Vico consistently attributes the capacity to attain truth to the faculty of critical judgment.[7] The amplitude and fecundity of the *ars topica* must be checked by the precision and sobriety of the *ars critica.* A subtle but important departure from this model occurs in *De antiquissima,* which suggests a fusion of the two *artes.* As in *De ratione,* Vico distinguishes *topica* and *critica* according to function. "Topics discovers things and piles them up. Criticism divides the pile and removes some of it: and thus the topical wits are more fertile, but less true; the critical ones are truer, but are sterile."[8] But Vico now faults not only the moderns, but also the ancients, ascribing to them an artificial separation of discovery and judgment. "Neither invention without judgment, nor judgment without invention can be certain."[9] *Topica* and *critica* are ideally one: "topics itself will become criticism."[10]

If Vico maintains a place for the *ars critica,* while exposing the pretensions of those who would use it to smother eloquence, he also pays tribute to modern science, which he judges to owe more to the experimental approach of Bacon and Galileo[11] than to Descartes or the Port-Royal logic. Occasionally it is said that Vico had little appreciation for Galileo. Isaiah Berlin writes that he "seems to have had no notion of what Galileo had achieved, and did not begin to grasp the effect of the new science upon the lives of men."[12] This is plainly false. In the second chapter of *De ratione,* Vico does not mention Galileo by name, but credits *astronomia* with detecting the "multiple faults of the systematic universe of Ptolemy."[13] Later texts speak of "the great Galileo" whose success in explaining natural phenomena occurred "before the geometrical method was introduced into physics" and the "sublime Galileo" who is credited with the observation of Venus and other astronomical marvels.[14] It is highly unlikely that Vico's choice of title for his magnum opus bears no relation to the *Due nuove scienze* of Galileo.[15]

Vico is willing to give Galileo and "the English" (whom he takes to oppose the introduction of the geometrical method into physics) full credit for fruitful deployment of the experimental method. This approval of the experimental method is connected with his defense of the *ars topica;* Vico in fact sees the experimental method as a particular application of topical reasoning. Against his Cartesian critics, Vico commends Herbert of Cherbury's *De veritate* on the ground that it is "truly nothing other than a topical art transported to the use of experimental physics."[16] The profitability of using topics in natural science is also a theme of *De ratione.* Vico attributes the success of modern chemistry, for example, to its ability to "faithfully, and so to speak, manually, reproduce a number of meteors and other physical phenomena."[17] What enables the genuine achievements of modern science is facility in *making,* rendered possible by an application of topical reasoning to the experimental domain. Thus Vico concludes the discussion of the *ars topica* in *De ratione* with an assertion that anticipates his famous *verum-factum* principle: "We demonstrate geometrical things because we make them; if we could demonstrate physical things, we would make them."[18]

Where, then, does Vico oppose the pretensions of modern physics, if he seems to approve of its non-Cartesian forms? How can he be said to offer a "genealogy" of modern science, if his essential sympathies are with Bacon against Descartes? We must look more closely at the stance Vico assumes toward Bacon in *De ratione*. It is undeniable that Vico admires Bacon enormously, in texts early and late. Yet Vico thinks that Bacon too is inspired by motives that are far from pure. Opening the *De ratione* with Bacon's name, Vico praises the *De augmentis scientiarum* for pointing to a world of new sciences that ought to be pursued. Yet he immediately adds that Bacon's procedure is informed by a desire for what is enormous and infinite. This desire, unregulated by prudence, has caused him to behave "in matters of learning in the same way as the rulers of the biggest empires, who once having obtained sovereignty in human affairs, try to outwit the things of nature herself, attempting to pave the seas with rocks, to sail through the mountains, and other such futile endeavors which are, just the same, forbidden by nature. For indeed everything that is given to man to know is finite and incomplete, like man himself."[19] Because Bacon lacks a sense of finitude and seeks to expand his own power without limit, he is driven to aim beyond what human industry can or should attain.

Against the Baconian lust for power, Vico holds that "we must exert ourselves to study physics as philosophers, so that we might order the soul. In this let us surpass the ancients, who cultivated the zeal for these things, in order to contend impiously with the gods for happiness."[20] The kind of vanity exemplified by Bacon is not uniquely modern. It is also present, Vico suggests, in pagan culture. This is only one of many loci, in writings early and late, in which Vico detects hidden points of contact that link secular modernity with ancient paganism. To study nature "philosophically" is "to quell human arrogance, if we indeed seek the truth in these things, which we desire so much. And if we do not find it, the desire for the truth will itself take us by the hand and lead us to God, who alone is the way and the truth."[21]

How can Vico be so critical of Bacon's motives, if he admires the works that he thinks a Baconian approach is able to generate? Vico consistently adheres to the principle that ugly roots can generate beautiful flowers; his interpretation of mathematics in *De antiquissima* will show this to be true in a different context. Another discourse of mastery that

Vico seeks to expose as illegitimately ambitious, disrespectful of natural contraints, is the attempt to reduce the life of ethical *praxis* to manuals or compilations of moral rules. Vico invokes an Aristotelian *topos:* "the deeds of men cannot be assessed by a straight and unbending rule of the mind; they must be viewed according to the supple Lesbic rule, which does not conform bodies to it, but alters itself according to them."[22] No matter how comprehensive our ethical manuals, practical life will present situations where no rules are at hand, or where there is a single rule whose particular application is unclear, or where there are many conflicting rules which might apply, or where the rule that usually applies demands an exception. There is no method that can reliably bridge the gap between universal and particular in the ethical life. Systematized routines, embodied in the *artes* that Vico admires and associates with the moderns, are no substitute for the virtues, better understood by the ancients.[23] "For in those things regulated by practical wisdom, it makes no difference whether you have many *artes* or only a few."[24] Practical wisdom (*prudentia*) "takes its deliberations from the circumstances of things, which are infinite; hence any comprehension of them, however wide, is never sufficient."[25] At best, rules will furnish access to the general features of a situation. But in practical affairs, wisdom is a matter of insight into particulars.

Attention to the particular and the contingent implies an acceptance of probability. "With respect to prudence in civil life, we should remember that occasion and choice are the mistresses of human affairs, and are most uncertain, governed for the most part by simulation and dissimulation, things which are exceptionally deceitful."[26] Only *prudentia* and its ally *sensus communis,* which "arises from probabilities," are sound guides in the active life.[27] Those who fail to see this point, perhaps having spent too much time in the classroom, "accustom themselves to clinging to general precepts: in actuality we find that nothing is more useless."[28] Vico paints a vivid portrait of the imprudent savant (*doctus imprudentis*) who approaches ethics as if it were a manual of adamantine propositions. He contrasts the type of the expert with three other types: the fool (*stultus*), the astute ignoramus (*illiteratus astutus*), and the wise person (*sapiens*).[29] The fool lacks knowledge of either general or particular. Theory and practice escape him alike; he "constantly pays the penalty for his rashness."[30] The astute ignoramus knows how to succeed in temporal affairs. But his ignorance of the most important things, evidenced by his consistent preference for the *utile* over the *honestum,* ensures failure. In Aristotelian terms, he does not possess *phronesis,*

but only its counterfeit, *deinotes.* Only the wise person possesses both
practical and theoretical wisdom, knowing how to rise from lowly occasions and chance opportunities to the highest good. "Wise people (*sapientes*), who through all the obliquities and uncertainties of human actions
aim for eternal truth, follow roundabout ways, because they cannot take
straight ones; and they execute plans which in the long run are for the
best, as far as the nature of things allows."[31]

By contrast, the distinguishing marks of the imprudent savant are
slowness in decision, arrogance in behavior, and incapacity for persuasive speech. Because he lacks experience in situations where plausible
arguments can be made *in utramque partem,*[32] his choices come slowly,
often too slowly. Vico scorns the critics who, "when something doubtful
is presented to them, say: 'Let me think about it.'"[33] Vico does not dis-
guise his distaste for the physicians of his time who would suspend action, waiting for the disease to progress into something more treatable.[34]
Because his education focuses on the analytical faculty, and neglects the
memory and imagination, the imprudent savant will not develop his
synthetic capacities. He will be unlikely to discover new or hidden things,
to notice the small but telling detail that can alter one's perception entirely. As a result, his judgment will often rely on incomplete and misleading descriptions of a situation. This deficiency in apprehension,
enabled by the substitution of precepts for *prudentia* and *sensus communis,* leads him to "erupt in actions both astonishing and arrogant."[35] Vico
identifies *sensus communis* as the rule (*regula*) of both *prudentia* and *eloquentia.*[36] Disregard for either produces the ineloquent bluster of one-
sided rationalists. "Led to judge before properly apprehending," they
"become arid and dry in expression and without ever doing anything set
themselves up in judgment over all things."[37] The decline of eloquence
and prudence are strictly parallel. Even when the "unscripted, anxious
stutterers" produced by anti-rhetorical ideals are able to apprehend and
judge rightly, they will not have acquired the habit of persuasive speech.[38]
This is the third failing of the imprudent savant. Vico is not referring to
an inability to dress humble language with ornament. He means that
persons without eloquence will be unable to communicate their wisdom, or to make it useful in social life.[39]

Insofar as he approximates the caricature of the imprudent savant,
the moral agent will fail to realize the good in particular situations. His
substitutes for *prudentia* pretend to take him "in a straight line from general to particular truths," so as to "burst through the tortuous curves of
life (*anfractuosa vitae*)."[40] Sometimes he may succeed—the very contin-

gency of life ensures that his demise is not guaranteed—but the usual outcome is failure. "Frustrated in their own plans, deceived by those of others, they usually give up."[41] An ethics based primarily on maxims is self-deluding and self-frustrating. One might suppose that Vico is denying any point at all to moral rules. He does not, however, exclude the possibility that some rules, for example, the commandments of the Decalogue, have the power to bind, admitting of no exceptions (although he would emphasize that their interpretation and application to particular situations is far from unproblematic). Moreover, Vico tempers his criticism of the Stoics in several places, praising them insofar as they "seriously and authoritatively teach about the *constantia* of the wise."[42] The ideal of rigor, embodied in an outlook that emphasizes the moral law, has a genuine role to play in character formation. "Rigor in human actions, meant to ensure that a person is constant to himself in all his doings and through all things, was best taught by the Stoics, to whom it seems the more recent sects of philosophers correspond."[43]

Since moral rules are not self-interpreting or self-applying, the ancient emphasis on virtue must be retained, against those who would arrogantly dismiss it. Thus Vico traces modern rigorism to a desperate and prideful attempt to escape from contingency, and mocks the Stoic habit of confusing its own conception of reason with the *regula veri*. It is also true, however, that Vico's genealogies characteristically endeavor to find some truth in the perspective that is being undermined. Hence Vico acknowledges that Stoicism and its modern analogues may be used to illuminate the central place of *constantia* in the life of the *sapiens,* although this *constantia* can never be reduced to scrupulous rule-following.[44] Vico considers the primary function of rules to be pedagogical. They serve as "an image of the divine cross-roads (*deorum compitalia*)" which "only indicate how and where one is to go, that is, via philosophy to the contemplation of the best nature itself."[45] To expect them to deliver mathematical certainty is a symptom of madness: "If you were to import the geometrical method into practical life," Vico writes, "'you would do no more than exhaust yourself in becoming a rational lunatic.'"[46] The path to success in practical reasoning lies not in demonstrative skill, but in the cultivation of prudence and eloquence.

Eloquence and Prudence

If Vico had only criticized the idea that ethics can be reduced to a core of iron propositions, arguing for the necessity of a non-rule-governed practical wisdom, he would be little different from Aristotle or Aquinas. What Vico adds to an Aristotelian perspective is his insistence that eloquence is the necessary counterpart of prudence. The analogy between prudence and eloquence is embedded in Vico's conception of the *sensus communis,* which he describes as the "criterion" of both.[1] How are prudence and eloquence essentially parallel? When they function properly, both address particular situations, consider the full range of circumstances, employ a stock of precedents, engage the passions, and demand sharp perception. *Quid sit agendum?* is the question that frames their inquiries. Situated in the contingent and the probable, where considerations can be adduced *in utramque partem,* each aims for truth while eschewing the need for apodictic argument.

Vico explicitly connects the rise of Cartesian pedagogies that devalue eloquence and the allied *ars topica* with the abandonment of an ethics centered on virtue.[2] The *ars topica* is necessary not only for the orator, but for anyone who seeks the twin desiderata of comprehensiveness and speed in practical reasoning. As the good doctor cannot waste time in treating a patient, so the effective orator must give immediate assistance to the accused.[3] Protracted analysis can, literally, be deadly. A distinctive characteristic of the *phronimos* is the capacity for making the right decision *without* the luxury of long deliberation. The moral agent requires the *ars topica,* no less than the orator, doctor, or lawyer.

By itself, however, the *ars topica* is not sufficient; it generates facility and plenitude, but not necessarily truth. This is a genuine danger of the *ars topica,* in Vico's eyes. He takes seriously the possibility that it will lead to a false eloquence, from which will arise a dangerous skepticism. Echoing Cicero and Quintilian, Vico observes that Carneades was a master of topical plenitude. "He would argue for both contraries, holding on one day, that justice exists, on another, that it does not, bringing forth equally decisive arguments, with incredible force. This was born from the fact that truth is one, probabilities many, and falsehoods endless."[4] A genuinely philosophical rhetoric must perceive the limitations of the *ars topica,* whose unchecked use may degenerate into sophistry.[5] It must situate *copia* as a means to an end beyond itself. The ability to summon all potentially relevant considerations does not guarantee truth, even if it is an important prerequisite.

Eloquence plays a vital role in the cognitive moment of practical reason. It is also necessary to effect the transformation of human desire, which is the ultimate goal of ethics.[6] Discovery and judgment are fruitless unless they issue in a concrete work of persuasion. Vico names philososophy and eloquence as the two things "capable of turning to good use the disorders of the soul, all the evils of the interior man which originate from desire, as it were from one source." For the wise, philosophy is an effective remedy. It replaces disordered desire with the virtues. In the typical case, however, eloquence is required. Even if it cannot actually inculcate virtues, "eloquence inspires the common person to perform the duties of virtue (*faciant officia virtutis*)."[7] A purely rational approach is not sufficient: "the mind (*mens*) may be ensnared by those delicate nets of truth, but the soul (*animus*) cannot be turned and conquered except by more bodily means."[8] The necessity for artifice cannot be eliminated, since the desires are never fully rational. The soul of the *vulgus* "must be drawn by corporeal images in order to love; for once it loves, it is easily taught to believe; once it believes and loves, it must be inflamed in order to will, against its ordinary lack of power."[9] Vico illustrates by reference to the oratorical case. "Unless the orator does these three things, he has not at all crafted a work of persuasion."[10] Similarly, in the domain of ethical praxis, practical reasoning must culminate in a work of self-persuasion that issues in action. As invention and judgment are useless without persuasion, so deliberation and choice are fruitless without action, the proper conclusion of a practical syllogism. Vico makes the Aristotelian point in a rhetorical key. An ethics that seems true in the abstract but lacks the capacity to persuade, to effect the transformation of desire, is a self-discrediting ethics. It is the kind of philosophy that Vico consistently rejects as useless and therefore harmful.[11]

One might wonder whether Vico's distinction between the wise and the vulgar reinforces the position that eloquence is exclusively for the stupid or corrupt, unnecessary in the ideal case.[12] The *sapiens* seems to need only philosophy in order to transform his passions into virtues. "Wise men induce their own souls (*animus*) by the will (*voluntas*), which is a most peaceful servant of the mind (*mens*); hence it suffices to teach them a duty, and they will perform it."[13] It is true that the *sapiens* does not need the type of eloquence appropriate for the *vulgus*. But this need not imply the total severance of truth from rhetoric. The *sapiens* discerns the perfect coincidence between beauty and truth without requiring an "extra" act of persuasion to motivate action. His aesthetic perceptions have not been rendered superfluous, but perfected to the extent that he finds it impossible to distinguish between what is useful and what is ethically desirable. The *utile* and *honestum* are perceived as identical, once the transformation of desire is complete. Fallen human beings approach this condition asymptotically. The *sapiens* in Vico's discourse does not correspond to a class of existent human beings. It functions as an ideal type that connects his texts with the Roman tradition that he treasures, and serves to remind his readers of their imperfection.

Vico consistently maintains that true philosophy is not separable from rhetoric. Eloquence is "wisdom speaking," he says, adapting a Ciceronian and Renaissance commonplace.[14] "Who is to be believed?" he asks. "Arnauld, who denies it, or Cicero, who affirms and professes that he was made eloquent from topics above all? Let others be the judge."[15] Vico leaves the judgment to others, because he wants to make it clear that his appropriation of the *ars topica* is more than a reactive defense. It is not a condemnation of the modern world as such, but part of a larger strategy that seeks to do it justice, while rejecting its wilder pretensions.

THREE

Critique of Descartes

Despite the widespread appreciation of Vico as an early critic of Cartesianism, the specific passages in which he explicitly attacks Descartes are rarely examined in any detail.[1] *De ratione* is certainly an anti-Cartesian text, but it does not once mention Descartes by name. It is in *De antiquissima Italorum sapientia*, composed a year after *De ratione*, that Vico first stages an explicit confrontation with Descartes. In this confrontation, Vico makes some relatively straightforward arguments that attempt to rebut specific claims made by Descartes. This approach, however, will give way to a genealogical strategy that seeks to unmask Descartes as a tyrant who is fundamentally uncandid about the origins of his thought.

In chapter 1 of *De antiquissima*, Vico characterizes Descartes as a "dogmatist," since he considers all truths, including those of mathematics, "doubtful until metaphysically established."[2] Unless their truths can be demonstrated from other truths known in metaphysics, non-metaphysical sciences are uncertain; they "cannot provide anything certain about the subjects which they treat."[3] These sciences presuppose some view about the relation between mind and body, but they do so without justification, until metaphysics supplies them with proper foundations. What can be done in order to discover the requisite foundations? Vico insinuates a similarity between the dogmatic seeker of metaphysical truth and someone awaiting initiation into a cult, referring to Descartes as the "great Meditator" who "bids the postulant for initiation to approach the holy of holies of metaphysics" with a mind purified from the prejudices that arise from the senses and from other sciences.[4]

"The dividing line between the skeptics and dogmatists," Vico declares, is the "first truth that the metaphysics of Descartes has revealed to us."[5] Vico considers the skeptic to share with the dogmatist the assumption that all truth requires a metaphysical justification; he differs from the dogmatist only in denying the existence of a *primum verum* from which other truths can be known. The first truth, according to Descartes, is *cogito ergo sum*. Vico mocks Descartes by referring to him as "Renatus" and doubts the originality of both his construction of the problem and his particular solution.[6] The use of the evil genius was anticipated by the Stoic in Cicero's *Academia;* the *cogito* was already enunciated by the character Sosia in the *Amphitruo* of Plautus. Far from being a dispassionate seeker of truth, Descartes is like the head of a cult who recruits members by dressing up old commonplaces in the garb of novelty. Vico does not claim that the *cogito* is false; he merely holds that "it is an ordinary cognition that happens to any unlearned person such as Sosia, not a rare and exquisite truth that requires such deep meditation by the greatest of philosophers to discover it."[7]

The non-originality of the *cogito* is not its fundamental problem. Descartes himself was quick to acknowledge that it had precedents, after a correspondent pointed out the presence of a similar argument in Augustine.[8] Fortunately, Vico's critique is not limited to an observation of its lack of novelty. The *cogito* is inadequate, Vico argues, because it is ineffective. It does nothing to persuade the skeptic that knowledge of anything beyond the appearances of consciousness is possible. The skeptic does not doubt that he thinks, but his bare apprehension of thinking does not furnish certain knowledge about the nature of thinking. "Although the skeptic is conscious that he thinks, he nevertheless is ignorant of the causes of thought, or by what means thought comes to be."[9] To have certainty about a thing is not to possess a mere acquaintance with it, but to know its inner constitution—which means, for Vico, to know its genetic source, how it is caused or derived. "For to know (*scire*) is to grasp the genus or the form by which a thing is made, but consciousness (*conscientia*) is of those things whose genus or form we cannot demonstrate."[10] Certainty about thinking would be attainable only if we knew the genus or form through which thinking comes to be. Since the *cogito* does not provide this sort of knowledge, it reveals nothing about the nature of thinking that is not already evident. It furnishes ordinary *conscientia,* but not *scientia.*

Perhaps recognizing the inadequacy of the *cogito* to satisfy the skeptic, philosophers use other means in attempting to discover the genus or form of thinking. The "subtlest metaphysicians of our time scratch one another and get pricked in turn" as they try to find what is missing in the *cogito.*[11] In what may be a reference to both Descartes and Malebranche, Vico characterizes the solution of the subtle modern meta-physicians as a kind of *deus ex machina*. They "resort to an occult law of God as to a device, explaining that the nerves arouse the mind when they are moved by external objects and the mind pulls on the nerves when it wishes to act."[12] Thought can either be aroused by the motion of corporeal nerves or produced by its own action, just as a spider can either be moved by the threads of its web or make the threads move along with it. Such models of the interaction between mind and body, however ingenious, only confirm the suspicion that their proponents "do not know the genus through which thought is produced."[13] Igno-rance of the genetic cause is tantamount to ignorance of the thing itself, unless one merely desires *conscientia*. But the skeptic need not deny the familiar data of everyday consciousness. His claim is that we lack *scientia* and hence ought to suspend assent "lest we add the problems of opinions to the difficulties of things themselves."[14]

Vico knows that the Cartesian dogmatist will reply that we have certain knowledge of our existence, since existence is grounded in the incontrovertible essence of thought. Against this, Vico maintains that *scientia* of the self cannot be gleaned from mere *conscientia* of thinking. At best, we have *conscientia* of our own existence. For a person to be "en-tirely certain that he exists"—to have *scientia* of his being—he would have to "make up his own being out of something that he cannot doubt."[15] But such self-making is impossible, since the person who thinks is both mind and body, "and if thought were the cause of my being, thought would be the cause of body." Thought is not a necessary cause of body, however, because "there are bodies that do not think." [16] Even if the dogmatist is correct to maintain some connection between thought and existence, he errs by assuming that the *cogito* can penetrate to the cause of thinking, rather than merely gesture to a sign whose cause re-mains opaque. "Thinking is not a cause of my being mind, but a sign (*signum*), and the sure sign (*techmerium*) is not a cause. For the careful skeptic will not deny the certainty of sure signs, but he will deny that of causes."[17] However true in itself, the *cogito* is a useless weapon against the skeptic.

If the primary truth of Descartes is unable to refute the skeptic, does it follow that we must embrace skepticism? Vico answers this question in the first chapter's concluding section, entitled *adversus scepticos*. Although we may be acquainted with things that present themselves to our consciousness, the skeptic argues, we are obliged to consider them as effects whose causes are unknown. Our ignorance of causes is not just a contingent fact. As the "genera, or forms, from which each thing is made," they necessarily elude our grasp in every instance.[18] Vico's response to the skeptic is twofold. First, in the next chapter, entitled *De generibus sive de ideis,* he cites instances in which we grasp these genera because we make them ourselves. Exemplary cases are synthetic geometry, painting, sculpture, ceramics, architecture. In these arts, skepticism would be utterly beside the point, although it can still secure a foothold in the arts of rhetoric, politics, and medicine, which are "conjectural" precisely because they do not teach the forms by which their subject matter is created. Vico's second response is to argue that "you may turn" (*regeras*) the argument of the skeptics against themselves.[19] Any effect of which we have *conscientia* has a cause. If these causes are truly unknown, as the skeptic argues, then they cannot reside within us; they are not innate ideas. If causes are not innate ideas, they must exist somewhere, in some locus or receptacle outside the self. This locus Vico names the "comprehension of causes, in which is contained all genera, or all forms, through which all effects are given."[20] Vico identifies the *caussarum comprehensio* with the *primum verum.* Since the *comprehensio* is infinite and necessarily prior to finite body, it is nothing other than God, "and indeed the God whom we Christians profess."[21]

It may seem that Vico does not provide an authentic *via media* between dogmatism and skepticism, but takes a stance that is perhaps even more dogmatic than Descartes. Vico appears to open himself to this charge not only by invoking God against the skeptics, but also by associating the first truth with an historically specific God. To counter this impression, we may observe that if Vico's stance were truly dogmatic, he would argue that his primary truth could be known with certainty, just as the *cogito* can be established *a priori.* This is precisely the position that Vico rejects near the end of the third chapter of *De antiquissima.* He does so by recalling an argument from *De ratione:* "we demonstrate geometrical things because we make them; if we could demonstrate physical things, we would make them."[22] Any authentic *a priori* demonstration of the existence of God would require the demonstrator to try to make God, which "would be tantamount to making himself the God of God, and denying the God whom he seeks."[23] The argument against the skeptics seeks to restore a "first truth," but it is not dogmatic. It eschews the attempt to give a self-evident justification of the *primum verum.* Vico's strategy is to provide a rhetorical inversion of the skeptic's position, not a demonstration.

In all likelihood, the skeptic would find Vico's position tainted with dogmatism, while the dogmatist would fault Vico for conceding too much to skepticism. Whether Vico's inability to please either the dogmatist or the skeptic constitutes an objection to his argument, or further indicates that his position is a genuine *via media* (middle ways are rarely recognized as such by their opponents), merits reflection. Vico concludes the first chapter of *De antiquissima* by a compressed recapitulation of his own alternative to dogmatism and skepticism. As the primary truth, God provides the norm by which we measure human truths. The human truths of which we can have *scientia* are those "whose elements we fashion (*fingamus*) for ourselves, contain within ourselves, and, by means of postulates, project indefinitely; and, when we compose the elements, then the truths that we know in the act of composing them, we make; and, because of all this, we grasp the genus or form by which we do the making."[24] A deeper understanding of the nexus between truth and making, here invoked in opposition to skepticism, will require more attention to the articulation of the *verum-factum* principle (to be given in due course).

In his second response to his Cartesian critics, Vico suggests that Descartes not only overestimates the power of the *cogito,* but also fosters the habit of neglecting ancient philosophy for the express purpose of promoting his own doctrines. "If at times an ancient philosopher is read, he is read in translation, because today, on the authority of Descartes, the study of languages is useless."[25] To the extent that we are influenced by Descartes, "we think up new methods, yes, but we don't discover any new things; our discoveries are stolen from experimentalists and dressed up with the new methods."[26] Although the initial impulse to impose order upon thinking may have been salutary, the actual effect of Descartes' rule was to create a state of affairs where "only his judgment must be employed and only the geometrical method."[27] As Vico had earlier accused Bacon of aspiring to dictatorship, he now suggests that Descartes' true intention is indistinguishable from tyranny. "Descartes had done what those who have become tyrants have always been wont to do. They come to power proclaiming the cause of freedom. But once they are assured of power, they become worse tyrants than their original oppressors."[28] Vico understands the Cartesian invitation to follow the *lumen naturale* as an attempt to justify the neglect of other philosophers. "Young simpletons readily fall under his spell because the long labor of much reading is tiresome, and it is a great pleasure to the mind to learn so much so quickly."[29]

Vico implies that Descartes, although perhaps a natural genius, owes much of his success to intellectual stimulation occasioned by precisely the texts that he discourages others from reading. In wanting his readers to believe that he had no significant predecessors or important teachers, Descartes "gathers the fruit of that plan of wicked politics, to destroy completely those men through whom one has reached the peak of power."[30] His Machiavellian cunning inspires him to lie about his origins: "although he can dissimulate the fact with the greatest art in what he says, he was versatile in every sort of philosophy."[31] Though Vico half-apologizes for saying these things "a bit too clearly and at some length" in the *Seconda risposta,* he portrays Descartes in the same terms more than a decade later in the *Vita.* Composed in the third person, the form of the *Vita* is intended to embody a stark contrast with the egocentric nature of Cartesian philosophy, whose natural expression is in the first person.

Vico vows not to "feign what Descartes craftily feigned as to the method of his studies simply in order to exalt his own philosophy and mathematics and degrade all the other studies included in divine and human erudition."[32] The uncandid fable of the *Discours de la méthode* stands in stark contrast with Vico's own narrative. "With the candor proper to a historian," he attempts to "narrate plainly and step by step the entire series of Vico's studies."[33] The *Vita* proceeds to identify "Renato" as a man "much too ambitious for glory" who "tried to make himself famous among professors of medicine with a physics contrived on a pattern like that of Epicurus."[34] Descartes was largely successful in achieving this objective; the highest praise of a philosopher has become "He understands the *Meditations* of René."[35]

The key to reversing this state of affairs, Vico thinks, is to show that in making self-serving claims about the relationship of reason to tradition, Cartesian discourses are designed to promote their own power. But how cogent is Vico's critique? Yvon Beleval has argued that Vico cannot be taken seriously as a reader of Descartes, on the ground that Vico may not have actually read any of his work.[36] It does seem, as Fisch and Bergin note, that Vico's immediate source for the Cartesian physics was the *Philosophia Naturalis* of Henri du Roy, whom Descartes repudiated.[37] The dangers, moreover, of confusing a polemic with a close and sympathetic study of primary texts are real. But Beleval's doubt that Vico ever read the *Discours de la méthode* is not to be taken seriously. Beleval wonders what language Vico would have read the *Discours* in, since he claimed not to know French. Aside from the possibility that the passage to which Beleval appeals in the *Vita* ought not to be taken literally, the obvious reply is that Vico would have read the *Discours* in Latin translation, for example, the *Dissertatio de methodo* as rendered by Etienne de Courcelles, published in 1644 in Amsterdam as part of the *Specimina philosophiae*.[38]

It may be true that Vico only begins to give a genealogy of Cartesian philosophy. One need not deny that contemporary readers who pursue such an aim ought to display more sensitivity to the Cartesian texts than Vico himself did. An important step in this direction has been taken by David Lachterman. When Lachterman speaks of the "Cartesian gift and need for dissimulation" and suggests that his "relations to his own roots or 'sources' are unsurprisingly *opaque*," he may be understood as expanding Vico's charge that Descartes lies about the origins of his own thought in order to exalt it.[39] Certainly the mode of suspicion employed by Lachterman in his approach to Descartes owes something to Leo Strauss and his students. But this indebtedness may be relatively shallow, since the Viconian strains of Lachterman's own "genealogy of modernity" are not far to seek.

The Roots of Mathematics

A preoccupation with "the lower" is the hallmark of genealogy. Genealogical narratives typically seek to expose the roots of the higher in the lower. Hence in his Preface to *Daybreak,* Nietzsche introduces himself as a "'subterranean man' at work . . . who tunnels and mines and undermines."[1] Vico's analogue to Nietzsche's *Unterirdischen* is Tacitus, whom he takes to possess an "incomparable metaphysical mind" that "descends into all the counsels of advantage" for the sake of contemplating "man as he is," in contrast to Plato's ambition to know man "as he should be."[2] In *De antiquissima,* Vico attempts to understand mathematics "from below" in Tacitean fashion. It is not that Vico is a straightforwardly anti-mathematical thinker, as some commentators have suggested.[3] On the contrary, he agrees that mathematics possesses a unique certainty, and he even suggests that it constitutes a participation in truth (although the mode of this participation is highly problematic, as we will see). But where does the certainty of mathematics come from? Vico answers this question by attempting to expose the origin of mathematics in the radical deficiency of the human mind. He seeks to humble the discourse that modern rationalism most exalts.

Mathematics takes its point of departure from human ignorance. "When man sets out to inquire into the nature of things, he realizes at length that he cannot arrive at that nature by any means, because he does not have within himself the elements through which composite things exist."[4] Mind is alien to nature, unable to know it because unable to make it, except in the most approximate fashion. Hence it seems limited to the possession of inherently doubtful *conscientia* rather than assured *scientia.* Vico describes this condition as not simply a naturally given limitation, but speaks of the "fault of the mind" (*mentis vicium*).[5] He understands the estrangement of mind from nature as something more than guiltless ignorance. It is an effect of human fallenness, a decline from a primordial state in which mind and nature were integrated. The remedy to this state of affairs is for the human mind to quit being receptive and to become creative, to mimic the God whose curse has rendered the mind ignorant and impotent. Hence man "turns this fault of his mind to good use" and creates "by abstraction, as they say" the two things that lie at the foundation of mathematics: "the point that can be drawn and the unit that can be multiplied."[6]

Although the mind in its postlapsarian state strives to imitate God, Vico does not think that it succeeds in creating realities. The point and the unit, as made by the human mind, are not *res* but *ficta*. "For the point, if you draw it, is no longer a point; the unit, if you multiply it, is not entirely a unit."[7] In addition to lacking reality, the work of human creativity is born out of pride. Man has "arrogated to himself a right" (*pro suo iue sumpsit*) that was not originally his—the right "to proceed from these fictions to infinity, so that he is allowed to project lines indefinitely and to multiply the unit countlessly."[8] Though unable to generate realities, human pride is successful in enabling the mathematican to generate "a kind of world of forms and numbers which he can embrace entirely himself."[9] This "kind of world" (*mundus quidam*) as Vico calls it— suggesting that he views the world of perfectly manipulable mathematical entities as a world in only a qualified sense—exists within the mind that has created it and hence can be known with full *scientia*. The externality of the objects to be known, which is what limited the mind in its previous condition to the attainment of nothing more than doubtful *conscientia,* has been overcome. "By lengthening, shortening, or putting together lines, by adding, subtracting, or reckoning numbers, he produces infinite works (*infinita opera*) because he knows infinite truths (*infinita vera*) within himself."[10] Under initially unpromising conditions, the mind has converted weakness into power.

What enables the human mind to make the transition from utter impotence to mathematical *scientia* is precisely its mimicking of the divine procedure. Human mathematicians "make the truths they teach" and operate "with their abstractions just as God operates with reality."[11] The procedural analogy to divine knowing certifies mathematics as the paradigm of purely human *scientia*. Vico considers this analogy to hold at both the level of problematic and theoretic. "Nor is it only in problems, but in the theorems themselves, which are supposed to involve contemplation alone, that there is need for construction. For when the mind gathers the elements of the truth that it contemplates, it cannot do so except by making the truth it knows."[12] Mathematics is a genuine *scientia operatrix*, Vico maintains.[13] Because it proves from causes, because it most thoroughly constructs its elements, it is most certain. "The most certain things are those which, redressing the defects of their origin, resemble divine knowledge in their operation, inasmuch as in them the true is convertible with what is made."[14] As God contains the elements and the generated *Verbum* entirely within himself, so the mathematician possesses the elements of his *scientia* and its constructions *intra se*. This position is not abandoned after the *De antiquissima;* Vico reaffirms it twenty years later in the *Vici vindiciae* of 1729, composed after the first version of the *Scienza nuova*. "Just as the geometer is, in his world of figures, a god (so to speak), so God Almighty is, in his world of spirits and bodies, a geometer (so to speak)."[15]

In exposing the roots of mathematics in the vice of the human mind—understood as the desire of human *curiositas* to "seek a truth denied to him by nature"[16]—Vico has put forward a narrative that is meant to shock and discomfit its typical practitioners. In this sense, the account is certainly "genealogical." But to what extent has Vico actually undermined mathematics? Is he attempting to subvert mathematical discourses, or does he simply intend to provide an alternative but still "respectful" account of mathematical truth? There is some evidence for the latter possibility. Vico consistently regards the *factum* known by the mathematician as *verum*. Mathematics is a primary instance of the principle *verum et factum convertuntur*. Moreover, he does not hesitate to describe arithmetic and geometry as "most useful" (*utilissimae*).[17] There is, nevertheless, a genuinely subversive element in Vico's grounding of mathematical truth in human ignorance and arrogance. Even though the mathematical mind might attain truths that it can know with certitude, Vico emphasizes that these truths have a shadowy reality. He considers them "fictions" created by intellect. They are not eternal verities to be contemplated timelessly, but truths that come to be through the agency of a creative process whose ultimate warrant is deeply suspect, however useful its fruits. Although he avoids a complete denial of its certainty or utility, Vico has in fact removed mathematics from its Cartesian pedestal.

It would be easy to conclude that Vico is simply a nominalist who has exposed the roots of mathematics as consisting in elements that are reducible to sheer linguistic convention. This is the route taken by Corsano and others. [18] Two considerations, however, prevent us from following this path. First, Vico does not hold that humans literally create mathematical elements out of nothing. They create them *tamquam ex nihilo*, "as it were from nothing." *Unum* and *figura*, the elements of arithmetic and geometry, are also viewed as "abstractions" that must be drawn from something existing prior to mathematical creation. *Figura* is abstracted from *corpus*, which itself is a dissection of *homo*.[19] The other division of *homo* is *animus*, which is carved into *intellectus* and *voluntas*.[20] From all of these dissections, "from these things and from all other things," *unum* is abstracted, along with *ens*.[21] Though the mathematician proceeds on the model of God's creation, *ad Dei instar*, his elements do not exist outside of the divinely created *elementa rerum* to the extent that they are real.

Second, the "fictionalist" account of mathematics in the first chapter of *De antiquissima* must be read alongside the more "realist" account given by its fourth chapter. There Vico suggests that the elements of mathematics may yet possess some ontological weight, despite the fact that from a genealogical perspective, they appear utterly unreal. Although Vico often adopts the Tacitean pose of viewing human phenomena "as they are," his ultimate aim is to harmonize Tacitus with Plato. Hence he holds *both* that mathematical elements are fictions when viewed "from below" (that is, from the standpoint of their human origin) *and* that the mathematical point can be understood as if "from above," as a participation in the "metaphysical point." The metaphysical point is a *res media* between God and material bodies, "unextended indeed, but capable of extension."[22] Imputations of a pure nominalism to Vico are difficult to reconcile with his view that truth, or its likeness, flows from metaphysics into geometry through the "perilous gateway of the point."[23] Although the geometer's point is a nominal definition, it is parasitic upon the definition of the point as the definition of a real thing, as considered by the "Zenonians." Hence the point is not merely an arbitrary fiction: "geometry receives its truth from metaphysics, and returns what it receives to the same metaphysics."[24] As much as Vico may appear initially to embrace a nominalism in mathematics, his teaching is that mathematical *elementa* are radically dependent upon metaphysics. To deny this, one must discount Vico's consistent affirmation that metaphysics is the "fount of all truth from which everything in the other *scientiae* is derived."[25]

Vico's positioning of mathematics at the pinnacle of the human *scientiae* may be regarded as an ironic agreement with Descartes. What mathematics gains in certainty and clarity, it loses in ontological significance, even if its objects retain the obscure reality of participations in metaphysical points. Descartes had compared human science, which ideally will become a *mathesis universalis,* to the light of the sun.[26] Vico, however, compares the artifice of the dissective procedure that he associates with mathematics to seeing by lamplight in the dark. Against his Cartesian critics, he declares that "knowing clearly and distinctly is a vice rather than a virtue of human understanding."[27] Vico's genealogical approach to mathematics attempts to deflate its pretensions to absolute knowledge while preserving its value as a participation in metaphysical truth.

This dual perspective applies to the synthetic geometry that Vico, like Hobbes, judges worthy of study, in contradistinction to the analytic geometry of Descartes. Synthetic geometry is an *ars* able to "teach the genera or modes by which its matters come to be"; it is therefore certain in both results and procedure. Because it makes its own genera, synthetic geometry is a pure exemplification of the *verum-factum* principle: "man possesses within himself the elements, which he teaches."[28] Analytic geometry, by contrast, is an *ars* that does not satisfy the *verum-factum* principle. "Analysis, although it produces results that are certain, is nevertheless uncertain in its workings, because it takes its subject matter from the infinite and descends from there to the smallest element. That all things can be found in the infinite is given, but in what way you are to find them there is not."[29]

This passage is mysterious unless we keep in mind the genealogical dimension of Vico's account of mathematics. The name for the ancient procedure that begins with the infinite and descends to particular conclusions is *divination.* Vico's intent is to unmask Cartesian analytic geometry as nothing less than a form of divination. In chapter five of *De ratione,* Vico emphasizes the role of chance in determining whether one is able to form an equation that will solve the problem at hand, and even (quoting Vergil) compares the analytic geometer to the "oracular priestess who, still resisting Phoebus, raves in great fury, and fiercely struggles to shake off the god from her breast." He ends the chapter by characterizing analysis as "a certain art of divining (*ars divinandi*) to which we have recourse as a kind of machine" and quotes Horace: we should not "allow the god to intervene, unless the plot deserves to be unraveled by such a supernatural character."[30] Fifteen years later, Vico holds substantially the same view. In the *Vita,* he reproduces a digression from an annual lecture which he delivered to his students so that "they might know how to make choice and use of the sciences for eloquence." In that digression, Vico contrasts the virtues of synthetic geometry—its figures and drawings "refine imagination" and "quicken perception"—with the habits encouraged by the practice of "teaching youth the elements of the science of magnitudes by the algebraic method." Vico lodges a fourfold complaint against this method: it strikes the perceptual faculty, confounds the memory, blinds the imagination, and ultimately destroys the understanding because "algebra professes to divine." Vico's curriculum would retain only a small place for algebra, making it an appendix of the mathematics course and recommending its use only when "to find required magnitudes our human understanding would be obliged to undergo desperate labor by the synthetic method." In such cases, one might excusably "take refuge in the oracle of the analytic" (*oracolo dell'analitica*).[31]

Why should Vico compare the "rational" *ars analytica* to the "magical" art of divination? The comparison has struck at least one commentator as "utterly fanciful." Gianturco observes that in fact "analytical geometry was not the product of the Dionysiac inspiration of a single hierophant of mathematics."[32] It seems clear, however, that Vico's intent is not to provide an historically accurate analysis, but to contend that practices which seem distinctly modern and rational contain hidden isomorphisms with practices that are pagan and magical. Something similar about the ancestry of pagan philosophical thinking in divination is suggested when in the *Scienza nuova* Vico will derive *contemplatio* from *templa coeli*. Vico is not denying that analysis is either true or useful. His point is that when learners are encouraged to use the method as a short cut, forsaking the longer road in order to avoid the hard but instructive work of synthesis, they are similar to diviners who obtain correct results without quite knowing how. What Vico holds, as Milbank notes, is that "when analysis is used unnecessarily or too exclusively it is akin to magical divination and superstition, [but] when it is used properly it is a door to genuine metaphysics."[33] Despite its potency for abuse, analysis impresses Vico to the extent that in the *Vici vindiciae* he describes it as a capacity that could not exist but for "an *ingenium* superior to human power."[34] Once again, "Tacitean" unmasking gives way to "Platonic" gestures toward the transcendent: "analysis is only possible (and guaranteed in its truth) as a participation in an ultimately inaccessible divine synthesis."[35]

FIVE

Verum-Factum

Vico's genealogical approach seems to oscillate between two poles. On the one hand, it sets out to expose a phenomenon or discourse as something humanly constructed, as a *factum* that has no unique or special claim to truth. On the other hand, it seems eager to acknowledge that cultural formations, even those susceptible to being unmasked as something other than what they pretend to be, manage to preserve a connection with truth insofar as they are participations in the divine *Logos.* Hence Vico holds a more positive view of the *factum:* "the true and the made are convertible" (*verum et factum convertuntur*). [1]

It may appear that the relation between genealogy and *verum-factum* is merely extrinsic, but Vico himself implies otherwise in his notion of a symbiosis between "Plato" and "Tacitus." There is an internal connection between Vico's understanding of the *verum-factum* principle and his genealogical, historicizing approach. Before the internal connection between Vico's genealogy and his metaphysics of the *factum* can be perceived, however, we have to attend closely to his particular explication of the *verum-factum* axiom in *De antiquissima.*

"For the Latins 'the true' (*verum*) and 'the made' (*factum*) are reciprocal or, in the common language of the Schools, convertible."[2] Thus the opening sentence of *De antiquissima Italorum sapientia* announces the *verum-factum* principle. Vico claims to have discovered this principle through a philological investigation of the origins of the Latin language. Since the Romans had no pursuits other than agriculture and war, up to the time of Pyrrhus, Vico reasons that whatever "relatively learned phrases" were contained in their language must have come from "some other learned race."[3] This race is the "Italians," made up of the Ionians and Etruscans. Among the Ionians, Vico asserts, the Italic school of philosophy flourished; the Etruscans excelled in cultic practice and architecture. Vico's project is to unearth "the ancient wisdom of the Italians from the origins of the Latin language itself,"[4] a task never before attempted, but one that he thinks merits inclusion among Bacon's *desiderata*. The goal is to discover a wisdom so ancient that it is practically new. That which is the "most ancient" promises also to be the "most modern."

De antiquissima presents itself as a study in philology, but Vico takes pains to distance himself from conventional philology, whether in its classical or modern humanist guise. Anticipating his critique of the "conceit of scholars" in the *Scienza nuova*, Vico reproaches Varro, Scaliger, Sanchez, and Scioppius for attempting to understand language with the assistance of "the philosophy which they themselves had learned and were cultivating."[5] By contrast, "we adhere to no particular school," not even that of Plato, despite his exemplary work in the *Cratylus*.[6] Vico disavows membership in a school as unseemly for a philosopher.

As Vico's early critics noted, it is difficult to take seriously many of the etymologies in *De antiquissima*. Considered as a study in philology, Vico's project fails, even by the standards of his own time. It seems more fruitful to read *De antiquissima* as Vico's attempt to present a new metaphysics—an essay prompted by the stimulus of philological reflection while transgressing its limits.[7] The core of the new metaphysics is the convertibility of *verum* and *factum*. As evidence for the claim that *verum* and *factum* meant the same, Vico cites other, ostensibly interchangeable terms that suggest an equation of thinking with a process of collecting or gathering. *Intelligere*, "to understand," was the same as *perfecte legere*, "to read completely"; both are encompassed in the phrase *aperte cognoscere*, "to know clearly." *Cogitare*, "to think," is the same as the vernacular *andar raccogliendo*, "to gather or collect," which may also be expressed by *pensare*. The term *ratio* meant both "reason," in the sense of what distinguishes men from brutes, and the "gathering" (*collectio*) of the elements of arithmetic.[8]

However spurious these correspondences are from a philological standpoint, they serve to illumine the *verum-factum* principle. Vico uses them to suggest a basic analogy between human understanding and the act of reading. "As words are symbols and signs of ideas, so ideas are symbols and signs of things. Hence, as reading is the action of one who collects the elements of writing from which words are composed, so understanding is collecting all the elements of a thing, from which its most complete idea may be expressed."[9] This idea is far from original. Galileo portrays his physics as an exercise in reading the book of nature;

Hobbes deliberately renders *nosce teipsum* as "read thyself."[10] As an assertion that "to know is to compose the elements of things"—to read their letters by gathering them into unities—*verum-factum* does not so much recover the ancient wisdom of the Italians as express a basic continuity between Vico and modern thought.

Vico proceeds, however, to place his own stamp on the notion. After linking truth and making in general, he immediately asserts that only God, strictly speaking, embodies the *verum-factum* principle. If the true is what is made, then "the first truth is therefore in God, because God is the first Maker."[11] Since God is infinite and complete, so is the truth he makes. No truth is outside God; he contains "the elements of things, extrinsic and intrinsic alike."[12] Because he makes these elements and contains them within himself, he can arrange them perfectly, with utter precision and control. His understanding of the *elementa rerum* is identical to self-knowledge. Human beings, by contrast, do not possess such understanding of the elements. Since the human mind does not contain the elements within itself, it can only think about things at one remove. "Thought (*cogitatio*) is therefore proper to the human mind, but understanding (*intelligentia*) proper to the divine mind."[13]

Vico deviates from the dominant tendencies of modern thought by advocating a philosophy of humility. He argues that the human mind, "finite and external to everything other than itself, is confined to the outside edges of things, never collecting all the elements."[14] Its cognition is only a "participation in reason," as opposed to a full mastery.[15] "Divine truth is a solid image of things, like a statue; human truth is a monogram or plane image, like a painting."[16] Against the dogmatists who would exalt it, Vico downgrades human truth. Unlike the skeptics, however, he does not intend to deny its claims altogether: "man is neither nothing, nor everything."[17] The human being is a *particeps rationis*. In the first instance, Vico's principle *verum esse ipsum factum* serves not to raise men to the level of God, but to mark the distinction between creature and creator. It articulates the ontology that most naturally complements the earlier deciphering of Bacon and Descartes as thinkers who are consumed by their own pride.

Unlike these moderns, the ancient pagans understand that human reason is essentially participatory, a sharing in something greater than itself. The wisdom of the Italians requires, nonetheless, a fundamental correction. Ancient models of the conversion of *verum* and *factum* picture God as a craftsman, a *demiourgos* who works at things external to himself.[18] This conception of God is incompatible with Vico's theological belief that the world is not eternal, but created in time from nothing. It is also at odds with Vico's understanding of divine truth as the arrangment of elements that are contained within God, rather than outside of him. Both reasons of piety and demands internal to his metaphysics require Vico to distinguish between "created truth"—a *factum* that, in some sense, exists separately from its producer—and "uncreated truth"—a *genitum* that is one in being with the *primus Factor*.[19] The second person of the Trinity is not a *factum* but the *Verbum,* begotten not made. "With truly divine elegance," the Scriptures call it "the wisdom of God, which contains within itself the ideas of all things and accordingly the elements of all ideas."[20] If Vico proceeds to associate human truth with construction, he does so only in a space that has been determined by Christian theology. *Verum-factum* is not a secular thesis, but a principle that requires the subordination of *verum* to *verbum* and *factum* to *genitum*.[21]

Such wisdom is directly accessible only through the science that Vico identifies as "revealed theology" (*theologia revelata*).[22] Vico takes revelation to be the most certain science, but distinguishes its certainty from that possessed by human *scientia,* since we cannot comprehend the "genus or mode by which it is true."[23] Human truth, if it is to be known with certainty, requires a comprehension of the genus, that is, an internal possession of the elements and the mode through which they may be combined. This is strictly possible only in the case of mathematics, where the elements are entirely derived from the human mind. It is analogously possible in the other disciplines, which Vico considers able to create images of the elements of things by means of the process he names "dissection" (*dissicere, dividere*). Through dissection, the human sciences can gain access to the elements and proceed to set them forth in a fashion that produces truth. As Vico puts it in the *Scienza nuova prima,* "by means of division, we must proceed from cognition of the parts and thence of their composition, to achieve cognition of the whole."[24]

The sharp distinction in procedure between revealed theology and human *scientiae* might be taken to imply the radical autonomy of the latter. Since the *factum* known by dissective and compositive methods seems to occupy a space entirely independent of revelation, is Vico not drawing an essentially secular picture of human knowledge? Some interpreters have read Vico in precisely this way. Closer attention to *De antiquissima,* however, shows that *verum-factum* is not a secular principle. Dissection presupposes the existence of something to be cut up, an ontologically prior *unum*. The *unum,* according to Vico, is nothing other than the *Verbum* itself. Rather than creating its own objects from nothing, human *scientia* aspires to know the elements contained within the *Verbum:* "God knows everything, because he contains within himself the elements, from which he composes all things; man, however, seeks to know them by dividing."[25] The distinction is not between two sets of elements, but between two modes of grasping the *elementa rerum.* One mode is proper to the infinite God, who possesses the elements *in se;* the other, to finite human beings who grasp them from the outside by means of dissections. Human *scientia,* to the extent that it attains truth, always involves knowledge of realities that at root are divine generations or creations, even if human reliance upon dissection ensures that such knowledge is inevitably refracted and distorted. Since the *factum* known by human *scientia* is always compromised by its own procedures, it can be nothing more than a partial approximation of truth, perpetually falling short of the divine *genitum.* Vico emphasizes that dissection carries with it a distortion of the whole: for the Latins *minuere* means "both diminution and division, as though the things we divide lose their original composition and are diminished, changed, and marred."[26] Despite this severe limitation, Vico grants human dissection the power to capture elements that lend themselves to being combined and arranged into a *factum.* To the extent that a *factum* is "solid," built up out of parts that fit together in a harmonious fashion, it may be considered as *verum.* (Aesthetic coherence is a sign of truth, metaphysical participation its ground.) The point that must not be lost—although inevitably it will be lost, since self-love naturally inspires love of things made by the self—is that this *verum* is nothing more than a "monogram" or "plane image" of the divine *verum.*

The *factum* can be known with certainty, insofar as it is made from elements of whose origin and derivation we can give a precise account. It is true (as distinct from knowable) to the extent that it participates in the divine *Verbum.* In *De antiquissima,* epistemological certitude and metaphysical truth are mutually opposed. From an epistemological perspective, the truths of mathematics are maximally certain; from a metaphysical perspective, they are minimally true. Ethics appears as the inverse of mathematics. Its proper objects (desire and the *telos*) are not amenable to dissection and hence are knowable in a mostly conjectural manner. This epistemological defect, however, is offset by their close relation to the metaphysical genera, the real elements of things. This complex attitude toward the *factum* gives Vico the freedom *both* to regard human makings with suspicion, especially when their makers begin (idolatrously) to value them as ultimate, *and* to maintain a conception of the *factum* as nothing less than the site in which truth is immanently or latently present.

We are now in a position to state with greater clarity what we earlier referred to as the "internal connection" between *verum-factum* and moral genealogy. Since they are not known by revelation, the mode of truth that is uniquely immune from human making, genealogies (on Vico's own premises) must be regarded as human constructs, narratives that are made by the historian/philosopher. In the *Scienza nuova,* Vico will explicitly consider his own narrative as a historiographical *factum.* If genealogical narratives are constructs, and yet possess some claim to truth, there must be a sense in which the *factum* and the *verum* coincide. The *factum* cannot be utterly *falsum;* if this were the case, genealogies would lose their bite. They would be reduced to the status of fables that have no claim on belief at all, something less than likely stories. ("Likely" is always elliptical for "likely to be true.") Perhaps the genealogist could embrace this consequence, admitting that his stories are in principle indistinguishable from errors. Nietzsche himself hints at such a thing. In the Preface to *On the Genealogy of Morals,* Nietzsche disdains the notion of "refutation" precisely because it presupposes the idea of truth and describes the relation between his genealogy and rival accounts as the replacement of "one error with the other." He hints at the possibility that his narrative is also a *factum,* every bit as much as the conceptions that he opposes, and therefore little more than an alternative way of erring. But does Nietzsche write as if he believes this to be true of his own genealogy? Arguably, he does not. In systematically behaving as if his genealogy is a superior account of the nature of morality, Nietzsche is committed to the belief that his *factum* is also a *verum.* One may hazard a generalization: if the theory and practice of a genealogist are to be consistent, he or she must affirm some version of *verum-factum.*

It is not that any and every *factum* is *verum.* Genealogy requires the sense that in many particular instances, the *factum* is akin to the *falsum.* To expose a taken-for-granted phenomenon or cultural formation as a construct—as something historically contingent that comes to be at a particular time and place, in the service of particular interests— is to subvert its claim to be accepted as true. Genealogies characteristically seek to expose a range of cultural constructs as "mis-made" or "badly made." All human *facta,* on Vico's metaphysics, are to an extent poorly made, bearing only a shadowy relation to authentic truth. Some makings, however, may be exhibited within a narrative (itself a *factum*) as participating more closely in divine truth than others. Insofar as this narrative has a claim to be true, the *facta* depicted within it are also candidates for participation in the *verum*.

What are the criteria for judging a historiographical narrative as true? With what justification can any genealogy, including Vico's own, make a truth-claim on its own behalf, while remaining aware of its own status as a *factum?* Vico will most thoroughly engage with such questions in his reflections on method in the *Scienza nuova*. Yet it is *De antiquissima* that first articulates the dual character of the *factum* as simultaneously *verum* and, because humanly originated, inadequate to the highest reality. Vico's understanding of the *verum-factum* principle will give him the confidence to strive for a synthesis of Tacitus and Plato that combines a genealogical, historicizing approach with a conviction in abiding truth.

PART 2

The Development of Modern Historical Consciousness in the *Diritto universale*

The Intention and Form
of the *Diritto universale*

Is modern historical consciousness a necessary presupposition of moral genealogy? The question is difficult, as the case of Nietzsche shows. If one associates "modern historical consciousness" with the "historical school" of the nineteenth-century German academy, then the notion that genealogy requires a distinctively modern sense of history becomes problematic. In his "unmodern meditation" *History in the Service and Disservice of Life,* Nietzsche takes Greek history-writing as his inspiration and his model. This may suggest that his genealogical project owes little or nothing to the modern historical approach, whose dominant German form conceals a profound hostility to life under the seeming exactitudes of detached scholarship. Other evidence, however, points in the opposite direction. The First Essay of *On the Genealogy of Morals* identifies the "historical spirit" (*historische Geist*) as precisely the quality whose lack ruins the English genealogists, but which Nietzsche himself possesses in abundance.[1] In the *History in the Service and Disservice of Life,* Nietzsche aligns himself with the program of a "critical history" that is unabashedly modern.[2] Nietzsche's criticism of historical scholarship in its German form, as exemplifed by Hegel and his epigoni, does not seem to be intended as a rejection of modern historical consciousness as such. He deeply admires the Swiss historian Jacob Burckhardt, whose example shows that one can possess the modern historical sense without succumbing to the deadening professionalism of the German university.[3]

Despite Nietzsche's professed affinities for the Greeks, one may venture that his moral genealogy is inconceivable apart from the discovery of historical consciousness in modernity. But how and when did "modern historical consciousness" come into being? Leo Strauss's observation that "the genesis of historicism is inadequately understood" seems as true today as it was in 1950.[4] In the preface to a later edition of *Natural Right and History,* Strauss made the suggestion that a study of Vico would deepen our understanding of historical consciousness, and serve as an antidote to the tendency to take it for granted.[5] The central contention of Part 2 of this volume is that Vico should in fact be read as an early (if not the earliest) expositor of a position that can legitimately be termed "modern historical consciousness." This happens first not in the *Scienza nuova,* but in the earlier series of texts that Vico grouped under the title *Diritto universale.*[6]

The "historicism" that emerges in the *Diritto universale* is not an anticipation of the scientific and scholarly study of history that claims to be "value-free." The *Diritto universale* is a preparation for the moral genealogy of the *Scienza nuova.* In some ways, Vico states his conclusions about secular modernity and its pagan counterparts more clearly and at greater length in the *Diritto* than in the *Scienza nuova,* although its stance is less characterized by a commitment to "unmasking" than that of the magnum opus. This chapter and the next three will show how Vico comes to adopt a profoundly historical, if not historicist, approach to justice and natural law. In the final chapter of this part, I will show how Vico relates the articulation of historical consciousness in the *Diritto* to what he calls "Christian jurisprudence." The program of Christian jurisprudence, Vico concludes, promises to succeed where prior approaches (including the Roman jurisprudence that he generally admires and regards as exemplary) have failed.

What inspires the composition of the *Diritto?* External motives would include both the conversations that Vico mentions in the work's *occasio scribendi* and the desire to secure a chair in law at the University of Naples—a position six times as lucrative as the chair in rhetoric that he was to hold for most of his life at the University of Naples. More important is what Vico identifies as the *caussa scribendi.* In thinking about the nature of law, Vico finds himself confronted with a question as old as Plato. Is justice rooted in nature, or is it a matter of convention, expressed in a legal code to be followed only when one lacks the means or ability to be unjust? Modern answers to this question, Vico thinks, can be reduced to two positions. First, there is the stance that Vico associates with "the skeptics" (*gli sceptici*), a category that includes Epicurus, Machiavelli, Hobbes, Spinoza, and Bayle. These thinkers, whether or

not they would understand themselves as skeptics, converge in denying that "right is in nature" (*ius esse in natura*). Justice is not natural; it
is based on fear, chance, or necessity. Second, Vico finds himself engaged with the project of modern natural law as represented by Grotius.
In *De iure belli ac pacis,* Grotius attempts to ground justice in a rational,
minimalist conception of human sociability. He does so by trying to
show that observation of the *ius naturale* is the necessary condition of
maintaining social order. This truth can be demonstrated with certitude, Grotius thinks, against Carneades' attempt to reduce justice to expediency. Hence he boasts that "with all truthfulness I aver that, just
as mathematicians treat their figures as abstracted from particular
bodies, so in treating law I have withdrawn my mind from every particular fact."[7]

Vico acknowledges and admires Grotius's immense erudition. In the
Proloquium of the *Diritto,* he praises him as the "jurisconsult of mankind."[8] Five years later, he will honor him in the *Autobiography* as one of
his *quattro auttori* "who embraces in a system of universal law the whole
of philosophy and philology, including both parts of the latter, the history on the one hand of facts and events, both fabulous and real, and on
the other of the three languages, Hebrew, Greek, and Latin; that is to
say, the three learned languages of antiquity that have been handed
down to us by the Christian religion."[9] Despite his status as first among
the "three princes of the natural law," however, Vico does not find that
he provides a satisfying resting place.[10] The relationship of Vico to Grotius
is more dialectical than mimetic. Grotius fails because he does not bring
his profound learning about particular laws and customs to bear in his
attempt to counter the skeptical reduction of justice to expediency. He
relies not upon his philological and historical knowledge, but upon
abstract and rationalistic arguments that do not persuade against the
objections of the skeptics. Hence he fails to articulate a convincing
response to the challenge of Carneades. His "system of universal law,"
however fertile a source of insights, needs to be replaced by an alternative conception of *diritto universale* that places historical facts and universal truths into a closer relationship.

As Vico understands him, Grotius treats the law of nations (*ius gentium*) and the natural law (*ius naturale*) as if they were not only distinct
but also separate and autonomous. Against this dichotomy, Vico will
attempt to exhibit the *ius naturale* as present within the *ius gentium,* which
in time becomes the *ius civile.* Vico will reject the notion that natural law is
profitably treated as if it were detached from the historical development of

customs and the laws that grow out of those customs. He will argue that natural law has both a metaphysical origin in eternal truth and an historical origin in the customs of human society. These dual sources can ultimately be traced to a single origin, to God himself, who will be identified as the "one principle and end of universal law."[11]

The attribute of God most closely connected to the *diritto universale* is his providence, whose ways (*viae*) are identified in the *De uno* as "opportunities, occasions, and accidents" that manifest themselves in human customs.[12] Far from being arbitrary or purely contingent, historical custom is the vehicle through which divine providence operates. Nature and convention are inextricably yoked; a proper grasp of this nexus enables one to discern the ground of justice in something more than expediency. This is the form of Vico's response to the position which, like Grotius, he associates with Carneades.[13] It serves to distinguish him from both the rationalist approach of modern natural law as represented by Grotius and the skepticism that he finds in Epicurus, Machiavelli, Hobbes, Spinoza, and Bayle. Lachterman felicituously characterizes the standpoint of the *Scienza nuova* as holding that "the customary, far from being at odds with human nature, will turn out to be the sole medium of its expression."[14] It is the *Diritto,* however, that provides the first and perhaps the clearest account of Vico's reasons for thinking that a correct understanding of law will regard it as *both* historical and conventional *and* immutable and natural.

Before we look at Vico's argument about the relationship between nature and convention, examining the development of his thesis in the context of justice, natural law, and the art of interpretation, we should pause to make some preliminary comments about the form and style of the text. The *Diritto universale* is the title that Vico gave to a group of writings undertaken in a three-year period. These are the *Sinopsi del diritto universale* (1720), the *De uno universi iuris principio et fine uno* (1720), the *De constantia iurisprudentis* (1721), the *Notae in duos libros* (1722), and the *Dissertationes* (1722). Vico envisages a tripartite system that will exhibit the origin, the cycle, and the constancy of the universal law.[15] The origin and the cycle are treated in *De uno;* the constancy in the two parts of the 1721 text entitled *De constantia philosophiae* and *De constantia philologiae.* Perhaps more important than the particular character of the system is simply the fact that Vico regards the *Diritto universale* as an authentic system. Vico's determination to embed historical inquiry within a system that claims to be both demonstrative and encyclopaedic confirms the suspicion that he not only takes a generically historical approach to the study of law, but does so in a specifically modern fashion.

The presence of "demonstration" in the *Diritto universale* is evident, although its precise function may be more difficult to determine. In the *Sinopsi del diritto universale,* Vico claims that on the basis of two definitions and five metaphysical truths taken as lemmas, he has "demonstrated" (*dimonstra*) the truths of things by reasoning "from their order, through their order, and in their order."[16] From the idea of order, Vico claims to demonstrate the existence of God, his nature as an infinite mind, and the analogy between principles of the sciences in the human mind and the principles of things in the divine mind. Having established this metaphysics, Vico is further able to demonstrate the principles of sacred history, Christian theology, and Christian ethics. (In the *De constantia philologiae,* Vico claims that although divine faith is superior to any demonstration, he can nonetheless demonstrate the *antiquitas* and *perpetuitas* of sacred history in a way that "approaches most closely to geometrical truth.")[17] The *De uno* proceeds along the lines indicated by the *Sinopsi,* spelling out the *definitiones veri et certi* and the five *assumptiones metaphysicae,* the *lemmata* that are footnoted throughout the text in much the same way (if not with quite the same frequency and consistency) that Spinoza cites prior definitions and postulates in the demonstrations of his *Ethica more geometrico demonstrata.* A comparison with Spinoza is not out of order.[18] Although Vico rejects Spinoza's determinism, he proudly quotes in the *Vita* a letter from Jean Le Clerc opining that the *Diritto* "is composed on a strict mathematical method."[19] Both the *Ethics* and the *De uno* begin with demonstrations *de Deo,* and both insist that there is nothing outside of God. The *Notae* to the *De uno* explicitly aver that "God is the first truth both in being (as they say) and in knowing," from which it follows that "the first metaphysical truth and the first logical truth are one and the same."[20] The *Scienza nuova*'s principle that *l'ordine dell'idee dee procedere secondo l'ordine delle cose* is an adaptation of Spinoza's axiom that *ordo et connexio rerum idem est ordo et connexio idearum.*[21] One can discern the workings of this principle not only in the *Scienza nuova,* but also in the *De uno,* whose expository order is meant to correspond to the logical order among concepts.

Comparisons to Leibniz are also relevant. In the *New Essays on Human Understanding,* Leibniz emphasizes the importance of the distinction between occasions and causes, holds for the existence of innate practical principles, and asserts the demonstrability of jurisprudence.[22] Vico, who regards Leibniz as one of the greatest geniuses of the age, maintains all three doctrines in his own manner.[23] He thinks that his truths are fully demonstrable, employs the distinction between occasions and causes at key points, and argues that the human mind contains *communes aeterni veri notiones* or *aeterni veri semina*. Lilla, despite his tendency to use Vico's anti-secularism (which he correctly emphasizes) as evidence for his status as an "anti-modern" (a dubious inference), rightly concludes that the *Diritto* means "to prove by modern means and in a modern vocabulary that God still watches over man."[24] Donald Kelley emphasizes the importance of juridical antecedents and goes so far as to hold that the *Diritto* "began by rejecting the natural-science model of thought."[25] Yet he also finds a parallel between Newton's *Principia* and Vico's description of his own treatise as a "principia of legal science" (*legitimae scientiae principiae*).[26]

Another aspect of the *Diritto*'s modernity is its commitment to the encyclopaedic ideal. The ideal is an ancient one, but Vico seems to take its modern renditions as exemplary. In the *Vita*, Vico praises his two modern authors for their encyclopaedic ambitions, even if he thinks that neither Bacon nor Grotius are fully successful in realizing them. Bacon provides a blueprint for the advancement of learning in all disciplines, but fails to be comprehensive in juridical matters: "as far as laws are concerned he does not succeed with his canons in compassing the universe of cities and the course of all times, or the extent of all nations."[27] Grotius takes a step further; he "embraces in a system of universal law the whole of philosophy and philology," although he does not put the two in their proper relationship.[28] By writing the *Diritto*, Vico hopes to succeed where Bacon and Grotius fail. He tries to "begin, to set out, and to complete a true encyclopaedia, that is, a mode of learning which is truly comprehensive, truly universal, and truly without offense—to which jurisprudence corresponds, as Ulpian defines it and the erudite agree."[29] It is not that Vico anticipates the secularized French notion of encyclopaedia; his "science of things human and divine" maintains contact with its ancient roots.[30] But he does seem to share the modern desire to construct a demonstrative science that is capable of comprehending its objects within a "system." This holds even if it is true (as Giuseppe Mazzotta persuasively argues) that his treatment of revelation limits his encyclopaedism to the extent that its construes the Bible as a divine text which cannot be subsumed within the human text.[31]

In certain respects, the *Diritto* attempts to defend an ancient and medieval view of natural law against modern dismissals. It is accurate to stress the "traditional" character of Vico's conclusions.[32] We will in due course note their important affinities with Augustine's *De civitate Dei*. But would Augustine approve of the particular strategy employed by Vico to reach those conclusions? Vico's willingness to embrace distinctively modern notions of intelligibility and system, as well as his relative confidence in the ability of human reason to decipher the historical process, sets him apart from Augustine.[33] This will ensure that Vico does not merely reproduce whatever notion of history can be found in Augustine. We will find him to articulate a doctrine of *modern* historical consciousness, a doctrine that will lead to the genealogy of the *Scienza nuova*.

Justice and Equity

Is justice a part of virtue, or is it the same as virtue? Vico begins his consideration *de iustitia* with this Platonic and Aristotelian question.[1] His answer is that "the force of truth (*vis veri*), or human reason, is virtue insofar as it fights self-love (*cupiditas*); the same virtue is justice insofar as it directs and equalizes utilities."[2] The internal connection between virtue and justice, Vico declares, is the "one principle and one end of universal law."[3] If justice is rooted in moral virtue, it may be regarded as natural.

But how can the natural, non-arbitrary character of justice be demonstrated against the skeptics who deny the existence of a conception of virtue that is not reducible to Machiavellian *virtù?* How can it be shown that "right is in nature" (*ius esse in natura*)?[4] Vico begins in a manner that seems far removed from anything resembling an historical approach to justice. Justice is a "common rule or measure" of bodies.[5] It is right proportion among things corporeal, a type of "eternal equality among fluctuating utilities" not itself reducible to body.[6] Vico follows Aristotle in recognizing two types of justice, commutative and distributive, and grounds these in the two types of mathematical proportion, arithmetic and geometric. To support the analogy between mathematical and legal proportion, Vico argues for a strong parallel between mathematical *aequalitas* and legal *aequitas*. Both types of equality are "most plainly demonstrated": as a sound mathematical method obtains geometrical proofs, so human beings "demonstrate" through actions what is just or unjust in a particular instance. Assent in theory and practice is "one in kind."[7] What generates the appearance of a difference between the two cases is the ability of the passions to distract the soul from perceiving the equitable. "When a man does not agree to perform a duty, he is overwhelmed by some disturbance of the soul (*perturbatio animi*) and fails to discern what is to be done. But once the disturbance is calmed and the soul recovered, the man repents acting badly. This does not happen in geometrical matters, for example, since in lines there are no desires or affections by which humans could be disturbed. For this reason the kind of assent in the practical life seems to differ from that in the theoretical life."[8] When the virtues of prudence, temperance, and fortitude are performing their function of fighting self-love, the discernment of justice in itself is no more problematic than the perception of numerical proportion. "What is equal when you measure it, is just when you choose it."[9]

This type of argument seems at best to establish the ideal existence of justice. But how can such justice have anything to do with human beings in whom the virtues operate imperfectly or not at all? If the moderation of *cupiditas* is the condition of equitable distribution of advantages, and if this condition is not satisfied in human beings who tend to be motivated by self-love, where does justice appear in human life? Vico takes this question seriously; like Hobbes and Pascal, he does not underestimate the extent to which humans are driven by vanity. To support the claim that *ius esse in natura,* Vico must argue that, despite his *cupiditas,* man is naturally social. In the *Scienza nuova,* Vico will take the claims "right is nature" and "man is naturally social" to amount to the same thing. If he can demonstrate the natural sociability of man, then he will have resolved "the great dispute."[10] Vico begins by arguing that, although humanity is fallen, it possesses certain "affections" that manifest themselves in facial expressions, which are the beginnnings of "expressive language."[11] To recognize distress in the face of the other, and to acknowledge this pain with a corresponding alteration in one's own countenance, is a tendency natural to human beings: "Man differs from animate brutes not only by reason and language, but also by his countenance."[12] The Fall did not obliterate this disposition. Even if it remains true that humans are primarily motivated by self-love, they also possess and exercise the ability to empathize with others through smiling and laughing. From the reality of commiseration, Vico infers that prior to any calculation of self-interest, "man will bring help to men."[13] Hence society is natural to human beings, made possible by the "sharing of advantages," which itself is grounded in expressive language.[14]

Here one can perceive the entry of historical consciousness into Vico's thinking about justice. The question "Is right in nature?" becomes a question about natural sociability, which in turn is resolved into a historical inquiry about the true nature of primitive humanity. Insight into the true nature of humanity, so crucial for refuting skeptical reductions of justice to power, cannot be answered independently of an account of its true origins. Vico expresses his principle that the *natura di cose altro non è che nascimento di esse in certi tempi e con certe guise* most dramatically in the *Scienza nuova,* but the axiom is implicit in the *De uno*—as when he speaks of the "ordo nascendi seu natura" of the three modes of the law (*dominium, libertas, tutela*), or when he seeks to narrate the "ordo nascendi sive natura" of "pure republics." Along with the concern to understand human origins comes the demand to exhibit the development of justice in history. Vico wants to show not only that humans *were* just, in some sense of the term, but also that they *are* just. As humans evolve from living in societies ruled by custom to nations governed by law, they come to possess an increasingly adequate concept of justice, as encoded in both the natural and civil law. Vico attempts to show this in narrating the historical expansion of the *aequum bonum.* Like natural sociability, equity in its primitive form is as old as humanity itself. It is, Vico says, the *fons* of the *ius naturale.* Its presence can be traced back to the first societies, in which goods were distributed not in a purely arbitrary fashion, but always in accord with some apprehension of the good. [15] Such an apprehension, while parochial, primitive, and distorted by the domination of *voluntas* over *ratio,* is nevertheless a genuine participation in equity, since Vico finds an aristocratic magnanimity in the strength of the first humans.

Vico's thinking about justice revolves around three axes: (1) its eternal, transcendental nature; (2) its presence at the origins of human society; (3) its manifestation in the ongoing development of the *aequum bonum.* If our conception of justice, to the extent that it possesses content, is dependent upon historical development, then how can Vico claim to refute the skeptic's contention that justice is not eternal but mutable, dependent upon and reducible to the accidents of time and place? The *De uno* faces this question in the chapter entitled "*utilitas* is the occasion, *honestas* is the cause of *ius* and human society."[16] Historical occasions are not the cause or sufficient reason of the idea of justice: "flux cannot generate the eternal, as bodies cannot generate anything above body."[17] Hence justice cannot be reduced to what promotes the advantage or interest of particular individuals; *utilitas* is neither the first nor final cause of justice. It is, however, the occasion that arouses the "will to justice." Through the pursuit of their own advantage, "men, naturally social and divided, weak and needy from original sin, are brought to cultivate society, that is, to celebrate their social nature."[18] Vico concludes that "as the body is not the cause but the occasion by which the idea of truth is aroused in the mind of men, so *utilitas* of the body is not the cause but the occasion by which the will to justice is aroused in the soul."[19]

Vico's use of the distinction between "cause" and "occasion" protects him from the reduction of justice to the sheerly conventional. It does so, however, by elevating instances that might strike others as mere historical accident to the rank of philosophically significant "occasions" on which human knowledge of justice depends. If Vico is to make this high valuation of occasion and custom plausible, he must construct an historical narrative that depicts the expansion of the *aequum bonum* in time, while maintaining its eternity. In the *De uno*, Vico refers to this process as the "cycle" of universal right. Before he narrates the cycle, he prepares the reader to accept an historicized concept of justice by inscribing within his encyclopaedia a fusion of "timeless" and "historicist" discourses. Thus Vico speaks both of the "society of truth" that pursues *veritas* for its own sake, in accordance with *honestas,* and the "society of equity" that is governed more directly by *utilitas*—only to assert their unity in practice.[20] He emphasizes the customary, affective origins of social order in the sections on *cognatio,* drawing a contrast with the effort to understand society through *cognitio,* obtained from the principles of "deep philosophy."[21] Both, however, will turn out to be identical to the common notions of eternal truth, the genera, which are both "from God" and "in us."[22] The "divine origin" of both the society of truth and the society of equity will ensure that "each is contained in the other."[23] The form of Vico's texts will mirror the substance of his central contention that ideal/natural and historical/conventional elements of humanity cannot be separated in practice, even if they can be distinguished in theory.

Our understanding of the historical dimension of Vico's treatment of justice may be deepened by attending to the *De uno*'s treatment of the categories of distributive and commutative justice. In chapter 64 of *De uno,* after having defended distributive justice against Grotius's critique of the Aristotelian notion, Vico proceeds to undermine any strong dichotomy between distributive and commutative justice: "iustitia rectrix in aequatrice, in rectrice inest aequatrix."[24] Distributive and commutative justice should be distinguished in theory, since the Grotian denial of the former tends to "proceduralize" justice without due regard for a substantive conception of the good, the *aequum bonum.* But in practice, Vico holds, the two go together. Public rulers are always forced to take account of private inequalities (if only to preserve their own power) and thus respect the imperative of commutative justice.[25] Conversely, justice among citizens is never exclusively a private affair, but always derives from a publicly proclaimed conception of equitable right that binds citizens in a common allegiance.[26] This implies for Vico that the proportions determined by distributive justice, far from being immune to historical development, are in fact dependent upon it, as subjects challenge the proportions decreed by the civil power in the name of equity. As Milbank observes, "the equitable involvement of distributive with corrective justice means that the latter is able to call the distributive foundations in question in the daily practice of 'private' justice. Hence all the changes in civil equity are prompted by protests on behalf of natural equity."[27] This is anticipated in the chapter on law in the *De ratione,* where Vico first charts the transition from societies based on civil equity to those dominated by the ideal of natural equity, and notes the advantages and disadvantages of each. In holding that humans approach ideal justice, *honestas,* through the tortuous paths of historical occasion, marked by conflict and *utilitas,* Vico makes human apprehension of the substantive *aequum bonum* essentially historical, even as it is regulated by an eternal, providential norm ("architectonic justice") that escapes full understanding.

If the foregoing interpretation is correct, the conception of justice articulated in the chapters on the "origin" of *diritto universale* (*De uno,* chapters 1–86) is incipiently historical. Vico describes these chapters as having described the "universal commonwealth" in a "metaphysical manner." To complete the description, Vico will need to give a more "empirical" rendering of the movement toward the *aequum bonum* that occurs in time. Hence he turns to the "cycle" of universal right, which purports to confirm "by means of the testimony of philology" what has "already been examined by philosophy." In Vico's sense of the term, "philosophy" requires "philology" for its completion; "demonstration" becomes historical narration. Rather than take this conception of philosophy for granted, one might be startled by its articulation in a "Platonic" treatise on universal law. History has been elevated from *res gestae* to the process through which human reason glimpses "one truth, one eternal reason, which dictates truth; one true good; one eternal choice, which commands it; one eternal justice, one God."[28]

EIGHT

Natural Law

In accordance with his initially "metaphysical" approach, Vico treats natural law by deriving it from its origin in virtue. "From the three parts of virtue," Vico declares in the *Sinopsi del diritto universale*, "are born three *ius* or *ragioni*: dominion, liberty, and protection" (*dominio, libertà, tutela*).[1] The corresponding chapter in the *De uno* speaks of the "genesis" of *dominium, libertas,* and *tutela* from the virtues. Dominion arises from the "prudent disposition of utilities, that is, a disposition made (*facta*) according to reason instead of cupidity or persuasion." Liberty arises from "the temperate use of utilities," or (as the *Sinopsi* puts it) "moderate choice in matters involving one's self and one's things."[2] Protection arises from the deployment of force in accordance with the virtue of fortitude, which Vico understands as the virtue of "forza moderata."[3] Both the virtues and the *iura* conform to the *De antiquissima's* notion of genera, in that both are generated from an origin, while having the power to generate offspring of their own. As the "three parts of justice," dominion, liberty, and protection constitute "the three sources of all the republics and the laws." Natural law is the *fons* of positive law.

Throughout the *De uno*, Vico calls attention to the trinitarian character of the natural law. As the virtues are mutually *complicata*, folded within one another, so are the three elements of the natural law. Both the virtues and the natural law can be traced back to the divine Trinity—the conception of God as infinite knowledge, will, and power (*nosse, velle, posse*) that Vico attributes (inaccurately) to the *Confessions*—and its human image as "finite *nosse, velle, posse* that tends to the infinite."[4] In its origin, the three parts of the *ius naturale* do not make up an idealized legal code, but constitute the transcendental elements of law itself. As Milbank writes, they are the "authoritative relations" that are "the three categories of possibility of law."[5] Their ideal status notwithstanding, Vico uses the language of becoming, of "genesis," in the initial description of dominion, liberty, and protection. In the first instance, Vico is speaking not of actual historical change, but of an atemporal emanation that generates a conceptual hierarchy. The exposition has the effect of stressing that *ius* is rooted in both virtue (*prudentia, temperantia, fortitudo*) and the metaphysical triad *nosse, velle,* and *posse.* The practical consequence is that dominion cannot be unbridled ownership, because it is regulated by knowledge (*nosse*) and prudence. Liberty is subject to will (*velle*) as informed by temperance, and protection is ideally governed by fortitude, itself derived from metaphysical potency (*posse*).

Vico abruptly switches to another depiction of dominion, liberty, and protection, proceeding from the side of "voluntary *ius.*" Dominion is the "*ius* of disposing things as you wish; liberty is the *ius* of living as you wish; protection is the *ius* of protecting yourself and your things, as you wish."[6] Taken by itself, this picture of the *iura* suggests that dominion, liberty, and protection are to be understood as "active rights," the exercise of which is a matter of the will, independent of reason.[7] But Vico introduces the gap only to close it, by pointing to the "one *fons* of necessary *ius.*"[8] To exist at all, the voluntary rights must be governed by *ratio,* or the noncorporeal standards of equity and *honestas.* In the absence of regulation by intelligence, rights lose their essential character. "For the greedy or luxurious are by nature slaves, not masters (*domini*); the immoderately free or licentious are by nature servants, not freemen; those secure by unjust means are not strong by nature, but violent and fearful."[9]

But is this "Platonic" strategy, designed to overcome the opposition between necessary and voluntary *ius,* finally satisfactory? Vico attempts to bridge the gap between the ideal and the real by turning to the genesis of actual rights. In the chapter on the "order of the birth or nature (*nascendi seu natura*) of dominion, liberty, and protection," Vico proclaims that the three rights are "inborn in man and born through occasions."[10] As part of the "immutable" natural law (*ius naturale immutabile*), the *ius* of liberty is eternal and existed before wars. But liberty was not "known and named" until nations began to wage war.[11] Prior to the introduction of wartime captivity and the enslavement of human beings, the right of liberty did not exist for human beings. Similarly, there was no human right of dominion before the first "division of the fields." Yet this does not imply that the *ius* of *dominium* is simply an arbitrary production. Vico finds Roman jurisprudence to appreciate both the eternal and historical character of right, and sees in its language an awareness that particular *dominia* are not "introduced but 'distinguished'" (*non intro-ducta, sed "distincta"*) by the first divisions.[12] Self-defense perhaps comes closest to a purely innate right, awareness of which is least dependent on historical circumstance. The right of self-preservation (*tutela sui*) exists "from the moment of birth." But *tutela* also has a temporal component, since it is acquired through the "judgment and authority of the senses."[13]

This understanding of rights as both eternal and temporal is a development of the conceptual framework articulated in *De antiquissima.* As elemental genera or divine archetypes, the ideal *iura* are both "from God" and "in us," not of our own making. Yet human knowledge of these elements relies on circumstance and occasion; it is a matter of historical construction. To be sure, humans are not the sole construc-tors of these rights; they cannot be, since *ius* is ultimately necessary and eternal. But voluntary *iura* are artifacts that participate in the *fons unus* of necessary *ius,* as the human *factum* participates in the divine *verum.* The *aequum bonum* is eternal, yet known to human beings only in time, through the creation of voluntary rights that aspire to equity. In the legal context, the "division of the fields" and "distribution of utilities" is par-allel to the "dissection of the whole" and the "composition of elements" in the *De antiquissima.* The content of the *aequum bonum* and the *ius naturale* comes to be known only through the (re)creation of elements and active disposition of utilities. This idea, basic to the structure of the *Diritto universale,* is a reworking of the dialectical relationship between construction and contemplation as expressed by *verum-factum.*

The point that Vico emphasizes about the historical character of *ius* is the "order" in which it evolves. A first glimpse of the *ordo* is provided in the case of the developing human being. Protection, as we have seen, is the *ius* "most intense" (*acerrimos*) in young children.[14] Adolescents exhibit the most concern with liberty, "which is conspicuous in adoles-cence and is often agitated by the soul's affections."[15] Liberty without restraint, like *voluntas* without *ratio,* gives rise to the "rule of cupidity" (*regnum cupiditati*).[16] After adolescence comes the mature rule of reason. "At last, at the age when cognition has unfolded, reason (*ratio*) is con-firmed in man." Once reason is acquired, it "moderates the protection of the senses (*tutela sensuum*) and the liberty of the affections (*affec-tuum libertas*), as if it were the ruler (*domina*)."[17] The end result is the supremacy of *dominium,* informed by *ratio* and accomplished by a pro-gression from *posse* and *velle* to *nosse,* from *fortitudo* and *temperantia* to *prudentia.*

An analogous passage from the moment of sheer force to the dominance of reason occurs on the historical scale, or so holds a conjecture fundamental to both the *Diritto universale* and the "ideal eternal history" of the *Scienza nuova*. Here Vico returns to the vocabulary of the tradition of the *ius naturale*. The *ius naturale prius* is identified with the "tutelage of the senses and the liberty of the affections," which Vico associates with the "first things of nature" (*prima naturae*) of the Stoics.[18] The *ius naturale posterius* is identified with the "*dominium* of reason, the equilibrium of the affections [genuine *libertas*], and the *tutela* of deliberation." These are the "consequent things of nature" (*naturae consequentia*) of the Stoics.[19]

After introducing the distinction between the *ius naturale prius* and the *ius naturale posterius*, Vico reviews his trinitarian theology, this time using the Augustinian triad *esse, nosse, velle* rather than the Campanellan triad *posse, nosse, velle* which he had erroneously attributed to Augustine in the second chapter of the *De uno*.[20] The effect is to identify the first element of humanity as either *esse* or *posse*, existence or potency, that aspires to the actuality of *nosse*, knowing. The middle term that links *esse* and *nosse* is *velle*. Through the exercise of the will, mediated by grace, humans can transcend "bare existence" and attain their contemplative *finis*. The gifts of divine *potentia, sapientia*, and *bonitas* endow the creature with "two parts of *ius naturale*: one, by which man wills his own being (*esse*); the other, by which man wills his own knowing (*nosse*)."[21] In small compass, then, Vico has distinguished between an initial state (*posse/esse, fortitudo, tutela, prima naturae, ius naturale prius*), a final state (*nosse, prudentia, dominium, consequentia naturae, ius naturale posterius*), and a transition. The transition from the *ius gentium* to the *ius naturale* is dominated by the *ius voluntarium* or *ius civile*.[22] The road from *esse*, "the first part of the *ius naturale*," to *nosse*, the "second part of the *ius naturale*" must pass through *velle*, which corresponds to the ideal *ius* of liberty. The role of *libertas* in Vico's thought is vital, precisely because he conceives liberty as ordered to something beyond itself. This historicization of natural law, accompanied by a teleology, is meant to oppose the Grotian partition of the "customary" *ius gentium* and the "rational" *ius naturale*. Vico uses roughly the same categories as Grotius, but views them as moments of a process rather than separating them into discrete parts.[23]

The *ius naturale prius*, then, is described as "the life of man in common with brutes."[24] This recalls the initial priority of self-preservation (*tutela sui*), although Vico now expands the category to include protection of the race. Even in primitive humanity, as we have seen, a social component exists, although the stress is on individual *utilitas*. The struggle to acquire useful things (*utilia*) and to avoid harmful things (*noxia*) generates the primary law of this stage: "man repels force by force" (*vim vi propulset*).[25] (Vico will later speak more fully of the *ius violentiae*.)[26] Nonetheless, the *prima naturae* include not only self-preservation, but also the procreation and education of children.[27] The life that humans share with brutes is not simply brutish; it includes aspects of the *conatus* toward truth and reason (here Vico explicitly cites the *De antiquissima*) that is denied to other animals.[28] The "seeds of truth" are present in humanity from its origins, despite the fact that primal *esse* is driven by *utilitas* more than *honestas*.[29]

Social life is more fully realized in the "life proper to humans," associated with the *ius naturale posterius*, "by which man wills his own knowing" and which is "nothing other than knowing" (*nosse*).[30] In the properly human life, social and intellectual goods are mutually implicated. Citing an example from Terence of paternal indifference and filial distrust, Vico concludes that father and son "live neither according to truth and reason, nor socially."[31] The superiority of the properly human life implies that "the second part of the natural law dominates the first."[32] Thus Pompey was able to resist the "natural" impulse to save his own life in favor of an equally natural impulse toward heroic action, and told his storm-fearing men that "to sail is necessary, to live is not."[33] The principles of the *consequentia naturae* are condensed in maxims, for example, "to act rightly is necessary, to live is not."[34] When the distinctively human mode of life is fully realized, *nosse* prevails over bare *esse*, and rational dominion perfects the rights of liberty and protection. "As we are endowed by divine power with bodily force (*vi corporis*) for the protection (*ad tuendam*) of this brute life, so for the protection (*ad tuendam*) of our rational life we are endowed by divine wisdom with the *vis veri*, from which virtue exists and is named, as we have seen above."[35] The later prevalence of *dominium* implies not the annihilation but the fulfillment of *tutela* and *libertas*.

Vico has outlined the initial and terminal stages of a process. A fuller description of the transition from *esse* to *nosse* is required. In the *Sinopsi*, and in the *De uno* 77, Vico deploys the Aristotelian vocabulary of "matter" and "form." The *ius naturale prius* is the "matter" of voluntary *ius*; the *ius naturale posterius* is the "form."[36] As a substrate, the *ius naturale prius* is logically compatible with all the particular instantiations of *dominium*, *libertas*, and *tutela*. It is relatively permissive, licensing anything that is compatible with the basic goal of self-preservation. In this respect, it is virtually equivalent to the *ius gentium*. Vico does not hold that the *ius naturale prius* is entirely vacuous, but suggests that its indeterminacy renders it open to any number of particularizations by voluntary or civil law. As defined by Ulpian (whom Vico quotes), the *ius civile* "neither departs entirely from the *ius naturale* or *ius gentium*, nor follows it in everything, but partly adds and partly subtracts from it."[37] The *ius naturale prius*, then, supplies material or "topical" possibilities;[38] the *ius civile* selects and adapts the material in accordance with particular purposes, purposes that serve the immediate interests of the ruling class while opening new horizons of equity, often despite the motives of the legislators.

If the *ius naturale prius* is the matter of voluntary *ius*, then it would seem legitimate to consider voluntary *ius* as the form of the *ius naturale prius*. Vico tends, however, to consider the *ius civile* as an extension of the *ius gentium*, as a type of matter that itself awaits formation by the *ius naturale posterius*.[39] As civil law limits the possibilities of the *ius naturale prius*, the *ius naturale posterius* "informs" voluntary law by placing it in conformity with eternal *ratio*. This lends it a restrictive character, which will ultimately culminate in the Christian prohibitions against vengeance and unchastity, unknown to the *ius gentium*.[40] Vico contrasts it with the *ius naturale prius* by declaring that it "does not permit, but either forbids or prescribes."[41] It is able to shape the matter given to it by the *ius naturale posterius* and to declare that some things, licit by the standards of the *ius gentium*, are unfitting for fully rational nature. Despite the contrast, both the *ius naturale prius* and the *ius naturale posterius* are said to be "immutable." The *ius naturale posterius* is immutable because it "gives just measures to liberty, dominion, and tutelage, and confers on them the eternal form of the just."[42] The immutability of the *ius naturale prius* is more difficult to understand. As Milbank comments, the *ius gentium* "clearly includes much that is far from 'immutable.'"[43] What Vico seems to have in mind is a set of rights whose natural participation in the *aequum bonum* renders them unable to be abolished by positive law. Thus Vico says that "from the *ius naturale posterius* the *ius naturale prius* is immutable, because what is licit by nature can be forbidden by law, but law cannot bring about what is by nature not licit."[44] For example, as Vico says in the *Sinopsi*, the law may prohibit a man from defending himself in a particular case, but legislative fiat cannot make self-defense itself contrary to nature.[45] The *prima naturae*, which Vico associates with the preservation of one's own *esse*, are "immutable" because they participate in, or are "informed by," the *consequentia naturae*.

It may seem, then, that Vico's appropriation of hylomorphic language is merely another way to say that human law participates in eternal law. But Vico is doing more than that. Against Grotius and others who separate the "natural *ius* of the philosophers" from the *ius gentium,* Vico stresses the continuity between the customs that harden into civil law, on the one hand, and the natural law on the other. The *ius civile* constitutes the link between the exigencies of first nature and the contemplative goods associated with final nature, the "divine life of man." At its highest point, civil law begins to approach the natural law, developing into what Vico, appropriating Gaius, calls "the natural right of the nations" (*ius naturale gentium*).[46] "Through the common customs of the race (*communibus moribus*), the right that has been unfolded (*explicatum*) is the natural right of the jurisconsults (*ius naturale iurisconsultum*), which is much different from the natural right of the philosophers (*ius naturale philosophorum*)."[47] The natural right of the philosophers takes itself to be purely rational, demonstrable *a priori;* the natural right of the jurisconsults emerges from the historical process. Guided by divine providence, operating within history as dictated by the things themselves (*rebus ipsis dictantibus*), "the common right of the peoples or nations approaches more nearly the *ius naturale.*"[48]

It is important to see that in contrasting the *ius naturale gentium* with the *ius naturale philosophorum,* Vico is not advocating an anti-philosophical approach to natural law. He is attacking the school of modern natural law, not philosophy as such. Since he thinks that his own science, which he will later call a "jurisprudence of the human race" (not at all unconsciously, *pace* Fassò), is capable of discovering the providential unfolding of natural right within the historical process, Vico cannot have thought that he was abandoning philosophy.[49] On the contrary, he views his new conception of jurisprudence as the consummation of philosophy. It blends philosophy and philology in such a way that it is both more demonstrative and more firmly anchored in history than that of Grotius. In doing so, he fulfills his desire, recorded in the *Vita,* to unite the "general maxims of justice" that he associates with medieval interpeters with the attention to verbal detail characteristic of the "humanist interpreters, whom he later perceived and considered to be pure historians of the Roman civil law."[50] But how is such a synthesis of the universal and the particular possible? Vico considers this question in the final sections on the "origin" of *diritto universale,* which make the argument that "the certain is part of the true" (*certum est pars veri*) and "authority a part of reason" (*auctoritas pars rationis*).

Verum-Certum

If the historical process is what closes the gap between the ideal and the real, the eternal and the voluntary, how does this occur? How can the universal *verum* of metaphysics and philosophy be related to the particular *certum* of history and philosophy? The two appear as irremediably opposed. *Verum* is the "perpetual and proper attribute of necessary *ius*," corresponding to eternal right.[1] *Certum* is the "perpetual and proper attribute of voluntary *ius*," corresponding to human might. "The law is harsh, but it is written," Vico quotes Ulpian.[2] To bring *certum* and *verum*, or might and right, into a harmonious relation seems impossible, as Pascal reminds us:

> Right without might is helpless, might without right is tyrannical. Right without might is challenged, because there are always evil men about. Might without right is denounced. We must therefore combine right and might, and to that end make right into might or might into right. Right is open to dispute, might is easily recognized and beyond dispute. Therefore right could not be made might because might challenged right, calling itself unjust and itself claiming to be just. Being thus unable to make right into might, we have made might into right.[3]

The wretchedness of the fallen creature ensures for Pascal that the gap between human justice and divine justice will be infinite. Although himself sensitive to the dominant role of *cupiditas* in the postlapsarian state, Vico is unwilling to accept this verdict, which he thinks leads to practical skepticism. He wants to argue that human justice, embodied in the particular *certum*, participates in divine justice, identical with the eternal *verum*. *Iurisprudentia*, as Vico conceives it, is the art of "accommodating *ius* to the facts."[4] It has the essentially practical function of uniting concrete *utilitas* with universal *honestas*. Thus Vico distinguishes between the *ratio legum* and *mens legum*. The *ratio* of the law is "the *conformatio* of the law to the fact"; the *mens* is equivalent to the "will of the legislator."[5] The *ratio* looks to eternal *honestas* and never changes; the *mens legis, seu voluntas legislatoris* looks to shifting *utilitas* and changes as utilities change, while taking its direction from the *ratio*.[6] Like the *sapiens* described in the early writings, the interpreter of the law (the "judge") must be able to negotiate a path through the obliquities and contingencies of practical life, without losing sight of the *finis*. As the social counterpart of individual prudence, *iurisprudentia* must take account of all the relevant facts in the political sphere. Thus Vico says that it embraces both *philosophia* and *historia,* and he praises the Roman jurisconsult for uniting the functions of the philosopher, pragmatic, and orator.[7]

If genuine jurisprudence is possible, it must be the case that, at least on occasion, the judge is able to unite the exigencies of particular situations with the demands of universal reason. As Gadamer writes, "The judge's decision, which has a practical effect on life, aims at being a correct and never an arbitrary application of the law."[8] For Vico, this has the vital consequence that the *certum,* though seemingly far removed from the *verum,* is actually a participation in it: *certum est pars veri.*[9] The *verum* needs the *certum,* if it is to have impact on actual human beings. "Right without might is helpless," because humans respond more reliably to authoritative coercion and rhetorical appeal than to unarmed truth. Legislators rely on the *certum,* "so they may hold with certainty, from the side of authority, the true that they cannot hold by appeal to human shame" (*pudor*).[10] But the *certum* also needs the *verum.* Unless they participate in necessary *ius,* voluntary *iura* "are nothing."[11] Without an element of the *verum,* authority is nothing but tyranny, and *iurisprudentia* an exercise in frustration, unable to construct a genuine mediation between universal and particular. "The certain is from authority, and the true from reason, and authority cannot entirely oppose reason, for then there would be no law, but only monsters of law."[12]

The consequence is that, while authority cannot be identified with reason, "authority is a part of reason."[13] This demands a certain respect for the deliverances of tradition: "reason cannot be given for all of those things which were established by our ancestors," Vico quotes Julian.[14] To demand "natural reason" from authority is foolish. "One should require civil reason from authority, that is common utility, which necessarily subsists to some degree in all laws."[15] As long as authority conforms to civil reason, it cannot altogether oppose eternal truth, since social bonds are ultimately grounded in reason and equity. "Civil reason, since it dictates public utility, is itself a part of natural reason."[16] The product of civil reason is an artifact—it is something humanly "made"—yet it is also a participation in truth. *Verum-certum*, it would appear, is an application or extension of the *verum-factum*.

Nonetheless, the distance between the authoritative *certum* and the rational *verum* must be acknowledged. The laws of civil reason are effective because they are harsh. Although the letter of the law preserves "civil equity," it kills "natural equity." Only its spirit gives life, through acknowledging the legitimacy of exceptions to the established rule. To penetrate the spirit of the law demands an act of interpretation, and Vico in fact identifies the original Roman jurisprudence as a certain "art of interpreting *ius*."[17] It is the tension between the *verum* and *certum* that generates the necessity of jurisprudential interpretation. The practical bent of jurisprudence does not divorce it from truth; any interpretation that aims at equity presupposes a wider scope for reason.[18] This conviction, foreign to legal positivism, is restated by Gadamer in a contemporary idiom. "The judge who adapts the transmitted law to the needs of the present is undoubtedly seeking to perform a practical task, but his interpretation of the law is by no means merely for that reason an arbitrary revision."[19] The *privilegia* decreed by the judge abrogate the *ius civile*, not arbitrarily, but in the name of natural equity. "For *privilegia* are indeed restrictions of civil *ius*, but explications of natural *ius*: for they are not introduced without some merit, so that one person is excepted by equity from the law of the rest and absolved from the laws that bind everyone else."[20]

Natural equity trumps civil equity, and Vico considers that "restrictions of civil *ius* are enlargements of natural *ius* and vice versa," recalling the earlier discovery of a dynamism between distributive and commutative justice.[21] This perspective seems to devalue civil law altogether, and might cause one to wonder why Vico attaches any significance to the *certum* as such. The key is to understand that, for Vico, access to natural equity is not available directly but requires the mediation of the historical *ius civile*. Human beings do not possess the *verum*, but the *certum*, which sets for them particular standards of equity that approximate the *aequum bonum*, even while falling short of it. Only through the emergence of the *certum* (which may be described either in terms of organic growth or artificial fabrication, depending on the case) are humans able to discern approximations of the natural *aequum bonum.* Legal "fictions," while in themselves ontologically null, nonetheless possess genuine value, because they widen our perception of the divine archetypes or genera. "Patrimony, heredity, republics are fictions (*fictiones*), insofar as we represent them as persons; but, as universal reasons, they are the genera of things and, since genera, true in the highest possible degree."[22] The *certum* and its manifestations in *lex* and *auctoritas* are decidedly artificial, but still provide access to the *verum.* Although some commentators find a striking difference between the metaphysics of the *De antiquissima* and the *Diritto universale,* it seems more likely that the *verum-factum* is present in the *De uno*'s conception of the relationship between the *verum* and the *certum.*[23]

Legal interpretation is a privileged vehicle through which equity is revealed in the course of human history. It is not that the process is infallible or immune to ideological corruption. Vico never forgets the distortive role of *cupiditas* in human affairs. His definition of justice implies that, as long as self-love plays a role in the distribution of advantages (*utilitates*), perfect justice will never be seen or achieved. Nonetheless, the interpretation up to this point has portrayed Vico as a fundamentally optimistic thinker who elevates history to the rank of truth-bearing construct, and thus makes historical consciousness a necessary condition of philosophical discernment. In the celebration of Roman jurisprudence's slow but steady progress in apprehending the content of the *aequum bonum* as it unfolds through customs and law, it seems that the subversive, genealogical aspect of Vico has all but disappeared. To rectify this impression, we must now attend more closely to another side of Vico, a side that harbors a deep pessimism about the ultimate ability of the City of Man to sustain itself.

Constantia and Christian Jurisprudence

Vico considers Rome to be the most impressive actualization of equity. It brings together the best of Athens and Sparta, combining a desire for reason and truth with an appreciation of authority and custom. Rome itself is the best evidence for holding that the philosophical *verum* is immanently present in the historical *certum*. This is true despite the fact that Rome is a society founded in pagan virtue, which Vico considers incapable of eliminating self-love. The *De uno* wants to exhibit man's greatness even in his concupiscence. Vico would agree with Pascal that man has "managed to produce such a remarkable system from it and make it the image of true charity."[1]

In many ways, the *Diritto universale* is a profoundly Augustinian treatise. Augustine is the *auctoritas* for Vico's thought on the Trinity, his anthropology of fallen humanity, his contrast between pagan virtue and Christian virtue, his belief in the unity of the virtues, and his commitment to the idea of providence as a *via media* between fate and chance. In reading Deschamps, whom he takes to "show by a geometrical method that the doctrine of St. Augustine is midway between the two extremes of Calvin and Pelagius, and equidistant likewise from the other opinions that approach these two extremes," Vico develops a disposition that enables him to explain the *ius naturale gentium* in a way that is both historically adequate and in agreement "with the sound doctrine of grace in respect of moral philosophy."[2] There can be no denying the considerable Augustinian presence in Vico's texts, early and late.[3]

Although the *Diritto* is not itself a genealogy in the full sense, it provides the materials out of which Vico will construct the genealogy that appears more clearly in the *Scienza nuova*. The chapters of *De uno* on the "cycle" of universal right provide the first clues to the complexity of his stance toward pagan culture. Vico identifies the original *ius gentium* as the law of the ruling groups (*ius gentium maiorum*), adding that in time it will embrace the *ius gentium minorum,* the law of the peoples who come after the foundation of civil societies.[4] The *ius gentium maiorum* is the right of private violence, "by which men without society (*homines exleges*) took things they needed with the power of their own hands (*manu capiebant*), would keep them for their own use, defend them with force, seize them for their own use and possession, and in the same way take them back by their own force when lost."[5] This law arises from the character of the rulers, from their "virtue." Such virtue is born out of "a false devotion to the gods," and is necessarily "imperfect."[6] Despite its origins in falsehood, the *ius violentiae* effectively tames the savage natures of the first human beings. Arising *ex patrum ordine,* it aims at "extinguishing any future use of violence," using force to counter force. The *ius gentium maiorum* is thus "certain but violent" (*certum sed violentum*).[7] Over time the violence of law will be tamed; civil right will become "certain and peaceful" (*certum et pacatum*).[8] But does civil law continue to bear the mark of its origin in the *ius violentiae*? Can pagan *ius* ever succeed in erasing the violence of its original character?

Vico emphasizes the progress in the movement "from the truth of violence" to the "modesty imposed by the true."[9] But in describing the conversion of the *ius privatae violentiae* into various "imitations of violence" (*imitationes violentiae*) that comprise the second form of the *ius gentium* (the *ius gentium minorum*), he implies that the violence lurking underneath the surface of pagan law can never be eliminated.[10] Vico considers the transition not as a movement from a state of violence to a condition of peace, but rather from a state of private violence to a condition of "public violence." Beginning with civil authority, and subject to its regulation, the *ius publicae violentiae* is more predictable and more benevolent than private violence. Its essential character, however, is indicated by its oaths, which are sealed by violence. Vico's conviction that pagan law can never escape its foundation in violence is illuminated by his conception of virtue. As the generative source of *ius,* virtue "exists and is defined" from the *vis veri,* the "force of truth" that fights against the corrupted nature of fallen humanity.[11] It is the form that reason assumes in fallen man: "human reason embraced by the will is virtue insofar as it fights cupidity."[12] Although this notion of virtue has some application to pagans and Christians alike, Vico notes an important contrast. Whereas pagan virtue restrains the affections without eliminating their parent, *ferocitas,* Christian virtue is the *vis veri* that "fights against cupidity and its parent, *philautia.*" Only such virtue can enable humans to convert *amor sui* into *contemptus sui,* Vico declares, echoing Augustine. This conversion requires "humility, the basis of all Christian virtue."[13] The *Sinopsi del diritto universale* describes humility as "the basis of moral virtue, and charity as its form, whose author and end is God."[14] Only virtue grounded in humility can replace *cupiditas* with *caritas.* Such virtue cannot be acquired through human action, but must come from above. It can be had only through divine grace, which alone guarantees true virtue.[15] Lacking grace, pagan virtue and the laws it generates can only mitigate the effects of an original violence. Since it is rooted in self-love, it cannot eliminate their cause.

Even in its most developed phase, pagan culture is governed by concealed violence. Is there an alternative to this state of affairs? Near the end of *De uno,* Vico writes that the "*ius naturale* was first born from the just law of—let me say it—libido and just violence, whence it became veiled under certain fables of legal violence, and then finally becomes manifest in open rationality and generous truth."[16] But can rationality become "open" and truth become "generous" as long as *cupiditas* retains the upper hand over *caritas*? Another mode of practice is needed. From the Roman *ius optimum* and its derivatives, "the fables of right and the unconcealed truth of nature would go forth into the practices of the Christian religion."[17] As impressive as they are, the reflections of the Roman jurists must be supplanted by a *iurisprudentia nova,* written by one who understands that "he who is wise, if he is to be constant in all things, must be Christian." The internal connection between jurisprudential wisdom and Christian piety, Vico says, "will constitute the continual argument of Book Two," namely the *De constantia iurisprudentis.*[18]

In line with the expectation generated by the conclusion of the *De uno,* the first part of *De constantia* expands the Augustinian argument about the difference between pagan and Christian virtue. Here Vico systematically connects the limitations of pagan virtue with false views of the ultimate end. In the section *de Christianae moralis veritate,* Vico declares that pagan views of the ultimate end are deficient because they result from a "false persuasion about human misery."[19] Vico stops short of an outright rejection of pagan ethics, however, characterizing its positions as ingenious conjectures, some of which approach the truth. His goal is to provide a critique of pagan thought in its Platonic, Stoic, Epicurean, and Aristotelian modes that preserves what is true in each.

Affirming several "dogmata" of Plato, Vico agrees that philosophy is a "meditation on death" (*meditatio mortis*) that tames *cupiditas* so that we might live according to truth and reason.[20] "Its end, its principal and highest fruit, is the union of mind with God."[21] Philosophy is inherently teleological, even as its own grasp of the telos is strictly limited. Vico credits Plato with distinguishing three types of lives: the "divine life of man" that contemplates eternal truth, the "human life" that participates in eternal truth through praxis, and the "brute life," where action is motivated by the falsehood of the senses.[22] The proper objective of humanity is to avoid brutish existence and to live according to *honestas*.[23] Although Vico will elsewhere criticize Plato for his ignorance of the Fall,[24] he does not judge any direct modification of Plato to be necessary here.

Vico proceeds to affirm three dogmata inherited from the Stoics. He accepts the ethical trichotomy of "good things, bad things, and indifferent things" (*bona, mala, indifferentia*) and endorses the equation of "living according to nature" and "following God."[25] Then he suggests an equivalence between the interpretation of antique *ius* and the moral principles of the Stoics.[26] The *indifferentia* are the "first things of nature" (*prima naturae*), which the *De uno* identifies as the cultural "matter" of the first natural law (*ius naturale prius*), to be given "form" by the consequent natural law (*ius naturale posterius*).[27] Vico identifies the *ius naturale posterius* with both the *consequentia naturae* and "natural reason."[28] Thus Vico grants that Stoic philosophy expresses the substance of natural reason and admires the Stoics for their moral seriousness. Their vanity, however, must be criticized. The Stoic *apatheia*, the "annihilation of the passions," is a "vain desire," born out of a desire to escape human fragility, and yet rendered impracticable by it.[29] Its ideal of the *sapiens* embodies a *falsa persuasio* about the true human end.

Vico continues in critical mode with the chapter on Epicurus. Here "lapses in moral doctrine" are identified, with no corresponding affirmation of dogmata.[30] The materialist ethics of Epicurus is self-refuting, Vico argues, because it has no place for its most important component. It cannot account for the moderation exercised by the *sapiens,* who chooses the pleasures that bring the least sorrow, and the sorrows that bring the most pleasure.[31] Vico eliminates in turn each of the possible homes for moderate choice in a strictly materialist ontology. The *delectus* or *modus* of bodies is not itself a body. Nor is it the void, the *inane seu nihil*. It cannot be a mode of the void, because *nihil* by definition has no attributes. Finally, it cannot be a mode of body, because this would imply that bodily things and those whose knowledge derives exclusively from bodies are wise.[32] The affirmation of the "most beautiful rule of custom" that enjoins the *sapiens* to seek moderate pleasures is incompatible with a materialist ontology.[33] Thus "Epicurus is refuted by Epicurus."[34] Even so, Epicurus also exhibits a measure of *constantia* that is characteristic of all philosophy; he combines a "crooked position" with a "straight method."[35] If one accepts the hypothesis that there is nothing in nature but body and the void, it makes perfect sense to define happiness as bodily pleasure. But no compulsion to accept the hypothesis exists, even when considered apart from its ethical consequences. Later in the *De constantia* Vico will allude to the fourth chapter of the *De antiquissima,* which contains an extended argument for the view that motion of material bodies requires an immaterial rule.[36]

In his consideration of Plato, the Stoics, and the Epicureans, Vico directly affirms some dogmata, while transposing them into a Christian teleology, and directly rejects some others, while striving to account for their attraction. Aristotle presents a more difficult case. Neither direct affirmation nor rejection seems adequate. Thus the title of the next chapter: "The dogma of Aristotle on ends corrected."[37] Vico begins by declaring that Aristotle confutes himself with a "golden passage" in his *Ethics* that affirms the superior happiness of the contemplative life.[38] Vico identifies several formal characteristics of ideal happiness, which he regards as common to Plato and Aristotle.[39] Ideal happiness is principally said of the interior man; it is identical with complete peace; it is enduring and always present; it requires the body only minimally; it unites man with God. It is doubtful that all of these criteria can be found in Aristotle, unless we have in mind a heavily Platonized Aristotle. But the essence of Vico's "correction" does not depend on the particular list of criteria. Aristotle's mistake is to divide theory and practice by establishing the practical life, "operation according to virtue" (*operatio cum virtute*), as "a separate end" (*alium finem*).[40] Unlike contemplation, this end is laborious; it requires bodily goods and luck. By Aristotle's own criteria, it cannot be the end of human endeavor, but only a means. In divorcing theory and practice by positing the latter as its own end, Aristotle obscures the strictly instrumental relationship of human activity to contemplation of the divine. Vico detects a tension internal to the *Nicomachean Ethics* and exploits it by suggesting that *operatio cum virtute* must be inscribed in a new teleology.

The "correction" of the Aristotelian dogma, then, is a rigorous insistence on the instrumental character of virtuous activity: "operation according to virtue is not the end, but a means to the end, so that with its frequent exercise cupidity may be extinguished."[41] The ethical life is an earthly purgative that prepares us for the contemplation of eternal truth with a pure mind. Vico is perfectly clear that full participation in contemplation is not possible in this life.[42] Nonetheless, action should be rigorously ordered to the eternal happiness that Vico identifies with vision of the divine essence. The indispensability of virtuous *operatio* should not lead one to confuse it with the single final end. "For, if the true is one, the true good must also be one; and if the eternal true is one, so is the eternal happiness to be striven after and contemplated (*spectanda*)."[43] From this unity Vico draws the corollary that the ultimate end of metaphysics, ethics, and politics must be the same.[44] Each is ordered to contemplation of the divine, even though such contemplation is available only "after this life."[45] Vico allows that even corrupt nature can enjoy a type of happiness, but insists that its condition is the possibility of imagining human society as it was before the Fall, as a universal brotherhood.[46] This is perhaps the most dramatic correction of Aristotle, with roots in both Stoicism and Christianity. The scope of the polis must be expanded to include all human beings, "not as individuals or solitaries, not as citizens of a single state, but as the universal human race."[47] Because such a conception of the end is so demanding, Vico argues that only *caritas* can teach the "praxis" of the "metaphysical good."[48] Because only "Christian wisdom" proposes "one end," it will teach a virtue "more eminent by far than that of all the pagans."[49] Vico argues from the Aristotelian assumption that of two ends otherwise similar, the end of wider scope will be more noble.[50] As Aristotle uses this rationale to affirm the superiority of the civil end to the moral end, so Vico uses it to affirm the superiority of the Christian end. Since it "diffuses the good to the universal human race," it surpasses the civil end.[51] The distinction between pagan and Christian virtue serves not to enshrine an ethical particularism, but to avoid the provincialism that Vico associates with pagan culture. If pagan ethnocentrism is to be surpassed, a new "Christian jurisprudence" is required.

It is plausible to regard the *Diritto universale*'s "Christian jurisprudence" as a rewriting of Augustine's *De civitate Dei*.[52] The majority of secular readings of Vico seem utterly unaware of the Augustinian passages in both the *De uno* and the *De constantia*. Even Lilla's interpretation, despite its emphasis on the theological side of his oeuvre, distinguishes Vico from Augustine in a questionable manner. "According to St. Augustine and his Catholic followers," Lilla writes, "the Roman

Empire fell under the moral weight of its own uncontrollable greed, pride, and sensuality. Although Augustine begrudgingly recognized certain civic virtues in the Romans, he insisted that the city was never a civilized place; in the final analysis the empire was nothing more than a proud, vicious state ruled by demons clothed as gods. Vico always distanced himself from this teaching, insisting that Rome be given her due."[53] This is misleading for two reasons. First, a more subtle reading of *De civitate Dei* would show that Augustine also insists that Rome be given her due. To say that Augustine sees Rome as nothing but darkness is to saddle him with precisely the Manicheanism that he so brilliantly overcomes.[54] Second, Vico does not "distance" himself from Augustine's view that Rome was itself dominated by its *libido dominandi*. Not only does the *De uno* draw Augustine's precise contrast between pagan virtue and Christian virtue, arguing that only the latter is true virtue, but the *Scienza nuova* as well juxtaposes the "power of Rome" with the "virtue of the martyrs."[55] Lilla correctly notes the exemplary status of Rome among the gentile nations, but takes no account of the passages in which Vico is highly critical of Roman culture.

Is it justified, then, to read Vico as more or less a pure Augustinian? Although it is certainly true that Vico wants to affirm Augustinian conclusions, it seems that he wants to do so in a way that is fundamentally non-Augustinian, if not anti-Augustinian.[56] Vico possesses a "modern" confidence in the ability of the human mind to penetrate the design of history and to depict its inner logic in a system. Although Augustine believes in the rationality of the divine plan, he is always quick to emphasize that humans are debarred from any real access to it. He asserts strict limitations upon historical knowledge. Vico, by contrast, thinks that history can be "scientifically" treated and deciphered, and set forth in an encyclopaedic form. One shudders to know what Augustine would think of a "rational civil theology of divine providence," as Vico will describe the chief aspect of the *Scienza nuova*. Vico himself seems to acknowledge his distance from Augustine when he claims to provide "*new* principles by which to demonstrate the argument of St. Augustine's discussion of the virtue of the Romans."[57] Vico is confident that even gentile history, scarred as it is by false metaphysics, possesses the unity of an intelligible *ordo*. Underneath the seemingly arbitrary character of choices made by the will, logic and order are always present. Leibniz's principle that "nature never makes leaps" applies to history. Customs are never "mere customs"; they are always expressions of nature. Like Leibniz, Vico seeks a *via media* between determinism and randomness. There is a certain degree of contingency in history, but it is not radical or inexplicable. Within limits, Vico thinks that history is predictable. Augustine, by contrast, holds that the future course of history is entirely unpredictable.

Vico possesses a modern form of historical consciousness, whereas Augustine does not. The historicism of the *Diritto universale* will be maintained in the *Scienza nuova,* the first version of which Vico published just four years after completing the *Diritto.* Assessing the logical and historical relations between the two texts is a complicated task. In lieu of a full analysis, we will offer three brief and inadequate remarks. First, while the *Diritto* contains both a doctrine of historical consciousness and quasi-genealogical suspicions about secular modernity, it does not integrate these two aspects very well. Second, the major difference between the *Diritto* and the *Scienza nuova* is not one of content, but of form. In the *Vita,* Vico says that he came to be dissatisfied with the *Diritto* because "he tried therein to descend from the mind of Plato and other enlightened philosophers into the dull and simple minds of the founders of the gentile peoples, whereas he should have taken the opposite course."[58] Third, the *Scienza nuova* will assume a sharper tone toward the secularity of modern culture. The *Diritto*'s implied critique of purely secular approaches to history will receive bolder expression in the *Scienza nuova.* In what follows, we will examine how the *Scienza nuova* takes over the historicism expressed in the *Diritto universale* and transforms it into genealogical narrative.

The Moral Genealogy
of the *Scienza nuova*

Vico, Genealogy, History

"*Historical refutation as the definitive refutation.*" Near the end of Book 1 of *Daybreak,* Nietzsche adopts this slogan as his own, comparing former attempts to demonstrate the nonexistence of God with a genealogical approach that reaches the same conclusion by a different route. "Today one indicates how the belief that there is a God could *arise* and how this belief acquired its weight and importance: a counter-proof that there is no God thereby becomes superfluous."[1] In Part 3, we will interpret the *Scienza nuova* as a "historical refutation" of the bases of pagan culture. Unlike Nietzsche, Vico considers Hebrew and Christian belief in a single, incorporeal, transcendent God to survive such a critique because—as Milbank suggests in his own reading of Vico as a genealogist—it constitutes such a critique.[2]

Some will immediately object that any interpretation of Vico as a moral genealogist is simply anachronistic, ascribing aims to Vico of which he knew nothing. Let us expand this objection, so that we may confront it directly. Vico mentions seven "principal aspects" of his new science. These are (1) a rational civil theology of divine providence; (2) a philosophy of authority; (3) a history of human ideas; (4) philosophical critique; (5) the ideal eternal history; (6) a system of the natural law of the nations; (7) origins of the universal history.[3] It will be noticed that in the list of *aspetti,* "genealogy" does not appear once. But does the absence of the label imply the absence of the thing?

At least one recent interpreter whom it would be hard to accuse of philological insensitivity has suggested a negative answer to this question. Giuseppe Mazzotta calls attention to the *Scienza nuova*'s view that Christianity is a triumph over "vain Greek wisdom," commenting that such wisdom "believed, like Rome, in its own power, and it ended up making of its philosophical theater a vanity fair."[4] Mazzotta does not hesitate to use Nietzschean categories in his reading of Vico: "classical political philosophy . . . is fired by utopianism, which is a will to power, a will to impose its own enlightened vision on the multitude." Mazzotta's contention that Vico constructs an "original and bold counter-discourse to modernity," animated by his "suspicious views of philosophy's own temptation of power and concomitant delusion about its pretended superiority over other forms of knowledge," is not far from the perspective of the present reading. Citing the desire to achieve a "systematic stripping away of the veils of power and deception," Mazzotta concludes that the *Scienza nuova* "encompasses a critique of philosophy's delusion of power: it unveils philosophy's claim to be the privileged and sovereign discourse of the modern age as well as its project to submit Christianity to its critical scrutiny."[5]

Another way to respond to the charge that reading the *Scienza nuova* as a genealogy of morals is irresponsibly anachronistic would be to look more closely at the *aspetti*. The third aspect of the new science is a "history of human ideas" (*storia d'umane idee*).[6] As we have shown in Part 2, Vico worked out the possibility of such a history in his prior engagement with modern theories of natural law. He describes the fourth aspect of his science as "born from" the third. Far from desiring knowledge merely for its own sake, Vico seeks to place the "history of ideas" in the service of "philosophical critique." Such critique, Vico claims, will offer "true judgments about the founders of the nations." [7] In beginning with Jove, it will "trace a natural theogony, meaning the genealogy (*generazione*) of the gods as it was naturally created by the founders of the pagan world, who were by nature theological poets."[8] Vico's aim is not merely to narrate, but to narrate for the sake of passing critical judgment, of bringing to light truths that had once been dark. Milbank writes that the "*Scienza nuova* is not *just* a genealogy. More fundamentally it is itself a judgment."[9] We concur with this verdict, but would add that the point of calling the *Scienza nuova* a "genealogy" is to distinguish it from a merely genetic account that aspires to be value-neutral. On the view taken here, the notion of genealogy *contains* the notion of judgment.

Far from indulging in false anachronism, it may be said that rendering the *Scienza nuova* in a genealogical key is better able to honor Vico's true intentions than interpretations which confuse him with later practitioners of the "genetic method" who attempt, positivistically, to tell stories about the past "as it really was." To claim that Vico constructs a genealogy of pagan culture is to say that he constructs a narrative with four salient characteristics, a narrative that is historical, suspicious, linguistic, and normative. First, the *historical* orientation assumes the form of an "archaelogical" investigation into prior cultural formations. The goal of the investigation is to illuminate cultural beginnings, not absolute origins.[10] Although Vico thinks that the development of culture possesses an order and intelligibility that can be apprehended by the human mind, he does not think that its origins can be understood apart from the divine. This assumption prevents Vico from crediting his science with the ability to attain an absolute origin that can be exhaustively and transparently known. Vico does not seek a single origin. His procedure is to look for clues which in themselves seem insignficant, but when pieced together are able to provide unexpected and surprising illuminations. It is a science that relies upon *ingenium,* the faculty of "connecting disparate and diverse things" by which man is "capable of contemplating and constructing (*facendi*) likenesses."[11] In its emphasis upon *ingenium,* which follows an appropriate method yet cannot be reduced to certain rules (*contra* Descartes), Vico's procedure might remind the contemporary reader of Foucault's comment that "genealogy demands relentless erudition" and that its "'cyclopean monuments' are constructed from discrete and apparently insignificant truths and according to a rigorous method."[12]

Second, Vico is always *suspicious* of previous historiography. He sets out to subvert received accounts, presuming they are ruses meant to conceal the roots of their own power. As Collingwood notes, Vico is among the first thinkers to raise the question: Can accounts of the past societies, written by members of those societies, be taken at face value?[13] His suspicion leads him to wonder whether the versions of myths that survive in extant texts are in fact corruptions of earlier myths that were a more faithful record of the societies out of which they arise. Although the most striking result of this suspicion comes in the "discovery of the true Homer," it would be misleading to suppose that Vico restricts his suspicious gaze to the Homeric question. What Mannheim calls the "unmasking turn of mind" may be found at nearly every juncture of the *Scienza nuova.*[14] Although Vico's first humans may have the innocence of youth, Vico shares little of this naiveté. His suspicion extends to everything. What Nietzsche calls "critical history" may turn out to be tame in comparison to the *Scienza nuova.* We will explore this dimension of Vico's science more fully in our analysis of the twin errors that Vico considers to plague all previous attempts at history-writing. These are the "conceit of nations" and "conceit of scholars."

Third, the specifically *linguistic* aspect of Vico's science cannot be overlooked. Well before Nietzsche and Heidegger, Vico places a large emphasis upon the value of etymological evidence in understanding the deep structure of historical cultures. He understands the force of the question that Nietzsche will pose: "What light does linguistics, and especially the study of etymology, throw on the history of the evolution of moral concepts?"[15] Etymologies of terms from natural language are important, Vico thinks, because they point to the history of things. They "tell us the histories of the things that words signify, beginning with their original and proper meanings and continuing with the natural progress of their metaphors according to the order of ideas, on which the history of languages must proceed."[16] The study of language is crucial, because "ideas and languages accelerated at the same rate."[17] Languages are valuable as "the most weighty witnesses concerning those ancient customs of the peoples that were in use at the time the languages were formed."[18] What Vico calls the "mental dictionary," the language spoken by the ideal eternal history, must always be related to, and derived from, the languages whose etymologies express the "same human necessities or utilities common to all" but "according to their diversities of place, climate, and, hence, nature and custom."[19] No investigation of the history of human consciousness is possible without close attention to the clues revealed by etymologies.

Finally, the point of Vico's science is ultimately *normative*. There is nothing of the disinterested, value-free social scientist in Vico. The stance that Vico assumes is not detached objectivity, but engaged commitment. Among other things, the *Scienza nuova* is a protracted exercise in eloquence, designed to rouse its readers to action against the forces that threaten to destroy humanity. Like Nietzsche, Vico is a physician of culture who diagnoses late modernity as a pale shadow of what came before, viewing it as a nihilistic force determined to crush everything that is noble. In some moods, he even seems to idealize the heroic morality of strength against the relentless levelings of modern ethics and politics. Unlike Nietzsche, however, he does not think that the path to cultural renewal is to be found in a rejection of Christian religion accompanied by a complex reappropriation of pagan culture. It lies, rather, in a form of *praxis* that takes its bearings from a truthful conception of the alliance between the "common wisdom" of the race—whose truth is denied by the "solitary philosophy" of the "Stoics" and "Epicureans"—and the "esoteric wisdom" of Plato and Aristotle, but *only* as revised and corrected by Christian theology. Vico would agree with Foucault that the point of "effective history" is to cut, but he would deny any necessary separation between historical genealogy and philosophical contemplation.

Our reading of the *Scienza nuova* as a moral genealogy will begin with his reflections on the conceits of modern method, whether in its "philosophical" or "philological" guise. It will proceed to give an account of Vico's alternative method, which Montanari has rightly described as an *archeologia del sapere*.[20] Both the application of this method to gentile history and the culture from which Vico draws the norms that govern the method's application will first be considered with respect to the "age of gods." We will proceed to show that Vico's history of the heroic age, bent on unearthing the inner logic that drives the struggle of the plebs against the patricians, should also be understood as a genealogy. It would be a mistake, however, to stop with the claim that Vico provides a genealogy of pagan culture in its "divine" and "heroic" phases. The claim is true, but it does not go far enough. The ultimate effect of Vico's narrative is to place modernity under suspicion. As we have seen in Part 1, Vico's early writings point to subterranean analogies between ancient paganism and modern secularism. We will examine the way in which Vico returns to this theme in the *Scienza nuova*. Vico's genealogy culminates in the claim that, despite the initial gains that seem to be achieved in the "age of men," a purely secular ethics that loses contact with the common sense of humanity is bound to degenerate into a new "barbarism of reflection."

Interpreting Vico as a moral genealogist will serve as an antidote to the widespread notion that Vico is simply a learned antiquarian who is fascinated with ancient myths and customs for their own sake. Our reading also aims to correct the equally misguided view of Vico as a Romantic who identifies himself with the folk mind and rejects modern civilization in the name of a nobler pre-civilized humanity. It will confirm the judgment of Mazzotta that "the view of Vico as a mere erudite hopelessly embroiled in the cult of calcified anachronisms, himself an anachronism in the modern world of technology and science that forever elude his grasp, is utterly false."[21]

TWELVE

Unmasking the Philosophers and Philologists

In 1724, Vico wrote an entire work devoted to exploding the errors of other accounts, calling it the *Scienza nuova in forma negativa*. Vico decided to suppress the text, which is now lost, on the ground that the "negative form of exposition, though intriguing to the imagination, is repugnant to the understanding, since by it the human mind is not enlarged."[1] The quest for a "positive" science seems to be incompatible with merely reactive endeavors. Nonetheless, Vico retains the Baconian conviction that a *scienza nuova* is not possible until the mind is purged of its idols. Thus both the *Scienza nuova prima* and the final *Scienza nuova* open with sections that aim to lay bare the defects of their predecessors. Vico locates the failure of past methods in certain human, all-too-human, tendencies of nations and their scholars. Philosophy, even at its best, disguises its true roots in myth, in order to promote its own discourse as self-sufficient. Philology, likewise, flinches from a hard look at origins, fearing what it might learn.

Vico does not simply file objections against his opponents. More profoundly, and more subversively, he "unmasks" them by exposing the root of their error in the "conceit of nations" and "conceit of scholars." These are not just products of ignorance, but devices of power that serve to promote local interests. They are cloaks that protect until seen through. Vico speaks of the two *borie* in the final *Scienza nuova*, whose form is typically aphoristic. To illuminate the argument, we must first turn to the *Scienza nuova prima*, where Vico articulates his critique more discursively.

74

The basic categories employed by the first book of the *Scienza nuova prima* (and the nearly contemporaneous sections of the *Vita*) are "vulgar wisdom" and "esoteric wisdom." Vico initially presents the failures of *sapienza volgare* and *sapienza riposta* as two distinct failures, although he hints at their common root in human vanity, and even implies an historicization of later rationalist philosophy by indicating that its errors can be exposed as natural outgrowths from the primal errors of divination and idolatry.[2] "Vulgar wisdom" is the wisdom of primitive gentile humanity. Although it is born out of the vice of *curiositas,* and contains the seeds of error, it nonetheless preserves the two great truths of providence and human free will.[3] It possesses the three "common senses" of religion, marriage, and burial, without which no human society is possible.[4] Vico will attend in due course to the distortions of vulgar wisdom, but, against the tendency of philosophers to violate the *sensus communis,* he stresses its truth. (It does not follow, as Lilla thinks, that Vico's "overriding aim is simply to defend primitivism against philosophy.")[5]

The failure of "esoteric wisdom" is presented in greater detail. In line with the axiom, memorably expressed by Nietzsche, that "one criticizes a person, a book, most sharply when one pictures their ideal,"[6] Vico first describes a model whereby the "certain origins of the humanity of nations" would be apprehended, together with "a certain acme, or state of perfection," which would enable the theorist "to discern the states and limits through which and in which the humanity of nations, like every other mortal thing, must pass (*correre*) and terminate."[7] In this ideal state, the integration of "immutable reasons" and "common customs" is complete. "The esoteric wisdom of the philosophers would lend a hand to and direct the vulgar wisdom of nations so that, in this guise, the most distinguished academics would agree with all the wise men of the republics."[8] The ideal is a union of theory and practice, contemplation and action. The perfection of the acme implies its embodiment in both the active life of nations and the human thinker.

Vico will periodically flash the ideal before the eyes of the reader. The Epicureans and the Stoics are judged to fall short of the ideal because they neglect vulgar wisdom. Vico takes the failure of the Epicureans to be primarily doctrinal. In the *De constantia,* Vico praises the practical maxims of the Epicurean *sapiens,* but criticizes the basic ontology on logical grounds and argues that it leads to an unhappy skepticism. The *Scienza nuova prima* echoes this argument, asserting that the Epicurean stress on "chance" makes justice into nothing more than transient utility.[9] The Stoics, by contrast, affirm the immutable side of *ius,* but "annihilate humanity by wanting it to be insensitive to the passions, and reduce men to despair of being able to practice their virtue with their maxim, harder than iron, that sins are all equal, so that beating a slave a bit more than he deserves is as much a sin as killing one's father."[10] These sects of Roman philosophy, far from supporting the practical integration of universal and particular that all *iurisprudentia* aims at, undermine it in opposite ways. With grim irony Vico exclaims that "so far do the sects of these philosophers concur with Roman jurisprudence, that one destroys its maxim, and the other renounces the practice that is most important to its principles!"[11] Epicurean ethics is all *prudentia,* no *ius;* and Stoicism is all *ius,* no *prudentia.* The result of both is a useless philosophy, with no special claim to truth.

Vico finds in Plato a genuine improvement over both the Stoics and the Epicureans. "The divine Plato alone meditated an esoteric wisdom that would direct man in accordance with maxims that he had taken from the vulgar wisdom of religion and the laws."[12] Lilla supposes that Vico "professes little admiration for the figure of Socrates," but it is Socrates whom Vico praises as the exemplar of *constantia.*[13] Accepting "the duty of a philosopher to live in conformity with the laws even when, for some reason, they have become excessively rigid," Socrates exemplifies a commitment to the union of vulgar and esoteric wisdom.[14] Nonetheless, even Plato ultimately blunders. The failure is not one of metaphysical doctrine or misplaced rigorism. It is the more subtle, and more pervasive, error of historical anachronism. "Yet Plato lost sight of providence when, through a common error of human minds—measuring the poorly known natures of others according to oneself—he elevated the barbaric and rough origins of gentile humanity to the perfect state of his own, most lofty divine knowledge (when, on the contrary, he ought to have descended or sunk from his 'ideas' back to those origins)."[15] (Note the connection between Vico's corrective suggestion and the procedure of the *Diritto universale.*) The primary failure of Plato, then, is his anti-historical procedure, which Vico considers as both cause and effect of ignoring providence. A consequence of the Platonic "erudite error," the decision to privilege "an ideal republic and a purely ideal justice," is the tendency to "twist and neglect" the *sensus communis.*[16] Vico finds the Platonic departure from vulgar wisdom most clearly reflected in the sexual communism that Socrates proposes in Book 5 of the *Republic.*[17]

A third failure of *sapienza riposta* occurs in the texts of Grotius, Selden, and Pufendorf. The humanist training of "the three princes of natural law"[18] seems to endow them with a historical sensitivity foreign to Plato. Despite this, however, the failings of modern natural law turn out to be more serious than those of Platonism. Like Stoic "fate" and Epicurean "chance," Grotius ignores providence and human freedom, the truths common to vulgar wisdom and Platonic teaching. He aspires to ground his quasi-mathematical legal science in secular reason, whose truth is entirely independent of the knowledge of God. (Here Vico alludes to the notorious *etiamsi*.)[19] Secularism is compounded by individualism. Grotius is not immune from the atomism common to the Stoics and the Epicureans. His Socinianism leads him to believe that humans were naturally good weaklings, "solitary simpletons who came into social life after it was dictated to them by utility. This is, in fact, Epicurus's hypothesis."[20] Vico praises Grotius for his learning and his synthetic aspirations, but does not hesitate to imply that he combines the worst elements of Stoicism and Epicureanism. Pufendorf is similar to Grotius. He commits the fundamental error of ignoring providence and "employs a hypothesis completely Epicurean or Hobbesian (which in this matter come to the same thing)."[21] Selden errs in a quite different fashion. He denies providence not by seeking a secular foundation for ethics, but by blurring the distinction between sacred and gentile history. In ignoring the separation between Jews and Gentiles, he posits implausible diffusion theories and excludes the space in which providence might work in nations lacking the benefit of revelation. His "excessive love for Jewish learning" causes him to miss the central question about how false religions manage to civilize in spite of themselves.[22]

"Denial of providence" will not perhaps strike the contemporary reader as a forceful criticism. But it should be kept in mind that Vico is attacking writers who claim to share certain theological premises. The anti-providential charge, if it sticks, unmasks at least some of Vico's opponents as disingenuous. Moreover, Vico sees the question of providence as coterminous with the question about primitive humanity. The charge that other writers deny providence has, in Vico's texts, the same sense as the charge that ignorance of vulgar wisdom leads to a flawed view of human origins and ends. "Since none of the three considered providence when establishing his principles, none discovered the true, hitherto concealed, origins of any of the parts that comprise the entire economy of the natural law of the nations—the origins, that is, of religions, languages, customs, laws, societies, governments, kinds of ownership, occupations, orders, authorities, judiciaries, penalties, wars, peace, surrender, slavery, and alliances."[23] From the failure to discern human origins, Vico notes three consequences. First, modern natural law engages in a false separation of the *ius gentium* and the *ius naturale,* without noticing that "this law arose with the customs of nations."[24] Second, it relies on evidence from philology, itself uncertain and beset by anachronism. Third, it assumes the truth of diffusion theories, overlooking the more likely possibility that law evolves from the demands of the *sensus communis,* without presupposing actual contact among nations, which "pass their early days in savagery and seclusion."[25]

Vico's strategy has been to narrate in turn the failures of Stoicism, Epicureanism, Platonism, and modern natural law. He pinpoints specific mistakes, notes their relation to broader failings, and draws contrasts to the ampler perspectives of Roman jurisprudence and Scripture.[26] He explains the lack of a suitable ethical *scienza* by reference to the fact that "we have up to now lacked a science which was, together, a history and philosophy of humanity."[27] Philosophers take philosophy for granted, unable to see themselves as products of a "human nature, from which arose the religions and the laws, by means of which the philosophers originated."[28] Philologists are little better, hampered by the poor condition of their sources, distorted by vulgar traditions. Vico proposes a dilemma: either the gentile world was created by the reflection of wise men, or it arose from "bestial men brought together by a certain human sense."[29] The first view is rejected summarily: "it is the nature of origins to be simple and crude in all things."[30] The second view is more plausible and appears to be taken more seriously by Grotius and Pufendorf. But their reconstructions of natural law from an original state rely on false philology. "Nothing is enshrouded in such doubt and obscurity as the origins of language and the principle of the propagation of nations."[31] Vico later poses the problem to reveal its ethical dimension, asking how "without language and with thought of nothing but the satisfaction of hunger, thirst, and the impulses of desire (*libidine*), [the first humans] attained any sense of humanity."[32] Both philosophy and philology seem radically inadequate to the task of discovering the origins of human language and ethics.

The critique of previous methods is substantially reproduced in the final *Scienza nuova.* Vico identifies anachronism as the problem, but presents it more vividly as an effect of human ignorance and pride. Two "axioms" (*degnità*) about the nature of the human mind explain the failing. "Because of the indefinite nature of the human mind, whenever it is lost in ignorance, man makes himself the measure of all things."[33] This and "another property of the human mind, that whenever men can form no idea of distant and unknown things, they judge them by what is familiar at hand," account for the tendency of present thinkers to mistake the authentic character of origins, in themselves "small, rude, and most obscure."[34] The error of anachronism, caused by ignorance, manifests itself in self-love, as the "conceit of nations" and the "conceit of scholars."[35] Every nation "has had the same conceit that it before all other nations invented the comforts of human life and that it conserves its memories of these things from the beginning of the world."[36] This form of arrogance generates the conceit of scholars, "who will have it that what they know is as old as the world."[37] Once he exposes this conceit, Vico can dismiss all previous approaches, from Plato to Bacon, insofar as they impose their own learning on "fabulous" beginnings.

The final *Scienza nuova* also contains the polemic against the Stoics and the Epicureans. Aphorism replaces the extended argument of the *De constantia philosophiae* and *Scienza nuova prima*. As a preliminary, Vico reminds us that "to be useful to the human race, philosophy must raise and direct weak and fallen man, not rend his nature or abandon him in his corruption."[38] In a single sentence, Vico condenses the view of philosophy scattered throughout his previous writings. Then he declares that "this Axiom dismisses from the school of our Science the Stoics, who seek to mortify the senses, and the Epicureans, who make them the criterion."[39] In the *Scienza nuova prima*, Vico holds that both culminate in the same error, but takes pains to emphasize the flaws proper to each sect. Now he only says that "both deny providence, the former chaining themselves to fate, the latter abandoning themselves to chance."[40] One difference is noted: the Epicureans "affirm that human souls die with their bodies." But the parallel is more important: "both should be called monastic, or solitary, philosophers."[41] This is all Vico needs to say about the Stoics and Epicureans. Once the objects of extended attention, they now deserve a summary dismissal. The "political philosophers, and first of all the Platonists" (the category does not exclude Aristotle, as Vico makes clear throughout) do not, by contrast, abandon vulgar wisdom. Since they "agree with all the lawgivers" on the "three main points" of providence, the conversion of passions into virtues, and the immortality of the soul, they merit admission into Vico's school.[42] Nonetheless, admission comes with an immediate rebuke. "Philosophy considers man as he should be and so can be of service to but very few, those who wish to live in the republic of Plato and not to fall back into the dregs of Romulus."[43]

Finally, Vico restates, as concisely as possible, the inadequacy of all existing philosophy and philology. He does so by simultaneously recalling two distinctions explicated in earlier texts: *scientia* and *conscientia, verum* and *certum.* "Philosophy contemplates reason, whence comes knowledge (*scienza*) of the true (*vero*); philology observes that of which human choice is author, whence comes consciousness (*coscienza*) of the certain (*certo*)."[44] This axiom "shows how the philosophers failed by half in not giving certainty to their reasonings by appeal to the authority of the philologists, and likewise how the latter failed by half in not taking care to give their authority the sanction of truth by appeal to the reasoning of the philosophers. If they had done this they would have been more useful to their commonwealths and they would have anticipated us in meditating this Science."[45]

Methods prior to Vico are unable to integrate vulgar and esoteric wisdom. They fail to unite the disciplines, philology and philosophy, that aim to penetrate to the essence of each. Vico emphasizes the difficulty he inherits from his predecessors, in order to prepare the reader for his own solution.

THIRTEEN

Knowledge as Archaeology

Near the end of Book 1 of the final version of the *Scienza nuova*, Vico proclaims that "the great fragments of antiquity, hitherto useless to science because they lay begrimed, broken, and scattered, shed great light when cleaned, pieced together, and restored."[1] Vico's science promises to achieve illumination through an archaeology of knowledge. In order to begin such an archaeology, one must emulate the wise person (*sapiens*) described in the *De antiquissima*. We must "reduce ourselves to a state of extreme ignorance of all human and divine learning, as if, for the purposes of this inquiry, there had been neither philosophers nor philologists to help us."[2] We must, "for purposes of this inquiry, reckon as if there were no books in the world."[3]

Vico begins the *Scienza nuova* with a preliminary display of his own erudition. Book 1 presents a chronological table, notes on the table designed to set the "materials" (*materie*) in order, and axiomatic elements intended to give the material "form" (*forma*). The initial exposition of the new science in fragments demands a principle that reduces chaos to order.

The principle is *verum-factum*.

But, in this dense night of darkness that hides the earliest antiquity, so remote from ourselves, there shines the eternal light, which never fails, of a truth beyond all doubt: that the civil world has certainly been made by men, and that its principles are therefore to be found within the modifications of our own human mind. Whoever reflects on this cannot but wonder that the philosophers should seriously have sought to attain *scienza* of the natural world, of

81

which, since God made it, God alone has *scienza;* and that they should have neglected to meditate on the world of nations, or the civil world, of which, since men had made it, men could attain *scienza.*[4]

Verum-factum is the one indubitable truth. As in the *De antiquissima,* only God has complete *scientia* of the natural world. Of the civil world, humans can have *scientia,* since in some fashion they construct it. Vico seems to endow history with precisely the same intelligibility as the *De antiquissima* attributes to geometry. As mathematicians create *tamquam ex nihilo* the line and the point, so human beings create the elements of the civil world.

> Indeed, we dare to affirm that he who meditates this science narrates to himself this ideal eternal history, insofar as he, in showing that "it had, has, and will have to be," makes the history for himself— since this world of nations has certainly been made by men (the first indubitable principle posited above), and since its guise must be found within the modifications of our own human mind. And when it happens that he who makes things is the same as he who narrates them, history cannot be more certain. Thus this Science proceeds exactly as geometry, which, when it constructs or contemplates the world of size from its elements, makes that world for itself, but with a reality greater by just so much as the orders concerning human makings or doings (*faccende degli uomini*) are more real than points, lines, surfaces, and figures. And this itself is an argument that these proofs are of a divine kind and should, O reader, fill you with a divine pleasure, since in God knowing and making are the same thing.[5]

Humans create the civil world, down to its very elements. The difference is only that the elements of the civil world are "more real" than the elements of geometry. In the *De antiquissima,* Vico argues that geometrical elements exist to the extent that they are "feigned" by the mind of the mathematician. How are civil elements more real than geometrical elements, if they too are manufactured by human beings? To answer this question, one must observe that Vico does not regard the "civil world" as entirely self-sufficient; he takes it to depend on the "metaphysical world" or "the world of human minds."[6] Civil elements, qua civil elements, are humanly created. But full specification of their ontology reveals their dependence on prior realities. It is *from* the "modifications of our own human mind," not themselves humanly made, that the elements of the civil world are "created" by human beings. "In our mind there are certain eternal truths that we cannot mistake or deny, and which therefore are not from ourselves."[7] This dependence of human making upon that which is not constructed by men recalls the participation of the *factum* in the *genitum* in the *De antiquissima*, as well as its conception of the *sapiens* who does not make but receives the *genera* of all things. In *De uno*, Vico explicitly says that the "principles of sciences" are both "from God" and "in us."[8]

How is human knowledge genuinely creative, if it ultimately depends on genera that we do not make? Any sound reading of Vico must liberate him from the notion that men autonomously create themselves and their world, and recover the sense in which Vico applies the model of "maker's knowledge" to the constructive activity of the historian. Ontologically, the civil world is entirely dependent on the divine ideas. But actual knowledge of the civil world is not obtained through preliminary introspection of the genera. It is acquired through construction. Vico's perspective from the *De ratione* to the *Scienza nuova* is thoroughly anti-Cartesian: the mind knows itself through its activities and cultural productions. This epistemological stance leaves room for the analogy between human knowing and divine creation. As in the *De antiquissima*, *verum-factum* signifies a process in which truth emerges through a process of selection and composition of elements into a whole. This is the obvious application of *verum-factum* in the *Scienza nuova*. "The great fragments of antiquity, hitherto useless to science because they lay begrimed, broken, and scattered, shed great light when cleaned, pieced together, and restored."[9] The new science is a massive exercise of *ingenium*, of gathering small clues and finding surprising connections that illuminate our knowledge of human origins and ends.[10] Only a bold reconstruction of the civil world can overcome anachronistic conceit and provide genuine *scienza* of human culture.

But not *only* human culture. The conception of culture as an artifact that subsists in isolation from the divine is utterly foreign to Vico. Here secular interpreters have tended to impose their own prejudices on Vico, overlooking the possibility that "culture" and "creation" are inseparable. The purpose of the new science is not just to know "the human." It also seeks knowledge of God. This is why Vico describes the principal aspect of his science as a rational civil *theology* of divine providence.[11] Vico wants to ascend from human things to the contemplation of God.

He does not postulate a secular world, but assumes a primordial connection between the human and the divine. The philosophers err by trying to contemplate God in the order of "natural things," an order whose elements are largely unknown to us. A more promising strategy is to focus on the human world, with the intent of discerning its relationship to the divine. This requires dual attention to "the world of human minds, which is the metaphysical world" and to the "world of human spirits, which is the civil world or world of nations."[12] From these worlds, more intelligible to human beings than the world of nature, the new scientist contemplates God.[13] (This reveals a sense in which Vico profoundly respects the Aristotelian imperative to begin with what is known to us.) Essentially the same schema is present in the *Scienza nuova prima,* where immediately after presenting the *verum-factum* principle, Vico distinguishes between "the most universal theory" and "most universal practice" in divine philosophy. The theory is the "metaphysics of human mind" that "leads it to God as eternal truth." The theory is actualized, "elevated" to the level of practice, when it is made to "contemplate the common sense of the human race as a certain human mind possessed by the nations, in order to lead it to God as eternal providence."[14]

Vico's deployment of the *verum-factum* principle intends to provide grounds for optimism about the ability of the human mind to know the civil world. Having been created by human beings, the *mondo civile* can be recreated by the new scientist. This is possible because the basic principles of the creation of the civil world are not arbitrary postulates, but "modifications of mind" that are common to the first humans and the later historian. Sometimes Vico seems to speak as if this subjectivity were relatively transparent, so that the new scientist need only to clothe himself in the garb of primitive humanity.[15] But elsewhere Vico makes clear that no simple act of imagination is possible.[16] If Vico's archaeology is to succeed in its aim of unearthing and reconstructing the elements of the civil world, it requires a rational procedure, a method.[17]

"Method" is the topic of section 4 of Book 1 of the *Scienza nuova,* which is dedicated to the "establishment of principles." Before elucidating Vico's conception of his science's method, as set out in section 4, some commentary upon the preceding sections of Book 1 is desirable. We must consider, first, the derivation of the Elements of the new science and, second, the deduction of the Principles from the Elements. The *Scienza nuova* retains the apodictic pretensions of the *Diritto universale;* it claims to "demonstrate" the rational civil theology of divine providence. Before demonstration can begin, however, appropriate starting points—the Principles—must be established. This, in turn, requires cognition of the Elements of the science. Knowledge of both the Elements and the Principles of the new science cannot itself be demonstrative. As Aristotle reminds us, there is a difference between dialectical movement *to* principles and demonstrative movement *from* them. Before we examine the movement to the Principles of Vico's science, as specified in section 3, we must consider the derivation of its Elements, as set forth in section 2. By what process does Vico acquire the Elements of the new science?

In the new science of Galileo, the process that attains knowledge of elements is *analysis*. The scientist resolves the whole into its constituent parts, its elements. Something analogous is true of Vico's new science, although Funkenstein is right to say that one looks in vain for an explicit acknowledgment of Galilean influence. The function of the Chronological Table and the accompanying Notes is to present the whole of Vico's science in a confused mode. In his explanation of the *dipintura,* Vico says that the "darkness in the background of the picture is the material of the science, uncertain, unformed, obscure, which is set forth in the Chronological Table and in the Notes upon it."[18] The process of resolution into elements begins with the notes themselves, which begin to "organize" the "materials" (*materie*), to set them in order. In order to complete the process, Vico must give "form" to the materials. Vico understands himself to have accomplished this task when he casts the Elements of the *Scienza nuova* as the 114 axioms that comprise section 2. The *raison d'être* of the Elements is "to give form to the materials" which have already been partially ordered by the notes on the chronological table. Vico considers the imposition of form upon matter to be equivalent to resolving the whole into its constituent elements.

But *how* does Vico move from a confused conception of the whole to its clear resolution into distinct axioms? What are the particular steps followed by his analysis? Vico says little that would address questions of this sort. Perhaps he means to underscore the "divinatory" character of analysis as such. In *De antiquissima,* as we have seen, he regards analysis as a useful but uncertain procedure that begins from the whole and moves toward its parts. Despite its puzzling character, there can be little doubt that "analysis" is an appropriate term for Vico's procedure in this context. In the *Scienza nuova prima,* Vico holds that "by means of division, we must proceed from cognition of the parts and thence of their composition, to achieve cognition of the whole that we wish to know."[19]

Through "division," the obscure materials of section 1 come to receive "form" by the axioms of section 2; the whole has been analytically re-solved into its Elements.

Yet another way of conceiving Vico's progression toward the axioms would be to recall his debt to Bacon. The *Scienza nuova* credits Bacon with the articulation of "the best ascertained method of philosophizing" in existence.[20] The movement from the "obscure, unformed, uncertain" *materie* to the philosophical and philological axioms is an ascent from the particular to the general. By reflection upon historical particulars that are chaotically set out in section 1, the general axioms of section 2 are brought to light. Vico regards the form of the third *Scienza nuova* as supe-rior to that of his earlier works, because it more faithfully ascends from the lower to the higher. Rather than begin by "trying to descend from the mind of Plato and other enlightened philosophers into the dull and simple minds of the founders of gentile peoples," it takes the opposite course of ascending from historical matter to the Elements.[21] Morrison's suggestion that Vico replaces the Platonic conception of ascent with his own notion of descent is misleading, since Vico adheres to the Baconian model of a continous oscillation between ascent from given particulars to general axioms and descent from general axioms to new particulars.[22]

Vico's account of the derivation of the Elements of his science is so confusing because it draws at once upon categories taken from Aris-totelian metaphysics (imposition of form upon matter), Galilean *scienza nuova* (resolution of whole into parts), and Baconian induction (ascent from particulars to general axioms). All three traditions have to be kept in mind when considering the relation between section 1 and section 2 of Book 1. To what use does Vico put the Elements, once he has them in hand? The point of acquiring the Elements through analytical resolu-tion, as the passage from the *Scienza nuova prima* suggests, is to proceed to their "composition, to achieve cognition of the whole that we wish to know." In a sense, the *Scienza nuova* is nothing but one continous process of composing the Elements, of placing them in constellations that reveal new truths about the "whole that we wish to know." Analy-sis into parts is a prelude to synthesis of the whole. As one might expect of a thinker who takes synthetic geometry as a paradigm, knowledge is fundamentally compositive rather than resolutive. Hence Vico describes the Elements as continually present within the new science. "And just as the blood does in animated bodies, so will these elements course through our Science and animate it in all its reasonings about the com-mon nature of nations."[23]

It is entirely legitimate to understand the Elements as rhetorical *topoi* that are continually applied and amplified in order to make "ingenious" connections that enlarge our understanding of human culture. Yet it seems that Vico's science is something more than an exercise in rhetorical *ingenium*. It also has pretensions to demonstration. If there is to be demonstration, there must be *principia*, starting points from which to demonstrate. Hence the general goal of Book 1 of the *Scienza nuova* is to establish the principles that constitute the starting point of demonstration. The Principles of Vico's science are set forth in section 3 of Book 1. But what are the Principles? How are they drawn, or "deduced" as Vico says in one passage, from the Elements?

The Principles of the *Scienza nuova* are stated with maximum concision in section 3 of Book 1. They are nothing other than the universally held customs of religion, marriage, and burial. The narrative that sets forth or "demonstrates" the development of human culture is to proceed from these starting points, which are "customary" rather than "philosophical." Vico does not, however, confine his conception of the "principles" of the *scienza nuova* to these human customs. Not only does he identify philosophical correlates of the three common senses at the end of Book 1; he also suggests that *verum-factum* itself is the master principle of the *Scienza nuova*. Vico does this not by inferring *verum-factum* from the Elements in a deductive manner, but by means of a strategy that, perhaps surprisingly, recalls the Cartesian establishment of the *cogito*. One can and should doubt everything that has hitherto been taught or suggested about the vexed topic of human origins. What remains after this process? "In a vast ocean of doubt, one small island appears, upon which we stand firm," Vico assures us. "In this dense night of darkness that hides the earliest antiquity, so remote from ourselves, there shines the eternal light, which never fails, of a truth beyond all doubt."[24] The indubitable truth is simply *verum-factum:* "the civil world has certainly been made by men, and that its principles are therefore to be found within the modifications of our own human mind."[25] The master principle of Vico's science is not a truth demonstrated from other truths, but the one thing we must affirm when everything else is put in doubt. Once again, a precise description of the path from Elements to Principles, from section 2 to section 3, seems difficult to give. Although he does use the term "deduce" (*dedurre*) to describe this movement, it seems unlikely that he intends this in a strong sense. The actual movement from the Elements of section 2 to the Principles of section 3 strikes the reader as more "dialectical" than "demonstrative."

With the principles in place, Vico concludes Book 1 with reflections upon the method he will use in narrating the course of human history. "Method" in this context is a general term which embraces the canons that Vico intends to observe in the new science's "demonstration" of effects from causes. What are these canons? The method of the *Scienza nuova* can be summarized in a list of imperatives.

(a) Begin where the subject matter begins, with the *principia,* the beginnings "beyond which it is vain curiosity to demand others earlier." These will be origins that are common to primitive humanity.
(b) Assume that developments from these origins unfold in a manner that is most economical—that is, most natural, orderly, and conducive to the preservation of the human race.
(c) Suspect the inherited versions of tradition. Seek to decode myths, to unveil the latent historical meaning behind the manifest sense. Employ a hermeneutic of suspicion, against the conceits of nations and scholars.
(d) Aim to understand the order of things through the order of ideas, and the order of ideas through the order of language.
(e) Test the *scienza's* findings by comparing them with imagined possibilities. Seek a negative answer to the question, Can the mind imagine more, fewer, or different causes than the ones it has actually found?
(f) Submit the *scienza's* findings to the criteria of vulgar wisdom, as embodied in the *sensus communis.*

These canons, of course, are far from transparent, and can only be understood in light of Vico's particular application of them.[26] Some initial commentary is nonetheless desirable. The imperative to "begin where the subject matter begins" signifies for Vico the first antidote to the anachronism of Grotius, Selden, and Pufendorf, who err by "beginning from the middle; that is, from the latest times of the civilized nations."[27] Modern philosophical historiography errs in parallel fashion. Brucker is criticized for beginning "when the philosophers began to reflect on human ideas," and not "when the first men began to think humanly."[28] The *Historia philosophica doctrinae de ideis,* whose form and presuppositions have proven so influential for modern historiography, is rejected on the ground that it "comes down to the latest controversies between the two wits of our age, Leibniz and Newton."[29] Vico's imperative should not be understood as disguising a yearning for absolute beginnings. The origins he seeks are specifically cultural; to penetrate beyond these to pre-cultural beginnings is impossible and vain.[30] The reason for proceeding historically is not a "disinterested" wish to know the past, or an infantile yearning for human natality. Rather, Vico takes seriously the notion that scientific knowledge is knowledge *per causas*. Any real investigation into the *nature* of a thing has to comprehend its origin and development. Vico assumes that a thing's present actuality is not fully intelligible until it is narrated as the end product of a sequence.[31] Nature and process cannot be prised apart: "the nature (*natura*) of things is nothing but their coming into being (*nascimento*) at certain times and in certain guises."[32] The connection between *natura* and *nascimento* is both etymological and conceptual. "The inseparable properties of things must be due to the modification or guise with which they are born. By these properties we may therefore verify that the *natura* or *nascimento* was thus and not otherwise."[33]

The beginnings must be common. The three principles of religion, marriage, and burial are identified as the customs that all nations have kept, "barbarous as well as human, though separately founded because distant from each other in time and space."[34] Vico desires not just a "foundation" that everyone *can* agree on, if they are rationally enlightened, but a starting point that is nothing other than the *sensus communis* of the race, the customs that all societies *actually* have in common, as a condition of their humanity. When Vico speaks of his beginnings as "eternal and universal," he does not refer to a priori propositions or invariable mental categories. He refers to cultural foundations, whose universality and necessity is established by reflection on the textual remains. (Once again, the archaeological metaphor is all-important.)

In tracking the development of nations from their origins, Vico forces himself to respect a principle of conservation. Here he is much closer to Leibniz than Newton, in the assumption that God produces the greatest number of effects with the least expenditure.[35] In fact, Vico gives a specifically theological rationale—divine omnipotence—for the statement that providence "must unfold its orders as easily as the natural customs of men."[36] The naturalness of means will be orderly, since providence "has infinite wisdom as counselor."[37] Orderly nature will always be teleological, since providence "has for its own end immeasurable goodness" and directs things "to a good always superior to that which men have proposed to themselves."[38] The methodological consequence of these assumptions is that Vico cannot assume special divine intervention in the course of gentile history. His history must, in some fashion, be empirically based.[39] The postulation of divine miracles to explain events is ruled out (here one may see an affinity to Leibniz).

In looking to philological sources for clues to human history, Vico cannot accept the inherited mythologies. These are all too likely to have been distorted by nationalistic pride. The conceit of nations ensures that the transmission of myths is almost always a corruption of their original sense.[40] And the conceit of scholars ruins the interpretation of myths by making them into philosophical allegories.[41] In order to decipher the myths as genuine histories of original customs, orders, and laws of the gentile nations, Vico has to employ a strict "hermeneutic of suspicion" against contemporary philology. Put positively, this means that philology is subordinated to philosophy (albeit a philosophy that is already in harmony with the *sensus communis*).

To reconstruct human beginnings, Vico makes a "history of human ideas" and a "philosophy of authority" two of the seven principal aspects of his science.[42] Vico notoriously expresses the synchrony between ideas and things in the axiom that recalls Spinoza, *Ethics* 2.7: "The order of ideas must follow the order of things."[43] The rationale for the parallelism is Vico's "neoplatonic" assumption that ideal genera are the causes of things. Any true science that wants to understand things in their eternal causes must comprehend ideas, as the causes of things. It is misleading to speak of ideas as merely the "window" through which we see things, or assume that Vico's interest in ideas is secondary to his interest in things.[44] "Things" for Vico are ultimately epiphenomena, the effects of divine mind and its human participations.

The history of human ideas is not, of course, a history of esoteric wisdom—recall the criticism of Brucker—but a "history of consciousness" or the history of "common ideas concerning human necessities or utilities."[45] Vico does not pretend to condense the meditations of philosophers into a single narrative. He wants to uncover the "cultural logic" that informs the religious and legal institutions of particular societies. To uncover this logic, he must pay attention to the surface, to the "public grounds of truth" that are embedded in language.[46] Thus another principal aspect of his science, a "philosophy of authority," assumes the form of an investigation into the mythic language of authority, the rhetoric that creates and sustains it. Initially, Vico seemed to regard the ideal and linguistic aspects of his science as distinct but mutually confirmatory. The *Scienza nuova prima* devotes one section to the origins of ideas, and another to the origins of language. Later Vico affirms more clearly the inseparability of thought and linguistic figuration, and so by the time of the third *Scienza nuova* reproaches himself for having "separately reasoned from these two sources about the method of deriving the matters of this Science, whereas he ought rather to have derived the principles from the two together; whence many errors of ordering came about."[47]

Vico assumes that language is the clue to the "order of ideas" and the "order of things" for at least three reasons. First, Vico wants to trace civil phenomena back to their source in the "modifications of mind," and language is the natural expression of mind. As the medium of the human mind, language is not the window dressing of thought, but its very substance. Language does not merely express something we already possess without language; it actually "brings thought into being." As Collingwood, whose rejection of linguistic instrumentalism was certainly influenced by Vico, writes: "an idea is had as an idea only insofar as it is expressed."[48] One must be careful not to read the insights of later thinkers back into earlier ones, but the substance of Gadamer's dictum, "being that can be understood is language," is implicit in the *Scienza nuova*'s treatment of cultural realities.[49] Vico affirms that "name" (*nomen*) and "nature" (*natura*) originally meant the same thing and rejects the notion that the human mind once had a nonlinguistic perception.[50] The giants become human for the first time when they are able to experience fear—that is, only when they can represent thunder semiotically, as "Jove," an angry and powerful being who disapproves of lewdness. The first language was mute, but Vico finds it impossible to conceive of anything except *homo significans*. "Thus the first language in the first mute times of the nations must have begun with signs, whether gestures or physical objects, which had natural relations to the ideas."[51] *Logos*, which means "both idea and word," is originally united with *mythos*, and mythologies are nothing but "the proper languages of the fables (as their name indicates)."[52]

Second, Vico is self-consciously aware that the new scientist's only route to origins is through the surviving texts. Despite the transcendental unity among the diachronic "modifications of mind," one cannot study primitive consciousness in any direct manner. We have access to the mind only as figured in language; human *facta* present themselves as *signa* that have to be read and decoded.[53] Thus Vico proceeds to uncover archaic mores and laws through a study of the "vulgar tongues," which are "the most weighty witnesses concerning those ancient customs of the *gentes* that were in use at the time the languages were formed."[54] All myth is somehow *vera narratio* that embodies the consciousness of an entire society. Neither ancient peoples nor their thoughts can be directly studied, but traces of both survive in the structures of their speech. Vico claims that his interpretations of myths will agree with things "directly, easily, and naturally," simply because they *are* histories of things, once deciphered.[55]

Third, rigorous attention to language—"philology" subordinated to the "metaphysical art of criticism," in Vico's terms—is a crucial, perhaps *the* crucial, part of the science's method. It must be stressed that for Vico philology cannot be truthful, unless its findings are submitted to philosophy.[56] Thus Vico proposes that the new scientist should continually ask himself whether the causes he uncovers are such that his mind cannot imagine more, fewer, or different causes than the ones he has actually found. The goal of the new science is to disclose natures by showing how "things were unable to have been born (*nate*) from any but their own births (*nascimento*), in those particular times and places and in particular guises, that is, from those particular natures."[57] This appears deterministic, but it should be kept in mind that Vico wants a *via media* between Stoic "fate" and Epicurean "chance."[58] The middle way is "providence," which is neither random nor reducible to the Stoic "eternal chain of causes" that "itself hangs upon the omnipotent, wise, and benign will of the best and greatest God."[59] Like Leibniz, Vico seems to suppose a type of "ethical necessity." Providence directs the world of nations in one way, the *best* way (i.e., most natural, orderly, and perfective of the race). This places a constraint on the meditation of the new scientist, who must ensure that he does not postulate causes or events that would do violence to the providential *logos*. The constraint is not burdensome, but ensures that the new science is a genuine participation in divine creating-knowing. The reader "will experience in his mortal body a divine pleasure as he contemplates in the divine ideas this world of nations in all the extent of its places, times, and varieties."[60]

This is the "philosophical" criterion that the scientist employs. It is presented as the culmination of a series of "sublime natural theological proofs."[61] The directive role of "esoteric wisdom" in Vico's own enterprise is considerable; he often takes pains to emphasize its necessity, even as he warns against its alienation from vulgar wisdom.[62] The other primary criterion is that the findings of the new science conform to the *sensus communis*. It should be observed that this is *not* a demand to respect existing norms or sensibilities. In an appendix to the second *Scienza nuova*, Vico says that his science "contains many discoveries about the things here reasoned, largely diverse from, and many of them quite contrary to, the beliefs hitherto entertained about them."[63] More important than the common sense of a particular group of people is the aesthetic coherence of Vico's own text. Vico knows that many of his readers, not having read his work "at least three times," are like tone-deaf auditors who "when they hear one or two of the more resonant notes on the harpsichord, do so with displeasure, because they fail to hear the others which, under the touch of a master of the keyboard, make a sweet and agreeable harmony."[64] Substantially the same criterion is stated in the body of the *Scienza nuova,* where Vico holds that a single inconsistency amounts to total incoherence.[65] *Sensus communis* is normative only in that it requires the new science to respect and build upon the truths of providence and free will that are taught by the best philosophers, and presupposed by vulgar wisdom.[66] The *sensus communis* cannot be ignored because its ultimate source is providence. Fallen humanity will sink even lower if it arrogantly despises common sense and tries to construct a utopia on the basis of pure reason. In making this argument, Vico underscores the gap between his archaeology of knowledge and modern conceptions of method that divorce reason from the *sensus communis.*

Pagan Consciousness in the Age of Gods

Vico identifies the "first principle" of the new science as "religion." In what sense is it "first"? It is not first epistemologically, in the sense of what is most knowable or most simple (which, for a Cartesian science, come to the same thing). Is it first metaphysically? Certainly his decision to take "God" as the starting point of *De uno* and his description of "religion" as *il primo principio* of the *Scienza nuova* is not accidental. There is at least a genetic connection. But "religion" and "God" are not the same: by the time Vico writes the *Scienza nuova*, he has decisively switched his focus from transcendental origins to cultural beginnings, in accord with the methodological axiom that "doctrines must begin from whence the matters they treat begin."[1] When Vico considers religion, marriage, and burial as his "three first principles," he considers them not as abstract truths or spiritual substances, but as "three eternal and universal customs."[2] Among these customs, religion is historically primary: "the world of peoples began everywhere with religion." Here Vico is not speaking solely of pagan culture; the claim applies to all the nations, the gentiles and the Hebrews. It is too facile to hold, as some commentators do, that the new science is strictly confined to the gentiles. The distinction between the Hebrew and Christian religions, which "both believe in the divinity of an infinite free mind," and the religion of the gentiles, "who believe in the divinity of a plurality of gods, each imagined as composed of body and of free mind" is a constitutive part of Vico's science.[3] What Hebrew and gentile religion have in common is that each plays a foundational role in the culture that grows out of it, and each acknowledges the existence of providence. Thus some of Vico's reflections on "religion" embrace both the Hebrews and the gentiles. Vico also emphasizes, however, the specific character of gentile religion as a system of idolatry, divination, and sacrifice whose untruth can be exposed from the vantage point of the Hebrew religion, whose reliance upon divine revelation ensures its ability to offer an alternative to these tendencies. In the following chapter, we will consider the significance of the Hebrews for Vico's science. Here we will argue that in the act of narrating the origins of gentile religion, Vico provides a genealogy of pagan consciousness in its initial phase, the "age of gods."

Vico's famous tripartite division of history into three ages—the age of gods, the age of heroes, and the age of men—along with the corresponding trichotomy of hieroglyphic, symbolic, and epistolary languages, are "two great philological truths" inherited from the Egyptians. These are, Vico says, "no less marvelous than their pyramids."[4] Evidence of a primordial age of gods is also found in Homer. Vico cites five passages in which the poet "mentions a language more ancient than his own, which was certainly a heroic language, and calls it 'the language of the gods.'"[5] Providing additional support from Latin antiquity is Varro, who "had the diligence to collect thirty thousand names of the gods."[6] These gods, Vico infers, functioned as symbolic expressions of "as many needs of the physical, moral, economic, or civil life of the earliest times."[7] What distinguishes the age of gods is its entirely theocentric character. The fables of the gods were "histories of the times in which men of the crudest gentile humanity believed that all things necessary or useful to the human race were deities."[8]

In the age of gods, "the gentiles believed they lived under divine governments, and that everything was commanded them by auspices and oracles, which are the oldest things in profane history."[9] Auspices and oracles—or more generally "divination"—lie at the heart of gentile religion. It would only be a slight distortion to substitute "divination" for "religion" in the parts of the *Scienza nuova* that treat of pagan religion. The problem is that to rewrite pagan religion as "divination" would omit its two other primary components, idolatry and sacrifice. Idolatry, or the identification of a part of nature (paradigmatically, the sky) with a god (paradigmatically, "Jove") is the precondition of divination, as well as its continuing effect. Sacrifice is its natural consequence, since Vico regards divination as a kind of witchcraft that demands "solemnizing" in rituals that are "savage and cruel." The common origin of idolatry and divination is followed closely "by that of the sacrifices made to procure or rightly understand the auspicies."[10]

To say that Vico offers a genealogy of pagan culture at its origins is to say that he exposes it as a system revolving around idolatry, divination, and sacrifice. It is not immediately obvious, however, that Vico narrates the origins of gentile religion with subversive intent. Vico does not in fact supply a crude or simple demythologization of pagan culture. He considers its myths to get some important things right. When Vico describes gentile mythology as *vera narratio,* he means to suggest that it is something other than unrelieved falsehood. At the very least, myth accurately narrates the self-understanding of its authors, although the new scientist has to work at deciphering the myths, since they have been corrupted by later generations. Hence Vico says that a "great labor" of his science is to recover the "public grounds of truth," which "with the passage of years and the changes in languages and customs, has come down to us enveloped in falsehood."[11] Greek mythology, properly deciphered, is seen to contain "true and severe histories of the customs of the most ancient peoples of Greece."[12] Like children, the first humans are incapable of deliberate deception. Since they lack irony, their texts do not contain a gap between their apparent intentions and their real motivations. If one is seeking to trace human self-understanding in its earliest forms, then myth is to be regarded as a source of the true. Both *logos* and *mythos* originally meant *fabula,* which itself is defined as *vera narratio.*[13]

Since they are based on ideas that are faithfully and unironically recorded as they are apprehended, gentile fables are bound to contain some truth. "Since it is impossible to create false ideas, for falsity consists in an incoherent combination of ideas, no tradition can arise, however fabulous, which did not at first have some inclination to the true" (*alcun motivo di vero*).[14] To say that myth records an accurate depiction of the pagan worldview, however, is not to say that this worldview itself is true, and in general Vico will argue that the "poetic metaphysics" of the first gentiles is substantively false. It cannot, however, be entirely false. Vico holds that the "vain science" of divination, on which pagan culture is based, "conceals two great principles of truth: first, that there is a divine providence, which governs the human things; second, that men have free will through which, if they so desire and if they act on it, they can escape that fate which, without such providential government, would otherwise be theirs."[15] In the clouds of the storms and the gleam of lightning, the gentiles "made out this great truth: that divine providence watches over the welfare of mankind."[16] The "vulgar wisdom" of the gentiles is wise because it glimpses the existence of providence, although it neither apprehends its true nature nor understands how it operates.

Primitive myth points to the truth, and even when it errs, it does so in a naïve manner. "False religions were born not from the imposture of others, but from their own credulity."[17] If gentile myth is both *sapienza volgare* and *vera narratio,* then what is left of the claim that Vico looks at pagan culture with a suspicious, genealogical eye? Given the vigor of Vico's defense of myth against those who would dismiss it as lacking any cognitive value, how can it be maintained that Vico means to subvert it? Before we answer these questions, an initial observation is in order. To notice the positive side of Vico's appraisal is not to doubt that Vico offers an authentic genealogy. Practitioners of the genealogical method are always free to acknowledge what is true or interesting in the perspective under attack. Even Nietzsche, who christens his *Genealogy* "A Polemic" and generally endeavors to be anything but fair to the opposition, admits that the priestly form of human existence is what enabled the species to acquire depth and become an "interesting animal."[18]

The positive side of Vico's narrative of gentile culture has led some to think that he identifies his own science with that of the primitive mind. This is not the case. Although pagan myth gets some things right, it does so in a questionable manner: it *conceals* truth under the form of what itself is not true. When Vico says that myth "makes out" the true, he means that it does so confusedly, in a fashion that is fundamentally distorted and tainted with the false. The gentiles have *un'idea confusa della divinità,* an idea which is mostly untrue, even if there is no question of a deliberate intent to err.[19] This does not imply, however, a total absence of culpability. Milbank astutely comments that Vico in fact invokes the idea of "a culpability beyond the level of deliberate intention, a culpability that is definitive of a whole culture, and not to be overcome within that culture."[20] Vico can make such a claim only because he writes from the perspective of a quite different culture that liberates him from pagan errors about the gods, as we will see in the next chapter. Here, however, we shall pursue the sense in which Vico considers the *vera narratio* of the gentiles to be systematically untrue.[21] We shall try to understand what Vico means when he contrasts the "truth of rational metaphysics" with the "false sense of poetic metaphysics," which is devised by "nations confused and stupid" who erroneously believe in the "false divinity of Jove."[22] To do this, we shall take our point of departure from the *Scienza nuova prima,* which squarely locates the roots of pagan religion in idolatry and divination. Before we consider the vital role of divination in the operation of gentile culture, we shall consider what Vico means by *l'idolatria*.

Idolatry is "the worship of imaginary gods, falsely thought of as beings of supernatural power who supported men in the extremity of their ills."[23] The beginnings of gentile culture are idolatrous because the gods it creates are imaginary. There is no question that Vico regards the pagan gods as imaginary beings, with no basis in reality. This may be established most economically by turning to the description of the "first nature" of humanity in the first section of Book 4 of the final *Scienza nuova*. The *prima natura* of humanity is a "poetic or creative nature." We may call it divine, because "it ascribed to physical things the being of substances animated by gods, assigning the gods to them according to its idea of each." [24] To call the first nature "divine" is hardly to romanticize it, since it operates by a "powerful deceit of imagination which is most robust in the weakest at reasoning."[25] Such natures are "all fierce and cruel," but "through that same error of their imagination" retain a "terrible fear of the gods whom they themselves had created" (*finti*).[26]

A more detailed consideration of the "natural theogony" is given near the beginning of the "Poetic Metaphysics." After the universal flood, Vico writes, the earth sent up dry exhalations that produced lightning and thunder. Some of the stronger *bestioni* in the mountains "were frightened and astonished by the great effect whose cause they did not know, and raised their eyes and became aware of the sky."[27] The gaze upward inspires the first human creation, an act of *poiesis* so sublime that it "excessively perturbed the very persons who by imagining (*fingendo*) did the creating, for which they were called 'poets,' which is Greek for 'creators.'"[28] The creation is the identification of the thundering sky as "Jove." In their ignorance, metonymically positing causes behind effects to produce "fables in brief" (*picciole favole*), the theological poets make themselves "the rule of the universe."[29] Through a "fantastic metaphysics," the first humans "become all things by *not* understanding them" (*homo non intelligendo fit omnia*).[30] By acknowledging the "sublimity" of the gentile fables, Vico may seem to endorse or approve of what gentile *poiesis* makes. To call the fables sublime, however, is not to assert their metaphysical truth. Vico never holds that the new scientist can or should make the perspective of the theological poets his own. As his reflections on method suggest, the new science is neither itself an act of mythopoesis nor disposed to accept the products of mythopoesis at face value (on the contrary, it views them under a hermeneutic of suspicion).

Although Vico does suggest a certain analogy between gentile *poiesis* and divine making, he does not say that both are equally true. The theological poets create "according to their own ideas," but this is meant to suggest only an analogy to divine making.[31] As Lachterman notes, neither the creation of the mathematician nor that of the theological poet can be a genuine creation *ex nihilo,* since the mind "has the relevant elements in it from the start."[32] "Jove" is not a creation out of nothing, but a magnified projection of the giants' own nature onto the sky. Though bigger and stronger, it is much like the giants themselves, "men all robust bodily strength, who expressed their very violent passions by shouting and grumbling."[33] The giants reduce the unfamiliar to the familiar, because "the nature of the human mind leads it to attribute its own nature to the effect."[34] Drawing upon their own violent and fierce natures, the first men "feigned (*finsero*) the sky to themselves as a great animated body, which in that aspect they called Jove, the first god of the *gentes* called 'major,' who meant to tell them something by the clap of his thunder and the hiss of his bolts."[35]

Vico's use of a cognate of *fingere* in this context recalls the *De antiquissima*'s conception of mathematical creation, to which the *Scienza nuova*'s analysis of gentile *poiesis* is strikingly parallel. Both mathematician and theological poet are said to "feign" what they make.[36] In both cases, Vico intends to suggest a basic skepticism about the reality of what is made, even if he proceeds to trace a sense in which the *factum* is a distorted participation in the *verum*. The gentile *factum* is a product of the imagination rather than reason; it derives from ignorance, not knowledge. "For God, in his purest intelligence, knows things and, by knowing them, creates them; but they, in their robust ignorance, did it by virtue of a wholly corporeal imagination."[37] The myth of Jove is the first and greatest divine fable, an image "so popular, disturbing, and instructive that its creators themselves (*che sel finsero*) believed in it, and feared, revered, and worshipped it in frightful religions."[38] But as the passage from Book 4 shows more clearly, the poets *falsely* believe in the gods they make, and hence idolatrously conflate the natural with the divine. It is *impossible*, Vico emphasizes, "that bodies should be minds, yet it was believed that the thundering sky was Jove."[39] Completely overwhelmed by their own creation, which was inspired by "fear created in men by themselves," the theological poets in the age of gods assume that everything they do and see is somehow Jove.[40]

Pagan idolatry generates a primitive system of ethics based on strength. In the age of gods, *bonus* and *fortis* mean the same thing; Jove is given the title of *optimus,* because he is *fortissimus.*[41] The fable of Jove is used "to teach the vulgar to act virtuously, as the poets have taught themselves."[42] Morality begins when the first humans imagine Jove to speak in a language of lightning bolts and thunderclaps that indicate the divine will (*numen*). Because Jove is *fortissimus* and therefore *optimus,* he is able to withhold the effects of his own power and "save" humans from destruction. "From this first great benefit he conferred on mankind, he was called *Soter,* or savior, because he did not destroy them (this is the first of the three principles that we have taken for this Science). And he was called *Stator,* or establisher, because he put an end to the feral wandering of these few giants, whence they became the princes of the peoples."[43] The fable of Jove establishes the first norms that govern interpersonal relations. In exchange for reverent submission, Jove agrees to "save" the giants and not vanquish them with his lightening bolts. If the giants relapse into bestiality, Jove will maintain his end of the bargain and destroy them. The implied contract begets not only the institution of promise-keeping, but also that of hierarchy, since the relation is constituted by the radical inequality of the two parties. One may even detect the beginnings of human selfhood in the ontology postulated by the fable. Before the fable of Jove, giants were little more than sites of drives to pursue pleasure and avoid pain. After the fable, they continue to house these drives, while perceiving an obligation to keep them in check. The fable of Jove constitutes the first step in the cultural creation of the morally responsible agent, whose ethical code springs out of a false myth about a violent god—a god whose action begets counterviolence that later developments of pagan culture can tame but not eliminate.

As Jove is both *optimus* and *fortissimus,* so the first human rulers are both strong and virtuous. Strength and magnanimity intersect in the "Herculean republics" in which "the pious, wise, chaste, strong, and great-souled cast down the proud and defended the weak, which is the mark of excellence in civil governments."[44] Ultimately, however, such strength is based on an idolatrous myth. Vico does not fall into the trap of romanticizing primitivism, of supposing that the first morality was anything other than superstitious and cruel, requiring the sacrifice of children to the gods.[45] Nowhere does Vico recommend a *return* to primitive morality. His aim is to reprove ahistorical thinkers who eulogize progress and condemn previous ages by reminding them that it was precisely a "fanaticism of superstition" that restrained the gentiles and made possible the rise of the republics, the precondition of philosophy.[46] The salvo against deists and freethinkers is not an endorsement of poetic morality.

The idolatrous failure to conceive a divinity that transcends nature, combined with the demand to know the will of the gods, leads to the family of practices that Vico terms "divination." "Idolatry shared its birth with that of divination, that is, a vain science of the future from certain sensible admonitions, believed to have been sent to man by the gods."[47] Divination is both intellectually false and morally questionable, since it originates from the vice of curiosity. Vico makes this clear in both the *Scienza nuova prima* and the axiom of the final *Scienza nuova* that locates the "beginnings of divination" in curiosity. What makes divination false is the fact that it looks to physical nature for signs of God, without any awareness of the possibility that God transcends nature. Vico does distinguish between the crude divination of the Romans and the "more refined" divination of the Chaldeans. Whereas the Egyptians, Greeks, and Romans base their auguries on the observation of thunderbolts and eagles—"the weapons and birds of Jove"—the Chaldeans practice a kind of astrology that looks to the shooting stars. Vico associates the relative superiority of Chaldean astrology with his identification of the "Eastern peoples" as the descendants of Shem, who fall into gigantism yet manage to preserve a somewhat less distorted memory of their humanity than the "Western peoples" (the descendants of Ham and Japheth).[48] Because of their comparatively less bestial origins, the Chaldeans will practice "a more refined divination from the observation of the movements of the planets and the aspects of the stars."[49] Even so, they share in the primal error of identifying the sky with Jove and hence adopting a practice of divination. The Hebrew culture uniquely resists this error.

The role played by divination in the origin of pagan culture, as Vico conceives it, is difficult to overstate. Divination is a "prime element" of the civil world; it is the key to the power of the first human fathers, who "must have been sages in auspicial divinity, the priests who sacrificed to take the auspicices or to make sure of their meaning."[50] The fathers are none other than the theological poets, the "sages who understood the language of the gods expressed in the auspices of Jove."[51] Divination is the source of jurisprudence, whose *interpretari* was originally *interpatrari,* "'to enter into the fathers,' as the gods were at first called."[52] Of the laws allegedly commanded by the gods in the first age (actually by those taking the auspices, as the new scientist knows, since the early pagans are confused and mistakenly attribute their own activity to the gods) the one that Vico identifies as "the first and most important" is marriage.[53] As the second principle of the new science, marriage is the key to what Vico calls "poetic morals." It is the soil out of which other ethical institutions grow. To say this is another way of emphasizing the centrality of divination for pagan culture, since marriage grows out of divination.

Although *la pietà* is the "mother of all the moral, economic, and civil virtues," it is only with marriage that the virtues begin to assume a recognizable form.[54] Moral virtue originates, Vico says, with *conatus,* the force that binds the nomadic giants into social existence.[55] The first manifestation of *conatus* is physical: human bodies cease their wanderings and come together in settlements. This restraint gives rise to "the virtue of the spirit," which curbs the "bestial lust (*libido*) from finding its satisfaction in the sight of heaven."[56] The first marriages occur when terror inspires the giants to abandon their habit of public copulation, leading each of them to drag a single woman into his cave. "Thus the act of human love was performed under cover, in hiding, that is to say, in shame; and they began to feel that sense of shame which Socrates described as the color of virtue."[57] The introduction of *pudore* complicates the picture. Fear, by itself, cannot account for the creation of pious monogamy.[58] Only the conjunction of self-preservative *utilitas* and natural *honestas* is adequate to explain why humans created deities that are capable of not simply violence, but genuine anger. Absent a sense of shame, the feral beasts might have continued to perceive natural phenomena like thunder and lightning, without apprehending them as anthropomorphic gods who express disapproval and threaten to punish if repentance is not forthcoming. These considerations show that Vico, far from simply multiplying entities, introduces shame into the account because he is supremely realistic, adhering rigorously to the axiom that "because of the indefinite nature of the human mind, whenever it is lost in ignorance, man makes himself the measure of all things."[59] If the first humans did not themselves possess the capacity to feel moral disapproval, they hardly would have been able to perceive its expression in anything external.

Religion and shame, then, are the twin sources of marriages, "chaste carnal unions effected under the fear of some divinity."[60] Human morality has its beginnings in religion, in the tacit agreement between Jove and the giant. Sometimes Vico writes as if marriage literally follows the establishment of religion, but this is misleading. Only *in* marriage is the pact between the giants and gods ratified. The tight connection between the first religions and the first marriages is manifested by the three "solemnities" (*solennità*) that accompany the latter. The first solemnity is the auspices, which by recalling the original thunder dictate that the wife adopt the public religion of her husband.[61] The second is the veiling of women: Vico derives *nuptiae* from *nubendo*.[62] The third, and perhaps most significant, is "a certain show of force in taking a wife, recalling the real violence with which the giants dragged the wives into their caves."[63] The violence of the original relation between Jove and the giant is re-enacted in the first marriages. The element of force is never fully overcome, but finds symbolic expression in later ceremonies. These three solemnities, which (as Lilla observes) seem to correspond to the virtues of prudence, temperance, and fortitude, are encoded in myths about Juno.[64] The depiction of Juno as both wife and sister of Jove is not an insignificant detail, but reveals that the first marriages must have taken place between brothers and sisters.[65] Juno's Greek name, Hera, inspired the first sovereigns to call themselves heroes. Vico finds etymological connections between Hera, *heri,* and *hereditas,* which must have meant a "despotic sovereignty."[66]

Vico traces *prudentia,* the first of the pagan virtues, back to divination. The first men were made prudent by taking direction from the auspices of Jove.[67] As rational philosophers conceive *phronesis* as a type of situational "reading," so the first prudence was a literal reading of the skies, for the sake of action. Justice arises from Jove—Vico derives *ius* from *Ious*—both in respect of the god-man relation established by the divine *soter* and *stator,* and in respect of a relative peace between human beings.[68] Temperance is acquired through the institution of marriage, where the giants learn to control their passions by learning to be "content with one woman for their lifetime."[69] Fortitude is the habit that derives from strength: the giants who abandoned their feral ways were necessarily the strongest. Vico proceeds to trace the beginnings of virtue in the myth of Hercules. The succession of Jove and Juno by Hercules in the natural theogony is not coincidental. It is the poetic expression of the truth that "piety accompanied by marriage is the school where the first rudiments of all the great virtues are imparted."[70] Virtue, originally the capacity for overcoming physical adversity, is born when Juno imposes the "twelve" labors on Hercules.[71] Vico rejects as a later corruption the conventional interpretation that posits feminine jealousy as the motive for the imposition of labors, and insists that the original signification of Herakles is *Heras kleos,* the glory of Hera.[72] Conquering obstacles by strength and winning glory are at the root of early virtue, which Vico equates with "poetic heroism." Vico notes that Plato raises his own "philosophical heroism," where the authentic hero transcends both man and beast through full command of the passions, above poetic heroism, which always involves a struggle with the passions.[73] He approves this elevation and elsewhere attributes it to Aristotle, without denying its mythical origins.[74]

The first marriages, sanctified under the auspices, are the occasion of the transition from feral giants into human beings who "with certain [i.e., particular] women produce certain children and thereby become certain fathers."[75] Marriage thus further articulates the notion of personal identity. It is also the origin of teleological community. Vico speaks of the "true natural friendship" of marriage and finds it to be the first human institution "in which are realized the three final goods: the noble, the useful, and the pleasant."[76] Finally, marriage serves to confirm the presence of hierarchical power relations and to reinforce the institution of promise-keeping via the prohibition of adultery. (The wife who breaks her pledge to her husband is treated with the same violence as the man who breaks his promise to Jove.) Given the tendency of the first husbands to claim "sovereignty" over their wives, one might detect the genesis of property rights. For the most part, however, Vico associates property with human burial—the third of the three principles of the *Scienza nuova*, which we will examine in due course.

Vico emphasizes that the very root of pagan culture—religion conceived as system of idolatry, divination, and sacrifice—is utterly contaminated by violence and self-deception. He is quick, however, to acknowledge the power of such a root to generate the institutions that are part of human civilization. There is a sense in which Vico's history is "progressive." From low beginnings, human society gradually rises to higher things. If there is genuine progress made by pagan culture, then why does it remain necessary to speak of Vico's narrative as a genealogy? Would it not be more appropriate to read the *Scienza nuova* as a celebration of pagan culture, rather than a subversion? To these questions, three things must be said. First, the apparent progressivism of Vico's narrative is not meant to portray pagan culture in a soft light. Its true intention is to glorify providence, to emphasize its greatness by showing its ability to transform a culture founded on utter credulity and falsehood into something that approximates truth. There is no tension between Vico's prosecution of *this* objective and our view that he casts a jaundiced, suspicious eye on the roots of paganism. Second, the progress is more apparent than real. Whatever beauty it may achieve at the highest point of its growth, the flower that springs out of corrupt roots is destined to perish. What Nietzsche says of Judaic and Christian culture may be applied, *mutatis mutandis,* to pagan culture. After an initial period of growth and splendor, it is doomed to degenerate into nihilism, unless it can be transformed at its core. One can acknowledge the presence of a progressive strand in the overall tapestry of the *Scienza nuova* without using it to blaspheme the whole.[77] These claims, here made polemically for the sake of anticipating an objection, will receive more substantiation in the final chapter. Third, the normative character of Vico's narrative should not be forgotten. Vico's characterization of pagan sacrifices as "savage and cruel" makes sense only if he is construed as offering a critique of those practices from a perspective that is alien to gentile culture. This perspective is the standpoint of Catholic Christianity, the standpoint from which Vico consistently distinguishes the Hebrews from the gentiles. Insofar as it takes Hebrew culture as normative, the standard to which the pagans must constantly be compared, the *Scienza nuova* constitutes an ongoing judgment *contra gentiles.* In both its origins and developments, pagan culture is judged as inferior to what is humanly possible with the assistance of divine grace. It is exposed as evil, in the Augustinian sense of the term; it is vitiated by the absence of a good that ought to be present. Even when it manages to approximate justice, it falls radically short, since what the Christian religion commands "is not merely justice but charity toward all mankind."[78] To defend this reading of the *Scienza nuova,* we will have to establish in more detail the important role played by "the Hebrews" in his thought.

The Hebrew Difference

What is the place of the Hebrews within the *Scienza nuova?* Is there a place? Many commentators have thought that the Hebrews are "exempted" from the new science.[1] The reasons for this view are obvious enough. Vico has increasingly little to say about the Hebrews as he writes the multiple versions of the *Scienza nuova.* The "rational civil theology of divine providence" is intended to narrate the origins and development of the gentiles, not the Hebrews. When they have not disregarded them altogether, commentators have tended to minimize the significance of Vico's scattered remarks on the Hebrews. These remarks are usually regarded either as fideistic assertions of orthodoxy, bearing little relation to the intellectual core of the new science, or as deliberately misleading statements intended to throw the Inquisition off the scent. In either case, the alleged exemption of the Hebrews from the new science serves to reinforce the widespread tendency to ignore what Vico actually wrote about them.

There is a sense, of course, in which the Hebrews are "exempt" from the new science. As Mazzotta observes, sacred history can never become an "object of study" in the same way that secular history is, since it ultimately stems from God's creation.[2] The *De antiquissima* already placed "revealed theology" outside Vico's hierarchy of *scientiae,* on the ground that the human inquirer is barred from the genus or mode by which it comes to be.[3] But to say that the Hebrews are exempt from the new science is not to say that they are absent from it. In the *Scienza nuova prima,* Vico holds that, apart from the demands of faith, "human necessity" requires that "the principles of this science be drawn from sacred history."[4] Similarly, "the principles of all gentile wisdom human and divine" are said by the *Vita* to have been discovered "in the bosom of the true Church."[5] The final *Scienza nuova* makes essentially the same claim when it contrasts the superior antiquity of *sacra historia* with the "most ancient profane histories that have come down to us."[6] Of the "state of nature under the patriarchs" out of which "the peoples and cities later arose," sacred history is able to "narrate in great detail," unlike the profane histories which have "nothing or little [to say], and that little quite confused."[7] The *Scienza nuova* aims to replace the existing gentile histories with a new history that is written from a perspective that draws upon the Hebrews, who "have preserved their memories in great detail from the beginning of the world."[8] Far from being absent from the new science, sacred history is the normative lens through which Vico looks at the profane history of the pagans.[9] As the *Scienza nuova prima* seeks to locate the "human necessity" for drawing the starting points of the new science from Scripture, so the final *Scienza nuova* proclaims its desire to give "human reasons in support of Christian faith, which takes its start from the fact that the first people of the world were the Hebrews, whose prince was Adam, created by the true God at the time of the creation of the world."[10] It is misleading to say that the Hebrews are exempted from the new science, unless one simply means that they are part of the *explanans* rather than the *explanandum*.

If sacred history is what enables Vico to describe and judge profane history, it must have something in common with it. If it were purely other, it would hardly be able to function as a norm. Yet its role as a vantage point from which judgment is delivered requires it to be qualitatively different from profane history. Vico's understanding of the relation between the two histories exhibits precisely this play of sameness and difference. In the *Scienza nuova prima,* Vico contends that "[sacred history] offers a more intelligible description than any gentile history of an original state of nature, or era of families in the beginning, in which fathers ruled under the government of God, which Philo elegantly named *Theocratia*," but says relatively little about just which particular aspects of sacred history prove illuminating where gentile histories are obfuscatory.[11] He suggests that "because of the two periods of slavery which the Jews suffered under the Egyptians and Assyrians, sacred history offers a weightier account of the antiquities of Egypt and Assyria than does Greek history."[12] But what is Vico's conception of *sacra historia*? How does it relate to Vico's narration of pagan culture as founded upon idolatry, divination, and sacrifice? To confront these questions, we must go back to the first part of the *De constantia iurisprudentis*.

The original state of mankind, to which sacred history alone attests, is that of *Ada integer,* who "would contemplate God with a pure mind and love God with a true spirit."[13] This prelapsarian state was one of perfect harmony: elders were given the same respect as parents, comrades as brothers, young men as sons. Varro manages to "conjecture" such a thing with his "formula of nature," but only dimly; Plato provides a surreal parody of it in Book 5 of the *Republic*.[14] Once the *sapientia integra* of Adam has been divided, and thereby corrupted, both the Hebrews and gentiles attempt to remedy this condition through sacrifices and honor (*honor*) given to God. But Vico insists on a distinction (*discrimen*) between the Hebrews and the gentiles.[15] The Hebrew sacrifices preserve something of the purity of the original Adamic contemplation; they are driven "more by purity of mind than purity of body." The gentiles, however, offer *honor* "only with purity of body."[16] Their *contemplatio* is derived from the *caelis templi*, the "temples of the heavens" that were marked out by the augurs.[17] This differentiates them from the Hebrews, who never confuse their piety toward God with the idolatrous worship of a heavenly body. Hence "the Hebrew people, who worshiped the true God, were not founded on divination," a fact that Vico identifies as "the principal reason for their separation from the gentiles, for whom idolatry and divination arise together as twins."[18]

Despite this crucial difference, the Hebrews and the gentiles alike inherit the effects of the Fall. "Now the worship of God had come from knowledge of the eternal true with pure mind in integral man, for it was always uniform. Whence, because man had been deprived by his own sin of knowing the true with a pure mind in the active life, the certain was substituted for the true."[19] Having lost the true in its pure form, both Hebrew and gentile religion attempt to recover it through the certain: "by laws are instituted certain gods, certain ceremonies, certain verbal formulae, so that religions acquire the character of the eternal, inasmuch as this is possible for man."[20] Here one may discern the origins of the famous axiom of the *Scienza nuova*: "men who do not know what is true of things take care to hold fast to what is certain, so that, if they cannot satisfy their intellects by knowledge (*scienza*), their wills at least may rest on consciousness (*coscienza*)."[21] The question is not whether the certain is to substitute for the true—Vico understands both the Hebrews and the gentiles as driven toward such a substitution—but how this is to take place. Laws instituted as a response to the felt absence of the true "correspond for the common run to the divine things which the philosophers teach by reason, and are the first and eternal truths which metaphysics establishes."[22] A metaphysics is latently present within the "religions founded by the peoples," just as the true is immanently present in the certain. There will be a difference, however, between a metaphysics whose object is supplied by the "true religion founded by the Hebrews, who conceive a single uncreated Creator of the world under no image (*sub nulla imagine*)," and a metaphysics whose object is determined by "the false religions founded by the gentiles, who venerate under the form of idols (*sub idolis*) the world, the soul of the world, the mind of this soul, or its motive force that is coeval with the world, acting by necessity and divided into the parts of the world, for example, Jove regarded as the motive force of the sky, Neptune that of the sea."[23] Both types of metaphysics are attempts by corrupt nature to "put together again" (*iterum coaluere*) the broken parts of what had formerly been *sapientia integra*. But the two forms of reconstruction will not be the same, since only the Hebrews manage to avoid the primal error of reducing the incorporeal God to parts of the world or to its immanent forces—Vico regards the latter as a more sophisticated variant of the former. The "contemplation of the highest things" (*altissimarum rerum contemplatio*) by the gentiles never entirely escapes its roots in the *templa caeli* marked out by the augurs.[24]

That Vico intends to make a connection between pagan religion and later metaphysics is strongly suggested by the following paragraph of chapter 4 of *De constantia philosophiae,* in which "the religion of the deists is demonstrated as false."[25] Less important than the particulars of the demonstration is its position in the sequence of Vico's thought. Later developments of gentile religion do not escape the blemish of its origins in idolatry and divination. Although Vico thinks that pagan corporeality is false, he does not find it unintelligible. He views it as a natural response to the demand to find a surrogate for the true in the certain. Since we can no longer cognize the eternal true with pure mind, it is not inexplicable that the gentiles would look to bodily, tangible things as a substitute. Whatever his Platonism, Vico recognizes that humans need bodily things if they are to know the highest truth. (The sect of philosophers who forget this and thereby "rend" human nature are the Stoics.)[26] Hence Vico explains the Incarnation as the ultimate response to the problem created by the severing of the certain and the true. Because it perfectly reconciles the *verum* and the *certum,* split by the Fall, the Incarnation restores in humans the capacity for the original Adamic piety.

Although he nowhere again purports to provide an *incarnationis demonstratio,*[27] Vico does not abandon this conception of Christ in his later works. Even the final *Scienza nuova,* which has struck many as taking scant account of what any Christian must regard as the central event of human history, implies that Christ is the ultimate reconciliation of the *verum* and the *certum.* In Book 4 of the *Scienza nuova,* Vico observes that Hebraic revelation begins with "internal speech," which is the "proper expression of a God all mind." It requires completion "by external speech through the prophets and through Jesus Christ to the Apostles, by whom it was declared to the Church."[28] The gentiles also aim for the *certum,* but less truthfully through the "auspices, the oracles, and other corporeal signs believed to be divine admonitions because they were believed to come from the gods, whom the gentiles believed to be composed of body."[29] Such institutions succeed in making out the truth of providence, but in a way that is contaminated with error. The remedy is to unite the inner truths revealed to the Hebrews with the external certitude that human beings desire by nature. In this first place, this remedy is the Incarnation itself. Secondarily, it is the "new order of humanity" which God permits to be "born among the nations in order that [the true religion] might be firmly established according to the natural course of human institutions themselves."[30] It is precisely in virtue of its ability to harmonize the *verum* and the *certum* that Vico speaks of "our Christian theology, which combines civil and natural theology with the loftiest revealed theology."[31]

The conventional view that Christ is utterly absent from the *Scienza nuova* is misleading.[32] This is not to deny that Vico spends more time on what he originally termed the *dubbi e desideri intorno alla teologia de' gentili.*[33] The novelty of Vico's science does not come from his theology, which tends not to be innovative, but from his distinctive analysis of pagan history beginning in the age of gods. It is important to see, however, that Vico's reading of pagan history depends in no small part on his understanding of sacred history. Mazzotta observes that the anti-religious tendencies of many of Vico's interpreters tend to promote "a systematic evasion of coming to terms with Vico's reading of the Bible and of Hebrew history, which is his way of reaching the core of religious consciousness."[34] The key to a more satisfactory reading of Vico on the Hebrews (a task which is still very much in its infancy) is to recognize that, while Vico emphasizes the separateness of the Jews and their freedom from idolatry and divination, he *also* regards the Hebrews and pagans as possessing a common origin. According to Vico, the "giants were scattered over the earth after the flood."[35] Originally created human by God—Vico specifically rejects the pre-Adamite heresy[36]—the descendants of the sons of Noah abandoned their religion, "dissolved their marriages and broke up their families by promiscuous intercourse, and began roving wild through the great forest of the earth."[37] Males pass the day pursuing females and fleeing from wild beasts; feral mothers abandon their children after nursing them. Since they "grow up without ever hearing a human voice, much less learning any human custom," the children are "quite without that fear of gods, fathers, and teachers which chills and benumbs even the most exuberant in childhood."[38] Vico also finds a physical dimension in the second fall of humanity. Allowed to "wallow naked in their own shit," the children "absorb nitrous salts into their bodies in greater abundance" and grow "robust, vigorous, excessively big in brawn and bone, to the point of becoming giants."[39]

From its feral and fecal beginnings, gentile humanity is eventually "refounded" as it rediscovers, albeit in distorted form, the institutions of religion, marriage, and burial. Unlike the gentiles, the Hebrews retain their ordinary stature and preserve the religion of their common father, since they never fell into giantism.[40] In this specific sense, Vico considers the Hebrews to have a distinct origin from the gentiles. This does not, however, entail the irrelevance of the Hebrews to gentile history. As Mazzotta notes, "the Flood marks the difference between the giantism of the founders of the gentile nations and the Hebrews who were of normal size. The difference between them is a difference in moral values, and the Jews, in their exception, are, paradoxically, the norm. The absolute heterogeneity between the three races is reversed into the perception of their common fate in a diaspora."[41] If the gentiles and the Hebrews come from the same God, why does Vico maintain a doctrine of distinct origins? As we have seen from the *De constantia philosophiae,* Vico places a large stress upon the freedom of Hebrews from divination. The final *Scienza nuova* not only preserves this doctrine, but elaborates it. One of the *principali cagioni* for dividing the world into the Hebrews and gentiles is that the religion of the former "was founded by the true God on the prohibition of divination, on which all the gentile nations arose."[42] Because they conceive God in a non-idolatrous manner, the Hebrews uniquely avoid the will to seek "knowledge of good and evil" through divination.[43] In a sevenfold enumeration of divinatory practice, Vico takes account of variations among different gentile cultures. Chaldean divination is not quite the same as Egyptian or Roman divination, and the ancient Germans worshipped their gods in forest clearings, rather than in regions of the sky marked out by the augurs. Such differences in detail, however, pale in comparision to the Hebrews. "But the Hebrews worshiped the true All Highest, who is above the heavens, in the enclosure of the tabernacle; and Moses, wherever the people of God extended their conquests, ordered the burning of the sacred groves enclosing the *luci* of which Tacitus speaks."[44] Hebrew culture is founded upon the rejection of divination, even if Christian languages inherit the tendency to refer to God as "the heavens."[45] (This is mostly innocent, however, since the Christian religion has never "produced a plurality of divinities," despite the "passing of years and of nations, not to say customs.")[46] Hebrew rejection of divination implies a corresponding recognition of the evil of idolatry—in principle if not always in practice, as the prophetic books remind us. Because God reveals himself directly to them, the Hebrews escape the fate of projecting their own natures upon the thundering sky. They conceive of God as pure mind, and therefore transcending nature as its creative source. Although Platonic philosophy glimpses the transcendent, creative character of the Good, the firmest support for the rejection of the Spinozist *Deus sive natura* seems to be revelation itself. (That revelation constitutes the primary source of resistance to the identification of God with nature is tacitly acknowledged by Spinoza himself in his determination to offer a radical critique of revelation.) Vico takes revelation already to know what the best metaphysics humanly confirms, but articulates in a comparatively obscure manner.

To the difference between false divination and true revelation corresponds a distinction between "bestial education" of the gentiles, enabled by "ordinary help from providence," and the "human education" of the Hebrews, made possible by "extraordinary help from the true God."[47] Since they have no truck with divination, the humanly educated priests of the Hebrews, the Levites, will be very different from the *mystae* who purport to explain the will of God through auspices and oracles.[48] This difference enables Vico to assess the characteristic institutions of gentile culture from a critical standpoint. Once again, however, the careful reader will be alert to the possibility of important parallels between Hebrew and gentile culture, since the existence of such parallels is implied by the capacity of the former to serve as a norm for judgment of the latter. Profane history tells us little or nothing about the original state of nature, which Vico identifies as the "family state," since its beginnings are obfuscated by the institutions of idolatry and divination. Sacred history, however, offers a "more intelligible description" of this state. What does this claim mean? Milbank suggests that "gentile history has been read as a kind of imperfect approximation to the semitic in that what has been stressed is theocracy, patriarchy, priestly rulers, a supreme god, an all-important role for written law, and the providential, temporal dimension of religion."[49] In the *Scienza nuova prima* Vico claims that "the first and oldest natural law of the gentes in the state of the families"—the protection of the weak by the strong in exchange for service, which Vico will call "asylum"—is "common to gentiles and Hebrews alike, but observed more thoroughly by the Hebrews than by the gentiles."[50] Even the briefest inspection of the structure of the *De constantia philologiae* will show that Vico takes the family state of the Hebrews as a paradigm for reconstructing what he calls the "obscure theocracy" of the Romans.

Perhaps the most striking feature of Vico's account is that it seems to regard both the Hebrew and pagan languages about the gods as essentially poetic, making use of imaginative rather than conceptual universals. The *De constantia* regards Moses not only as the supreme philosopher, lawgiver, and historian, but also as the first poet.[51] Following St. Jerome, Vico also emphasizes that most of the Book of Job is written in "heroic verse."[52] In the *Scienza nuova prima,* Vico describes the original Adamic language as "wholly poetic, surpassing in sublimity that of Homer himself," a fact that he adds "even philologists" recognize.[53] But can Vico so closely assimilate the Hebrew and pagan languages, while maintaining the normative status of the former? Milbank poses the question with characteristic urgency: "how, given its poetic-religious character, did Vico consider that the Adamic language as perpetuated in Hebrew contrived to avoid idolatry, divination and sacrifice, or the whole apparatus of mystification which Vico considers to have been the vehicle for gentile political violence and the obscuring of the historical record?"[54] A full answer to this question would require a detailed intepretation of the *De constantia philologiae* (the text which contains Vico's most elaborate remarks on the history of Hebrew culture), along with a judgment about the extent to which its themes survive or fail to survive in the later texts.

In lieu of such an interpretation, we may cite Milbank's own complex reading as an exemplary starting point. His main contentions can be summarized as follows: (1) Although the Hebrew language was originally poetic, like the gentile language, it avoids obfuscating the basis of culture by resisting the temptation to idolatrize nature and to invent semidivine men who are falsely represented as descending from the gods.

Genesis "records strictly human protagonists, human inventors."[55] (2) While the Hebrews rely upon a priestly caste for the intepretation of laws, like the gentiles, their history is uniquely open about recording the institution of its caste (the Levites) that does not resort to concealment for the sake of protecting their power.[56] (3) By naming God and yet leaving him unknown (*sum qui sum*), the Hebrew language preserves a more authentic sense of both the presence and absence of God.[57] (4) Whereas the gentile divine language is constituted by an original withholding of threatened violence (recall the conception of Jove as *soter* and *stator*), Hebrew language in its prelapasarian form "registers the notion of a *more primitive* meaning originally conceived as God's gratuitious creation of the world from a charitable and in no sense violent impulse."[58] (5) The charitable origins of Hebrew culture lead to its more equitable development, as attested by its different agrarian law (the "law of Jubilee"), its more humane treatment of vagabonds, and its resistance to the notion that the father has the right of life and death over his sons. Such a right is reserved for God, as Vico interprets the story of Abraham and Isaac to suggest.[59] (6) Although it is not abstract or metaphysical in its poetic phase, Hebrew language nonetheless possesses the capacity to articulate interior notions of an "inner law" or "purity of heart" that are impossible for the early pagan language to comprehend.[60] (7) Vico's claim that the Hebrews possess a superior memory means not that they are better recordkeepers, but more radically that "the Bible supplies the vital interpretive key which tells us how pagan mythology is to be unravelled."[61]

Vico simultaneously unmasks gentile theology as a false system of idolatry and divination and understands it to possess a modicum of truth. It dimly "makes out" the reality of providence, without adequately understanding its nature or its operation (in sharp contrast to the *scienza nuova* itself). Hebrew culture provides the unique counterexample to the claim that human culture necessarily originates in idolatry, divination, and sacrifice. If sacred history is the norm of the new science, why does Vico have relatively little to say about the Hebrews in the *Scienza nuova,* especially in its final version? It is difficult to know with certainty. Probably he thought that a science capable of giving "human reasons" in support of biblical faith would be a more potent apologetic than a text which cites Scripture at every turn. Milbank suggests that Vico decreases the number of references to the Hebrews because "only the most intellectually gifted of Vico's contemporaries would have been able to accept his entire vision as having genuinely apologetic intent." Despite his orthodoxy, he "would have had to fear the imputation of heresy."[62] Reading the *Scienza nuova* in light of the earlier writings suggests that Vico's conception of the Hebrew difference is a crucial part of what gives the new science its normative edge, and thereby qualifies it as an authentic genealogy of pagan myth.

From Achilles to Socrates

Vico does not conceive the distinction between "age of gods" and "age of heroes" as a rigid dichotomy. Within the first republics, "the age of gods coursed on, for there still must have endured that religious way of thinking according to which it was the gods who did whatever men themselves were doing."[1] "Heroic nature" continues to be theocentric, defining those without the auspices as subhuman. Heroic *ius* is still based on strength; it is the *ius* of Achilles, "who referred every right to the tip of his spear."[2] Governments in the heroic ages are theocratic senates that strive to maintain a firm distinction between patricians of divine ancestry and plebeians of bestial origin. (The division is already embodied in the structure of the families, which Vico calls "monastic republics.")[3] Justice is a matter of civil as opposed to natural equity. Strict adherence to legal formulae, held sacred and cloaked in secrecy, prevails at the expense of the plebs. *Qui cadit virgula, caussa cadit:* the laws cannot be observed too scrupulously in the "punctilious" time of the heroes.[4] In the interest of conserving their own power, the patricians withhold knowledge of the sacred laws from the plebs. Vico infers that "sacred" and "secret" originally meant the same thing.[5]

The first republics are established when the fathers unite to protect their own interests against the *famuli,* who grow increasingly discontent as the fathers begin "to abuse the laws of protection and to govern the clients harshly," thereby departing "from the natural order, which is that of justice."[6] Having grown "weary of being always obliged to serve their lords," the mutinous *famuli* unite to form "the first plebs of the heroic cities."[7] The coalition of individuals into classes that transcend family boundaries lays the foundation of the republic. Against Bodin and others, Vico emphasizes that these republics were not monarchic but aristocratic in form, because they were ruled by the union of noble families. The "kings" of the first republics are simply men chosen by the nobles, men "fiercer than the rest and with greater presence of spirit."[8] As Vico imagines it, the republic is the natural and necessary outcome of struggles in the family state. "Without human discernment or counsel," the nobles discover that "they had united their private interest in a common interest called *patria,* which, the word *res* being understood, means 'the interest of the fathers.' The nobles were accordingly called 'patricians,' and the nobles must have been the only citizens of the first *patriae* or fatherlands."[9] Vico emphasizes the spontaneous rise of the republic, quoting Pomponius's axiom that *rebus ipsis dictantibus, regna condita.*[10] Against Hobbesian accounts, Vico denies that the republic is, or could be, "born from the force or from the fraud of a single man."[11] Precisely because it emerges *without* conscious calculation, Vico locates its cause in providence and claims that "beyond any design of [the fathers], they came together in a universal civil good, which we call 'republic.'"[12]

The gathering of the family fathers into a single class that Vico will refer to as "nobles," "heroes," or "patricians" is accompanied by the first glimpse of class consciousness among the plebeians, the *famuli* who now understand themselves, however dimly, to be united by a common interest. As distinct classes arise, so does the possibility of laws that govern relations between the classes. The "first agrarian law" functions to subdue the rebellious *famuli* with the lowest possible cost of the fathers. "For the nature of the strong is to surrender as little as possible of what they have acquired by valor, and only so much as is necessary to preserve their acquisitions."[13] Thus "bonitary ownership of the fields" is granted to the plebs. Maintained only by "perpetual physical possession" of the fields, bonitary or "natural" ownership can be revoked any time, at the whim at the fathers.[14] The law is designed not to benefit the plebs, but to codify the power of the nobles and sanction the punishment of those who rebel. The *ius violentiae,* as Vico terms it in the *Diritto universale,* is not the law of the philosophers, but a weapon by which the strong organize their power.[15] Heroic ethics remains a morality of strength designed to perpetuate the authority of the fathers. It is not that the heroes understand themselves as arbitrary dictators. On the contrary, within the universe of moral discourse inhabited by noble and plebeian alike, heroic domination is eminently justified. "Since ownership (*dominio*) follows power (*potestà*), and since the lives of the *famuli* were dependent on the heroes who had saved them by granting them asylum, it was lawful and right that they should have a similarly precarious ownership, which they might enjoy as long as it suited the heroes to maintain them in possession of the fields they had assigned to them."[16]

The nobles dominate the plebs not simply by control of economic resources, but also—and more importantly—by their ability to define the terms in which both classes understand themselves. Although Vico does not ignore the link between power and economic factors—"the aristocratic republics keep the wealth within the order of the nobility, for wealth adds to the power of this order"[17]—he assigns a far more prominent causal role to the language that enables patrician rule. Power is maintained by a disproportionate allocation of resources, as in Marx, but the resources are more cultural than material in character. They are primarily linguistic, consisting of unwritten laws based on the auspices. The ruling nobles are priests who keep the auspices secret not only from foreigners, but "even from their own plebs, whence indeed it was everywhere called sacred doctrine, for sacred is as much as to say secret."[18] To preserve their own power, the nobles must conceal their deliberations from the plebs. Secrecy is "the soul through which aristocratic republics live."[19]

At the heart of the secret language is myth, which provides the stock of resources that heroic man uses to understand his world. The identity of the heroes is constructed out of the "divine" language created by the first humans, in which everything is imagined to be a god. The "heroic" language is a modification of the divine language; a distinction arises between the "immortal gods" and the heroes themselves, who are lesser gods or "sons of Jove, as if they had been generated under his auspices."[20] Understanding themselves in relation to both their divine parents and the *famuli* of bestial ancestry, the heroes possess the naiveté that Nietzsche associates with strength.[21] They define the plebs as inhuman not out of a conscious desire to oppress fellow human beings, but simply because they *are* nonhuman in the world of auspicial signs, which the heroes inherit and take for granted. Natural piety, as much as a deliberate will to maintain their own position, moves the heroes to exclude the *famuli* from the original "principles of humanity"—the sacred institutions of religion, marriage, and burial.

The heroes define plebeian nature by negation, imagining an ontological difference between themselves and anything that is other. They also articulate a positive conception of plebeian identity in myths that represent them as "poetic monsters"—"men in aspect but brute beasts in their customs."[22] The heroes employ images as the mechanism of apprehension, since their minds are not sufficiently developed to abstract intelligible universals. Bearing the marks of their crude origins, the heroes can only create "poetic characters" or "imaginative genera or universals, to which, as to certain models or ideal portraits, to reduce all the particular species that resembled them."[23] These are constructed according to what is most familiar—the human body and its parts, the senses and the passions. To represent the plebs, the heroes understand their distinctive characteristics not by conceptual universals, but by imagining a different "subject" for each attribute and then combining the subjects to create poetic monsters that unite the human and the bestial. The monsters do not "represent" a prior understanding, but simply *are* the plebs, as perceived by the heroes, who actually *think* in poetic characters.[24] Like the gods created in the natural theogony, the poetic monsters "arose from a necessity of this first human nature, which (as we demonstrated in the Axioms) is unable to abstract the forms or the properties from subjects."[25] The contrast is with the mental operations of developed human nature, which can be described in Aristotelian language that posits the abstraction of universals from matter apprehended by the senses and their combination or division in an existential judgment.[26]

In support of his account, Vico cites and interprets ancient myths about monsters. The satyr Marsyas is a monster who is flayed alive by the patrician Apollo, the god of "civil light." Vico discovers in this myth a clue to "the savagery of heroic punishments."[27] The satyr Pan tries to seize the nymph Syrinx, and "finds himself embracing reeds." The reeds, along with the clouds embraced by Ixion in his attempt to charm Juno, signify the "lightness" and "vanity" of natural marriage.[28] (The contrast is with civil marriage, marriage with the auspices.) From the clouds are born the "centaurs, that is to say the plebeians, who are the monsters of discordant natures of which Livy speaks."[29] The patricians use the fables to convince the plebs that they "were all monsters because they practiced marriages like those of wild animals (*agitabant connubia more ferarum*)."[30] Vico notes versions of the *Odyssey* in which Penelope prostitutes herself to plebeian suitors and gives birth to the monster Pan.[31] Another "monster of two diverse natures" is the minotaur, born from a union between noble and plebeian.[32] The Law of the Twelve Tables defines children "born of noble women without the solemnity of nuptials" as monsters to be thrown into the Tiber.[33] In Sparta, such children are imagined as "ugly and deformed offspring" who are "cast down from Mount Taygetus."[34]

Monsters are not the only figure used by the heroes to define the plebs in antithesis to themselves. Vico notes that the heroic *viri* see the plebs as women.[35] Doves are attributed to the "plebeian Venus" because they are base in comparison with eagles and swans, attributed to the "heroic Venus."[36] Plebs who challenge the established order are punished, as the plebeian Vulcan is "kicked out of heaven by Jove, and left lame."[37] Tantalus is a plebeian "who cannot reach the apples (which rise beyond his grasp) nor the water (which sinks beneath the reach of his lips)."[38] The plebeian Midas "dies of hunger because all he touches turns to gold,"[39] and the plebeian Linus "contends in song with Apollo and, once conquered, is slain by the god."[40]

These and other myths perform the social function of defining both patrician and plebeian identity. Vico explicitly assigns a causal role to the myths. The nobles use them to "hold the plebs in subjection to their heroic orders."[41] Comprising the hieroglyphic divine language, the first myths are pictorial and nonverbal (*mutus,* Vico conjectures, came from *mythos*).[42] The heroic language continues to use images, particularly heraldic emblazonings, but adds a verbal component in poetic song.[43] Thus Vico links himself with traditions that associate the civilizing process with the "lyre of Orpheus," and claims that musical metaphors in which diverse sounds come together in harmony are also civil histories that signify the union of the nobles, or the genesis of the first cities (which are composed entirely of nobles, since the plebs are denied citizenship). The patricians use the power of song to charm the plebs into accepting the structure of the aristocratic republic, and the notion of humanity on which it is based. The songs assume the form of fables, comparisons that remind the plebs of their own condition. Vico cites the example of Menenius Agrippa, who uses the fable of the belly and the members to "reduce the rebellious Roman plebs to obedience."[44]

What enables the subjection of the plebs is a language that uses the tropes of metaphor, metonymy, and synecdoche.[45] Irony seems to play no part in the linguistic strategies of the strong, magnanimous, and naive heroes. Vico hints that irony is a plebeian discovery that emerges in fables used by the plebs to protest their status.[46] These plebs, subsumed under the poetic character "Aesop," take the first steps in the articulation of an identity that is not simply a function of the heroic language. Vico quotes the following lines from Phaedrus:

> Attend me briefly while I now disclose
> How the art of fable telling first arose
> Unhappy slaves, in servitude confined,
> Dared not to their harsh masters show their mind,

But under veiling of the fable's dress
Contrived their thoughts and feelings to express
Escaping still their lords' affronted wrath.
So Aesop did; I widen out his path. [47]

The plebs are still under the spell of heroic discourse. Aesop is an ugly slave, possessing none of the "civil beauty" that was "considered to come only from solemnized marriages," contracted exclusively by the heroes.[48] Nonetheless, Aesop is able to initiate the construction of a new language that will culminate in self-knowledge. The elements of the new language are civil "counsels" that are "dictated by natural reason as useful to free civil life."[49] Because the counsels ascribed to Aesop aim at equity, later humans will associate him with "fables having to do with moral philosophy."[50] The association is anachronistic, because the plebeian mind is still too crude to understand the intelligible genera of philosophy. Aesop's counsels therefore assume, by necessity, the form of comparisons, as opposed to maxims or precepts. Hence the fable of the lion's share employs images, not discursive argument, to evoke the injustice of distributive inequality.

The patricians naturally resist the plebeian counterlanguage, and they construct myths that depict the fate of dissenters in graphic detail. Vico describes some of these in the "mythological canon" at the end of the section on "poetic economy."[51] After Aesop comes Solon, the second major poetic character of the plebs. Against the view that Solon was a lawgiver endowed with esoteric wisdom, Vico holds that he "must have been a sage of vulgar wisdom, party leader of the plebs in the first times when Athens was an aristocratic republic."[52] Solon's distinguishing feature is the ability to distill the various morals of multiple fables into maxims that exhort the plebs to realize their own humanity. The best known of these is the imperative to "know thyself." Vico writes:

Hence Solon was made the author of that celebrated motto, "Know thyself," which, owing to the great civil utility it had brought to the Athenian people, was inscribed in all the public places of that city. Later the learned took it as a great counsel concerning metaphysical and moral things, as in fact it is, and thus Solon was held to be a sage in esoteric wisdom and made prince of the Seven Sages of Greece. In this guise, because from this reflection there sprang up at Athens all the orders and all the laws that form a democratic republic, and through the first peoples' mode of thinking in poetic characters, these orders and laws were attributed by the Athenians to Solon, just as the Egyptians attributed to Hermes Trismegistus all inventions useful to civil life.[53]

"Solon" represents the apex of the plebeians' transformation of the heroic language into a discourse that begins to express their own humanity. The emergence of this discourse is accompanied by the death of the heroic language itself. "As the heroic or poetic language was founded by the heroes, so the vulgar languages were introduced by the vulgar, whom we will discover to have been the plebs of the heroic peoples."[54] The vulgar or "human" language consists of "articulate speech"[55] and is written in "vulgar letters," as opposed to poetic characters that are painted and sung. Vico insists that such a language is required for the transition from counsels and imaginative genera to maxims and intelligible genera. Vulgar languages "are composed of words, which are genera, as it were, of the particulars previously employed by the heroic languages."[56] Vico makes clear that articulate speech is a necessary condition of intelligible genera: "the rational or philosophic universals" are "born by means of speech in prose."[57] Articulate speech, then, differs from the heroic language in two important respects. First, it uses intelligible genera, as opposed to the imaginative universals of fables. Second, it is public, since composed in vulgar letters. These two qualities render it especially suitable for the promulgation of public laws, "with which uncertain right (*gius incerto*) is determined and hidden right (*gius nascosto*) is made manifest."[58]

The creation of the human language and the emergence of "Solon" are difficult to distinguish. Vico hesitates to assign sole causality to either linguistic process or natural aspiration, but implies that the two cannot be untangled. "Through this mastery of language and letters, free peoples must also be masters of their laws, for they impose on the laws the sense in which the powerful are drawn to observe them, even against their will, as we have noted in the Axioms."[59] However this may be, the emergence of public laws encoded in the human language serves as the necessary condition of the full achievement of equity by the plebs. It is not sufficient. Since the nobles strive to retain as much power as they can, there is always an interval between written laws and the embodiment of equity in the popular republics.[60] Thus Vico speaks of Solon as only the "beginning" of the process that changes the form of the republics. The patricians continue to interpret the laws to their own advantage. To achieve genuine equity, the plebs must not only pass laws and change the form of the government, but also control the mechanism by which laws are interpreted. They must assume judicial power, which ensures that the laws are interpreted and applied according to the ethical maxims of "benign" jurisprudence, as opposed to the "severe" jurisprudence of the patricians.

In the Greek history, Solon is followed by Socrates, whom Vico identifies as the "father of all the sects of philosophers."[61] Socrates improves on Solon by developing and perfecting the science of induction of universal from particular that Solon himself uses, if only implicitly, in the distillation of comparisons into civil counsels. Such a "dialectic with induction" is necessary, for "the Roman plebs, in the same way as those of Athens, passed new laws every day for single occasions, because they were not capable of universals."[62] These plebs, despite their stupidity, are the precondition of philosophy. "By means of the vulgar genera, both of words and letters, the minds of the peoples grew quicker and formed powers of abstraction, whence later there came the philosophers, who formed intelligible genera."[63] In line with his conviction that poetic wisdom is the "sense" and esoteric wisdom the "intellect" of the race,[64] Vico insists that "laws certainly came first and philosophies later."[65] Thus Vico writes the history of morality by placing Socrates after Aesop and Solon, and holds that the sequence is more than temporal succession.

> It must have been from observing that the enactment of laws by Athenian citizens involved their coming to agreement in an idea of an equal utility common to all of them severally, that Socrates began to adumbrate intelligible genera or abstract universals by induction; that is, by collecting uniform particulars which go to compose a genus of that in respect of which the particulars are uniform among themselves.[66]

In this way, a "justice reasoned on maxims of Socratic morals"[67] emerges, *a poco a poco,* from the plebeian revolts against the heroic morality embodied in "poetic wisdom." Plato and Aristotle further articulate Socratic ethics, without escaping its roots in social and political custom.[68] (The features of "Plato" and "Aristotle" that Vico emphasizes, in summary form, are precisely those analyzed at length in the *Diritto universale.* This suggests that the "content" of Vico's ethics in the *Scienza nuova* has barely altered since the *Diritto universale,* even if Vico is now able to provide a clearer genealogy.) Rational ethics must be seen as

essentially historical, for it would not exist—and has never existed—
except as an outgrowth from the soil of myth and fable. Against Poly-
bius, who maintains that "if there were philosophers in the world there
would be no need of religions," Vico concludes that "if there had not
been religions, and hence republics, there would have been no philosophers in the world, and if human things had not been thus conducted
by divine providence, there would have been no idea of either science
or virtue."[69]

I have dwelled mostly on the "Greek" movement from Aesop through
Solon to Socrates, because it most concisely indicates the "deep structure" of Vico's history of morality. Vico takes the basic structure, con-
stituting part of the *storia ideale eterna,* to apply universally. Historical
events unique to a particular society are conceived as occasions, not
causes, of the emergence of equity. The final cause is providence; the
efficient causes are simply the modifications of the language that, at
any given time in any particular society, articulates and determines the
limits of humanity. This is the rationale for concentrating on the tran-
sitions from (1) the heroic domination of passive plebeians in the first
aristocratic republics to (2) an inchoate apprehension of human nature
by the plebeians to increasingly adequate expressions of self-knowledge through (3) fabulous comparisons, (4) public laws, and (5) rational
philosophy.

Although the transformations of human consciousness of identity
are most clearly narrated in the Hellenic case, Vico finds parallels in
Roman history. Often the "occasions" of Roman history are better docu-
mented. Vico dwells, for example, on the first census as the means by
which the Romans conferred bonitary ownership on the plebs, without
citing a parallel event in the Greek case. The "causes," however, are
strictly parallel. The "lyre of Orpheus" that linguistically binds the heroes
has its counterpart in the Roman fasces.[70] Immediately after narrating
the heroic use of song to subdue the Greek plebs, Vico asserts that in
similar fashion Appius sings "to the Roman plebs of the force of the
gods in the auspices, of which the nobles claimed to have the science,
and thereby keeps them in obedience to the nobles."[71] "Aesop" is visible
in any number of Roman myths that Vico decodes as plebeian com-
plaints. Moreover, Vico thinks of early Roman law as itself "fabulous."[72]
The essential feature of "Solon"—the emergence of public laws and vulgar letters without the full achievement of equity—is embodied in the
Law of the Twelve Tables, which grants "quiritary ownership" to the
plebs but denies them "civil ownership" by reserving testament and

marriage to the patricians—as well as the auspices on which both depend.[73] When liberty is achieved in Athens and in Rome, the underlying causes are the same. Thus Vico draws a parallel between Pericles and Aristides in Athens, and Sextius and Canuleius, the tribunes of the Roman plebs.[74] The new science must attend to political events, without assigning them primary causality. The particular institutions of the class struggles in Rome—heroic contests, plebiscites, tribunes, formation of *comitiae*—may be unique to Roman history, but the causes of their formation are universal, since they are based in human nature and the "modifications of mind." The Greek and Roman histories are mutually illuminating; the latter is a "perpetual historic mythology of the many various and diverse fables of the Greeks."[75]

As for Socrates and Greek philosophy, Vico is able to locate a significant parallel in Roman jurisprudence. A *legal metafisica* of a highly (and not coincidentally) Platonic flavor emerges via the abstraction of eternal truths from the intentions of particular lawmakers.[76] It is not that Vico is blind to differences. He finds, for example, the Athenian movement from law to philosophy more rationalistic and less organic than the Roman transition, which is more stable and enduring, because its *verum* is more self-consciously mediated by the *certum*. But the fundamental analogy between "legal metaphysics" and "philosophy born from the laws" still obtains. Thus the "universal" character of advanced Greek philosophy is embodied in the "central maxim" of Roman jurisprudence: *legibus, non exemplis, est iudicandum.*[77]

Our explication has sought to account for the peculiar importance that Vico assigns to myth in the history of morals. It is now time to turn to the "age of men" and the "barbarism of reflection" that appears to be its inevitable consequence.

Modern Nihilism and the Barbarism of Reflection

It is evident that the author of the *Scienza nuova* is something more than a descriptive historian who only wants to narrate the "facts," while remaining studiously neutral about their ethical implications. Vico makes no pretense to "value-free" objectivity; his genealogy makes extensive use of inherently normative categories. As a physician of modern culture, Vico sets himself the task of diagnosing the causes of its sickness and suggesting appropriate remedies. Three consecutive axioms in the *Scienza nuova* indicate the "declinist" aspect of Vico's thought.

> Men first feel necessity, then look for utility, next attend to comfort, still later amuse themselves with pleasure, thence grow dissolute in luxury, and finally go mad and waste their substance.[1]

> The nature of peoples is first crude, then severe, then benign, then delicate, finally dissolute.[2]

> In the human race first appear the huge and grotesque, like the cyclopses; then the proud and magnanimous, like Achilles; then the valorous and just, like Aristides and Scipio Africanus; nearer to us, imposing figures with great semblances of virtue accompanied by great vices, who among the vulgar win a name for true glory, like Alexander and Caesar; still later the melancholy and reflective, like Tiberius; finally the dissolute and shameless madmen, like Caligula, Nero, and Domitian.[3]

The second axiom picks out the anthropological determinants of the human age, which itself may be divided into three phases. Men are first benign, then delicate, and finally dissolute. The first phase of the human age is dominated by the benign humanity of Aristides, Scipio Africanus, and—as we know from an earlier axiom—Socrates.[4] Up to this point, history seems to be a story of progress. Decline manifests itself only in the second phase, when human nature turns delicate. Here men focus on their own pleasure and elect ambitious demagogues who exploit popular hedonism for the sake of their own power. Unprincipled rule is not so much a condition as a problem, for which providence has a first, internal remedy—the figure of the "monarch." The monarch, as ideally imagined by Vico, is strong enough to keep human nature intact, and sufficiently just to ensure the maintenance of equity.[5] While Vico often praises monarchy, and clearly wishes to see it as a plausible response to social fragmentation, he is not blind to its defects. The third axiom above locates the essential attribute of Tiberius as melancholia, a property scarcely conducive to stable rule. Even if a less choleric monarch is chosen, he may not win popular assent. He may be ineffective against peoples who are "rotting in that ultimate civil disease and cannot agree on a monarch from within."[6]

The implication is that both demagogic and monarchical government are functions of delicate human nature, able to escape the downward trend only with difficulty, if at all. Hedonism passes into *luxuria,* and the way is prepared for the third and final phase. This is the point at which human civilization, so laboriously acquired over such a long period of time, collapses into shameless dissolution, creating a climate in which semi-beasts like Caligula and Nero are able to flourish. The rule of brutal dictatorship is temporary; providence will eventually need to use its other two "remedies" (*rimedi*). The first is conquest by another nation. "He who cannot govern himself must let himself be governed by another who can," Vico declares, adding the corollary that "the world is always governed by those who are naturally fittest."[7] Should this remedy fail, providence "has its extreme remedy at hand."[8] This is the remedy appropriate to the "extreme ill" of utter individualism, where people are more beasts than citizens. Here we must allow the professor of eloquence to speak for himself.

> For such peoples, like so many beasts, have fallen into the custom of each man thinking only of his own private interest and have

reached the extreme of delicacy, or better of pride, in which like wild animals they bristle and lash out at the slightest displeasure. Thus no matter how great the throng and press of their bodies, they live like wild beasts in a deep solitude of spirit and will, any two hardly being able to agree since each follows his own pleasure or caprice. By reason of all this, providence decrees that, through obstinate factions and desperate civil wars, they shall turn their cities into forests and the forests into dens and lairs of men.[9]

In the company of Vico, our contemporary communitarians are rhetorical pygmies, not to say minute philosophers. The extreme remedy prompts a *ricorso* to the age of gods. It is the fate of beasts "made more inhuman by the barbarism of reflection than the first men had been made by the barbarism of sense."[10] From the rubble, Vico conjectures, a few survivors will emerge and social humanity—or more simply, humanity—will begin again. Vico evokes the "primitive simplicity of the first world of peoples, who are religious, truthful, and faithful."[11] Since providence is above all ethical, she "brings back among them the piety, faith, and truth which are the natural foundations of justice as well as the graces and beauties of the eternal order of God."[12]

Is there something inevitable or predetermined about the decline characteristic of the age of men? Does Vico think it possible to reverse or even retard the trajectory from benign equity through delicacy to dissolution? Must readers of the *Scienza nuova* resign themselves to a quietism, if not indeed a fatalism of sorts? Although the image of Vico as a physician of culture is fundamentally sound, it is potentially misleading in one respect. Rather than prescribing his own solution, as an ordinary doctor would, he consistently attributes all remedies to the action of providence. The impulse of philosophers to promote their own discourses as remedies to decline is *hubris,* arrogance that itself is part of the problem. Despite his confidence in the ability of humans to contemplate the world of nations in the divine mind, Vico does not suppose that he knows, better than providence herself, the appropriate treatment for souls that have been corroded by the collapse of the city.

One might compare Vico to the later Heidegger, who confessed that "only a god can save us."[13] The quietist reading is not, however, without its problems. In the *Pratica della Scienza nuova,* Vico addresses the suspicion that his work lacks a practical dimension:[14]

This entire work has so far been treated as a purely contemplative science concerning the common nature of nations. It seems for this reason to promise no help to human prudence toward delaying if not preventing the ruin of nations in decay. It consequently seems to be lacking in the practice that all sciences should have which are called "active," as dealing with matters that depend on human choice.[15]

The statesman, instructed by contemplating the course of nations, will be able to use "good orders, laws, and examples to recall the peoples to their *acme* or perfect state."[16] Since it is unlikely that the statesman will himself *be* a philosopher—elsewhere Vico disposes of that Platonic dream—the *Pratica* proceeds to describe a more specific role for the philosopher that "can be completed within the academies."[17] This "requires that the academies, with their sects of philosophers, should support not the corruption of the sect of these times, but the principles upon which this Science has been founded," which Vico now gives in their "philosophical" guise: "there is divine providence; that human passions must be moderated since they can be; and that our souls are immortal."[18] These principles do not negate but reformulate the *sensus communis,* which the philosopher must respect and embody in his own person, as implied by Vico's citation of those who "speak of nothing but *honestas* and justice" without acting virtuously.[19] One must check the characteristic hubris of the academic philosopher *without* lapsing into anti-intellectualism. The responsibility of the academics is to teach the young that the civil world has been made by men, and that it has "just such matter and form as men themselves have."[20] Vico uses the hylomorphic metaphor to draw a series of contrasts between the wise and the *vulgus,* concluding that nations are "secure and flourish in felicity so long as the body in them serves and the mind commands" and that the young stand at the "crossroads of Hercules," faced with a choice between "the road of pleasure, with baseness, scorn, and slavery" or "the road of virtue, with honor, glory, and happiness."[21]

Vico suppressed the *Pratica* from the final version of the *Scienza nuova.* Some commentators have inferred from this decision that Vico was ultimately a fatalist, holding that his final intent was to write a book whose import is solely contemplative, with little or no practical dimension. If this were the case, however, the continued presence of the polemic against monastic philosophers in favor of the "political philosophies" of Plato and Aristotle would make little sense. The citation of

"Plato, who conceives a fourth kind of republic, in which good honest men would be supreme lords,"[22] would be an empty gesture toward a possibility that can never be instantiated, not even analogically. The rhetorical effect created by the sudden interruption of the cascade of triads that comprise Book 4 would be utterly pointless. And Vico despises nothing more vehemently than rhetoric that is pointless or otherwise divorced from truth. Philosophy became corrupt precisely when there "arose a false eloquence, ready to uphold either of the opposed sides of a case indifferently."[23] The function of the true eloquence, by contrast, is to embody the true philosophy, to use it to prompt virtuous action, which, Vico considers, religious sentiment by itself cannot do in the age of men.[24]

Vico's omission of the *Pratica* from the final edition, then, is not sufficient evidence that he means to leave us with fatalism. The *Scienza nuova* is, among other things, an exercise in eloquence whose labyrinthine beauties are designed to move as well as to teach and delight. Like any other fable, the *storia ideale eterna* aims to inspire virtue. It does so by evoking a vision of humanity in which the "esoteric wisdom of the philosophers will conspire with the vulgar wisdom of lawmakers."[25] The questions that must be asked are the following: Why are the dominant modern philosophies inadequate for this purpose? What makes the prevailing esoteric wisdom unable to enter into a harmonious relationship with the common sense utilized by wise legislators? Is there a kind of philosophy able to overcome its apparent tendency to promote skepticism and barbarism?

Vico takes the philosophy most characteristic of the age of men to be that of the "Stoics" and "Epicureans." In the *Seconda risposta,* Vico already blamed the Stoics for playing a causal role in the decline from civilization to barbarism. After the golden age of Hellenic civilization,

> The school of the Stoics arose, and in its ambition it aimed to disrupt the established order and to replace mathematics with their pompous maxim: "The wise man has no mere opinions." And the republic of the learned had nothing better by which to benefit. Instead, a quite opposite order, the skeptics, arose who were completely useless to society. They found occasion for scandal in the Stoics, since they saw that the latter were asserting doubtful propositions as true, so they set themselves to doubt everything. The republic of the learned was destroyed by the barbarians, and only after long centuries was it restored on the same basis, so that the

domain of philosophers was the probable, whereas truth was the
domain of the mathematicians.[26]

Stoicism leads to skepticism, which in turn leads to barbarism. The
other dominant branch of rational philosophy, the "Epicureans," Vico
considers equally useless to society. In the *Vita*, Vico condemns the
Stoics and the Epicureans for promoting "a moral philosophy of solitaries: the Epicurean, of idlers inclosed in their own little gardens; the
Stoic, of contemplatives who endeavor to feel no passion."[27] He concludes that "there is nothing more contrary to the principles not merely
of Roman jurisprudence but of civilization itself than those of these
two schools."[28] When Vico refers to Stoics and Epicureans, he never
refers exclusively to the ancient schools. He also means to evoke their
modern counterparts—Descartes and Spinoza on the Stoic side, Locke,
Hobbes, and Gassendi on the Epicurean side. Vico's hostility toward the
"monastic, or solitary philosophies" is well known. But how does Vico
actually criticize them? Aside from the excursus in *De constantia philosophiae*, Vico largely avoids making discursive arguments that intend
to show contradictions in their metaphysics or epistemology. His characteristic critique is *genealogical*.

Vico endeavors to give a genealogy of the dominant modes of
modern thought by exposing their roots in pagan consciousness. Milbank suggests, astutely, that Vico considers rational pagan discourse
to bear the marks of the original language of idolatry, divination, and
sacrifice from which it emerged.[29] This contention is present in all
three phases of Vico's thought. As we have seen, the *De ratione* makes
connections between Cartesian analysis and pagan divination. [30] The
De antiquissima suggests that the misapplication of universal categories, which Vico takes to be characteristic of both Cartesianism and
Aristotelianism, is an atavistic reversion: "to speak with universal words
is proper to infants and barbarians."[31] In the *Diritto universale*, Vico
traces anti-religious modern cosmologies back to the idolatry of nature,
finds the origins of philosophical contemplation in the practice of divination, and regards modern approaches to ethics that neglect divine
grace as only more sophisticated renditions of pagan virtue, which is
ultimately imperfect, because grounded in self-love. Vico reproduces
these contentions in the *Scienza nuova*. Near the beginning of the final
version of that work, he claims to have "derived new principles by
which to demonstrate the argument of St. Augustine's discussion of
the virtue of the Romans."[32] Near the end of the text, he draws the

strongest possible contrast between the "virtue of the martyrs" and the "power of Rome."[33]

The *Scienza nuova* also contains subversive historicizations of rationalistic, anti-theological metaphysics, even if these are not fully developed. Let us consider four representative loci in the final version of the *Scienza nuova*. First, there is Vico's approach to the question of the immortality of the soul. Vico considers that belief in this doctrine, while justified, has little to do with metaphysical proofs. It is grounded in the universal human practice of burial. Made pious by fear of the gods, the giants began to bury their dead in graves, "surrounding these graves with so much religion, or divine terror, that the places where the graves were, the Latins called 'religious places' par excellence. Hence emerged the universal belief, which we established in the *Principles* (the third taken by our Science), in the immortality of human souls."[34] Just as "religion" is equivalent to "belief in a provident divinity" (prudence) and "marriage" is synonymous with "moderation of the passions" (temperance) so "burial" refers both to a primitive custom and a propositional belief about the endurance of the human soul (fortitude).[35] These identities make sense only when one remembers that Vico consistently treats the metaphysical doctrines of "esoteric wisdom" as organisms that grow out of the soil of vulgar myth. Absent the custom of burying their dead in sacralized graves, gentile humanity would not have posited the immortality of the human soul, and the philosophers would not have anything to demonstrate. Vulgar wisdom is the original source of true doctrines about the nature of humanity. The role of the philosopher is to strengthen vulgar wisdom, to make it explicit and purge it of error. Vico does not take this form of dependence to entail the "reduction" of philosophy to myth. Without the reciprocal aid of philosophy in later times, the *sensus communis* itself will disintegrate. The right kind of philosophy, Vico thinks, is able to serve as a rational completion of human custom, not its antithesis. Thus burial is the common sense that serves as the occasion for the doctrine of the immortality of the human soul. (It is not its "cause"—Vico reserves this term for the providential pedagogy of the divine ideas.)

As a second example of Vico's genealogical suspicion of modern philosophy, we may cite his perspective on the relations between philosophical contemplation and the institution of divination. The "history of human ideas" begins with "contemplation of the heavens with bodily eyes." The Romans "used the verb *contemplari* for observing the parts of the sky whence the auguries came or the auspices were taken.

These regions, marked out by the augurs with their wands, were called temples of the sky (*templa coeli*), whence must have come to the Greeks their first *theoremata* and *mathemata,* things divine or sublime to contemplate, which eventuated in metaphysical and mathematical abstractions."[36] Once again, Vico attempts to expose the roots of advanced gentile thought—viz. the ability of the mind to contemplate intelligible objects—in the soil of myth and ritual. Superficially, these things seem far apart, but Vico considers the duty of *ingenium* to make illuminating connections between seemingly disparate things. The dependence of pagan metaphysics upon myth, Vico declares, gives the "civil history of the saying 'From Jove the Muse began' (*A Iove principium musae*).[37]

Can pagan thought ever escape from the myth of Jove? Vico is clear that rationalist metaphysics in its Stoic guise cannot. This brings us to our third instance of Vico's application of a genealogical method in the *Scienza nuova.* Although Vico persistently harps on Stoic individualism and unrealism about human nature, his most fundamental criticism is that Stoic determinism, far from being an achievement of rational thinking about the universe, is little more than a corrupted degeneration of the Jove story. Vico decodes Stoic determinism as "a dogma of Jove subject to fate."[38] In keeping with the original myth of Jove, the Stoics divinize and idolatrize nature, lacking any sense of a transcendent creative being. As Milbank observes, "any notion that Jove might be beyond nature is lost sight of: Jove/nature is regarded as a power of unknown extent which can only affect human beings so far as he himself submits to the processes of the signs or to that 'restraint' which is the chain of fate."[39] Yet insofar as the Stoic cosmology subjects Jove himself to the "eternal chain of causes," it actually loses what is true in the original myth. Vulgar wisdom apprehends, if only dimly, a sense of divine freedom: "in fact Jove and the other gods held council concerning the affairs of men and freely determined them."[40] As the "Spinozists of their day," set against the *sensus communis,* the Stoics "make God an infinite mind, subject to fate, in an infinite body."[41] Vico does not consider this twist on the myth of Jove to be a genuine escape from it. Since their notion of the divine remains entirely immanent, the Stoics fail to see that "their eternal chain of causes, to which they will have it the world is chained, itself hangs upon the omnipotent, wise, and benign will of the best and greatest God."[42]

The ontology of the Epicureans, whether in ancient or modern versions, is similarly trapped within the confines of pagan myth. The central thesis of Epicurean materialism, according to Vico, is that it "attributes to God body alone, and chance together with body."[43] By rejecting the notion of providential care in favor of random chance, the Epicureans also forget what was true in the original *mythos*. Yet their basic metaphysical beliefs can be exhibited as substantively identical to those of the giants. The initial phase of poetic metaphysics creates gods who are entirely corporeal, full of bodily passion; the theological poets originally conceive Jove as a "great animated body" bigger and badder than themselves. Epicurean ontology retains this aspect of the Jove myth, projecting it onto the entirety of nature, while eliminating the notion of providence. This explains Vico's tendency to regard Epicurean materialism as a philosophy designed "to satisfy the circumscribed minds of children."[44] Its metaphysics is no more demanding than the ontology accepted by the giants, the children of the race. When Vico writes that "the philosophy of Epicurus had begun to be cultivated in Pierre Gassendi's version," he means to suggest a double atavism: Gassendi can be reduced to Epicurus, who in turn can be exposed as reproducing a distorted version of ancient myth.[45] Vico brings to light connections between early paganism and advanced philosophy for the sake of calling the latter into question.

The conclusion of Vico's genealogy of Stoicism and Epicureanism is that neither philosophy apprehends the proper relation between vulgar and esoteric wisdom. Common to each is a kind of self-deception, a delusion that *logos* can escape from *mythos* by forgetting or opposing the customary wisdom of religion and the lawgivers. The *Scienza nuova* restates and elaborates the *Seconda risposta*'s view that Stoic and Epicurean doctrines, if taken seriously, lead to individualism and skepticism. "As the popular states became corrupt, so also did the philosophies. They descended to skepticism. Learned fools fell to calumniating the truth."[46] It is not too much to say that Vico intends to unmask Stoicism and Epicureanism as anti-civil ideologies.

At this point, one may wonder whether our thesis that Vico seeks to expose the insufficiency of pagan thought in general stands in need of serious qualification. Vico's attitude toward Plato and Aristotle, after all, is considerably different. We have already suggested that readings of Vico as straighforwardly anti-Socratic are misguided. Vico does not perform a genealogy of Platonism and Aristotelianism in the age of men. Instead, he regards them as the *più sublimi filosofie* that agree with and further articulate the doctrines of the lawgivers, especially those concerning providence, virtue, and immortality. The "political philosophies" of Plato and Aristotle promise to "raise and direct weak and fallen man, not rend his nature or abandon him in his corruption."[47] In a Platonic guise, esoteric wisdom can assume a positive relation to vulgar wisdom. Vico writes the *Scienza nuova* itself as a work of esoteric wisdom, formulating and defending the original principles of humanity in terms appropriate to philosophical discourse. In holding that poets are the "sense" and philosophers the "intellect" of the human race, Vico suggests both are necessary for humanity (just as the necessity of both *topica* and *critica* was argued in *De ratione*). While Vico certainly wants to pay tribute to the poetic age, against the anachronistic tendencies of rationalism, he does not posit a necessary devaluation of discourses based on the concept. In his examination of the fables, Vico understands himself "to have discovered the outlines" of all esoteric wisdom, "as if in embryos or matrices."[48] He does not confuse the *embrioni o matrici* with the thing itself. "In the fables the nations have in a rough way and in the language of the human senses described the *princìpi* of this world of *scienze,* which the specialized studies of scholars have since clarified for us with ratiocination and maxims."[49] Vico would not take his own work of philosophical reflection to escape the latter category, despite its novelty.

Vico's positive construal of Platonic and Aristotelian philosophy seems to imply that the problem is not pagan thought as such, but particular philosophies that contravene the *sensus communis.* Yet such a reading would be too facile. Vico does not find a simple return to Greece either practicable or desirable. He perceives the limitations of Greek philosophy, even at its best, and finds Roman jurisprudence superior in important respects. (The latter, too, is finally an unstable compound, insufficient to avert the barbarism of reflection.) What is more, he actually approves of "modern" intentions to improve upon Greek philosophy. The Epicurean materialism of Hobbes leads him astray, but Vico finds much to admire in his hope "to enrich Greek philosophy by adding a great part which it certainly had lacked," namely, "the study of man in the whole society of the human race."[50] The attempt is laudable, even if the particular "result was as unhappy as the effort was noble."[51] Vico's admiration for *il divino Platone* is perfectly genuine, yet always qualified by the awareness that Plato falls victim to the seductions of anachronism. These are most visibly reflected in his own proposals for an ideal republic, which Vico considers to be animated by ignorance of the Fall. [52] Aristotle serves to correct Plato in some respects, especially in his reflections on the particular virtues. The *prudentia* that Vico defends against modern quests for certainty owes more to Aristotle than Plato. In discussions of justice, Aristotle is often the main authority, despite the "Platonic" understanding of justice as the virtue that orders the others. Nonetheless, Vico is no more a pure "Aristotelian" than he is a standard "Platonist."[53]

Vico admits "Plato" into his school, even as he excludes the Stoics and the Epicureans. But who runs the school? Are Plato and Aristotle admitted to teach or to learn? Vico does not make an exception for either when he speaks of "vain Greek wisdom" near the end of the *Scienza nuova*. Even the best of Greek philosophy has to be humbled by a Christian emphasis upon divine grace, transcendence, and *contemptus sui*. If anyone is the master of Vico's school (other than Vico himself), it would be St. Augustine, whom Vico came to think of as his *particolare protettore*.[54] Somewhat like Aquinas perhaps, Vico disavows membership in any school of pagan philosophy. But he does not lack exemplars, as the Augustinian passages scattered throughout the *Vita* show. The reliance on St. Augustine, attested in the *Vita* and visible from the *De antiquissima* to the *Diritto universale* and the *Scienza nuova*, suggests that Vico intends to set forth "Providence" as a distinctively Christian alternative to either "fate" or "chance."

Our interpretation of Vico as a non-Nietzschean, Catholic genealogist is superior to the prevalent secular readings because it does the least violence to the full range of his texts. It portrays him as the Augustinian Christian that he claimed to be, without denying (indeed, while emphasizing) the innovative character of his work with respect to historical understanding. It underscores the importance of the Hebrews in his narrative, while respecting Vico's desire to be as fair as possible to the "false religions" of gentile culture, the mythical structures that are flawed but real participations in the religion of the true God, used by providence in the education of the race. Finally, in the most drastic contrast possible to the secular reading, it is able to adopt Vico's conclusion as its own. "*Insomma, da tutto ciò che si è in quest'opera ragionato, è da finalmente conchiudersi che questa Scienza porta indivisibilmente seco lo studio della pietà, e che, se non siesi pio, non si può daddovero esser saggio.*"[55]

CONCLUSION

To portray Vico as a genealogist of morals is to invite questions about the relation between his thought and that of Nietzsche. The problem is that Nietzsche's texts are immensely complicated, bristling with as many interpretive difficulties as those of Vico. One can imagine a triptych whose left panel would interpret Vico, whose right would consider Nietzsche, and whose center would be devoted to ascertaining the relations between them. In the absence of such a thing, what can be responsibly said?

Reading Vico as a genealogist not only illuminates the intention of the Viconian texts, but also has the effect of exposing the nonnecessity of Nietzsche's "natural history of morals." Vico's narratives present a vivid counterexample to the claim that genealogy is necessarily Nietzschean. In one of his few comments on Vico, Foucault gestures in this direction, while stopping short of embracing the Italian author as an alternative to Nietzsche.[1] But the question must be raised: If Vico and Nietzsche both apply the genealogical method, is there a case to be made for the superiority of one application to the other? Do we simply have two employments of the method, between which one might arbitrarily choose? Or, without pretending to have knockdown arguments that would settle the matter, can we supply grounds for preferring one alternative to the other?

Let us begin with what is likely to be more evident—the case for Nietzsche's superiority. Nietzschean genealogy is appealing because it seems to require fewer assumptions about the religious origins of humanity, the nature of truth, the role of providence in history, and other features of Vico's thought that will strike some readers as scandalous. In dispensing with any commitment to the "metaphysically higher," Nietzschean genealogy possesses all the attractions of austerity. The widespread disbelief in historical teleology as represented by Hegel only increases Nietzsche's credibility. It is not difficult to find particular instances where the Nietzschean diagnosis of piety as a cloak for the will-to-power of individuals dominated by *ressentiment* simply rings true. Nietzsche's characterization of modern liberalism as a secularized vestige of religious morality—"apart from the Church, we too love the poison"[2]—is not without plausibility.

Much of the writing against Nietzsche in the recent past only strengthens the impression that Nietzsche is vastly superior to the majority of his critics. Philippa Foot, for example, dismisses Nietzsche in a few pages, faulting him for "introducing quasi-aesthetic criteria which are irrelevant" in the context of moral evaluation.[3] But does she understand the writer she would criticize? Part of Nietzsche's point is to demolish the distinction between the aesthetic and the ethical that Foot takes for granted. When Foot triumphantly says that "First of all, I would like to point out that everything depends on his theories and observations of human nature," she seems not to recognize that Nietzsche's aim is to complicate the category of "human nature," if not dissolve it altogether.[4] Foot provides only one example of what seems to be true generally. What passes for high-octane analysis of Nietzsche in Anglo-American circles rarely manages to penetrate his thought.

But can we do any better? How can we criticize Nietzsche without simply caricaturing his thought? Perhaps the best way is to think from a perspective as large as Nietzsche's own, a standpoint that contains the capacity for sophisticated historical analysis while remaining alert to the question of truth. Rather than seeking to invent such a thing, we have argued that Vico already supplies a perspective that constitutes a genuine rival to Nietzsche. But is it possible to state more clearly the advantages of a Viconian position over a Nietzschean standpoint? Three comments suggest themselves.

First, Vico's perspective easily accommodates a range of features that are arguably necessary for genealogy, yet which Nietzschean approaches have to struggle to make room for. Alasdair MacIntyre has argued that in systematically denying the reality of authorial intention, post-Nietzschean genealogy cannot even formulate the problem of "the relationship between the intentional and nonintentional in linguistic use and more generally the relationship of the person who judges and acts to the preexisting linguistic and social conventions in and through which he or she judges and acts."[5] The total denial of selfhood by post-Nietzschean genealogy sits uneasily with a feature of genealogical writing identified by MacIntyre which any reader of Foucault or Deleuze will immediately recognize: "Behind the genealogical narrative there is always a shadow self-congratulatory narrative."[6] Peter Berkowitz has also argued—in my view, compellingly—that "at crucial junctures Nietzsche's genealogy rests upon the very distinction between doer and deed that he claims . . . is an absurd and harmful invention of slaves."[7] We do not say that Nietzscheans are simply unable to reply to the sort of criticism offered by Berkowitz and MacIntyre. It does seem, however, that the radical rejection of selfhood leads to conceptual problems which do not arise for a thinker like Vico. Although he rejects the Cartesian ego and emphasizes the sense in which the self bears the marks of historical development, his genealogy does not reject the very idea of the self.

Despite Vico's preservation of selfhood, is there still not a sense in which he is equally vulnerable to the wider problem faced by genealogists, viz. their inability to find a place for themselves within their own narratives? In one of his few direct treatments of Vico, MacIntyre has argued that the Viconian notion of historical development "seems to leave very little, if any, room for the appearance of a great original philosopher in Vico's own age."[8] Given the secularism, rationalism, individualism, and anti-historical stance of the human age, MacIntyre contends, the appearance of the *Scienza nuova* itself is inexplicable on Vico's own terms. Hence he concludes that "Vico's thought does not in fact belong to that of the age which he chronologically inhabits."[9] The reply to this is to recall that Vico distinguishes various moments within the age of men. He regards his own thought as exemplifying the alliance between vulgar and esoteric wisdom that is uniquely possible to achieve within the age of men, even if such an equilibrium is constantly threatened by atavistic reversions to paganism. Vico's thought would in fact belong to the age he chronologically inhabits, although it is properly associated with the part of the human age that precedes any point of inexorable decline. Hence Vico escapes the problem that MacIntyre associates with post-Nietzschean genealogy.

Second, Vico's genealogy is much fairer to the opposition than that of Nietzsche. Despite his asseveration that "slave morality" provides humanity with depth, Nietzsche is so consumed by his own hatred of religious tradition that he is largely unable to see Jews and Christians as anything other than purveyors of lies and malice. Against Foucault, Berkowitz has claimed that Nietzsche's genealogy is anything but gray, meticulous, and patiently documentary. In practice it is painted in black and white, disdaining to name names or date events. Because it shows little concern for "details, variations, and anomalies, it would be more accurate to call his genealogy inspired guesswork, suggestive speculation, or a likely tale."[10] Perhaps something similar applies to Vico. There is plenty of guesswork in the *Scienza nuova,* especially regarding its etymologies, some of which seem "made" rather than "true." Nonetheless, Vico does attempt to provide empirical and philological backing for his theses in a way that Nietzsche does not. Although it is not the case that Vico was a Romantic, he does have genuine sympathy with the poetic mind. He gives it full credit for the invention of myths which, though false in themselves and dangerous if allowed to develop without correction from a perspective that understands transcendence, play their proper role in the upbuilding of civilization. The severity of his criticism of secular modernity does not blind him to its achievements, especially in the realm of technique. One might say that Vico exemplifies the largeness of spirit that Nietzsche wanted to possess.

Third, there is the vexed question about the actual relation between Nietzsche and nihilism. Certainly Nietzsche intends his genealogy as an antidote to the nihilism that he takes to threaten what is best about the culture of Europe. Readings that casually impute nihilism to Nietzsche himself scarcely deserve to be taken seriously; by intent and profession Nietzsche is a great anti-nihilist. It is difficult to escape the suspicion, however, that his thought ultimately reinforces nihilism.[11] Some contemporary Nietzscheans have attempted to find a kind of harmony between post-Nietzschean genealogy and the values of the Enlightenment, but it is unclear whether liberal social or political institutions can survive Nietzschean genealogy. There seems to be little reason to suppose their immunity to "the kind of critique that gives ethical insight into institutions through explanations of how they work and, in particular, of how they generate belief in themselves."[12] Certainly Nietzsche himself had some doubts on the matter. In general, Nietzsche's successors seek to evade the consequences of their own theory, characteristically ending up as apologists for a secular social order. (Nietzsche, by contrast, was not afraid to look into the abyss, as the end of his life suggests.)[13] Reading Vico suggests the possibility of a genealogy that leads neither to a grim acceptance of nihilism nor a reversion back to the Enlightenment.[14]

Against our entire approach, it might be objected that Vico avoids the difficulties faced by post-Nietzschean genealogy, but only at the cost of accepting metaphysics and hence being something less than an authentic genealogist. Some have asserted, dogmatically, that genealogy is necessarily incompatible with metaphysics. Increasingly, however, readers of Nietzsche have recognized that genealogy is not at war with truth, but actually presupposes truth. What motivates the genealogical project is a desire to be rid of illusion, that is, to tell the truth in some sense of the term. Rigorous suspicion and objective truth are not opposed, but mutually confirming.[15] But if one speaks of truth, then one ipso facto introduces the possibility of something like "metaphysics." At the very least, it is difficult to see how genealogy as a method *entails* the rejection of metaphysics. Bernard Williams would probably accept this point, but nonetheless maintain that a proper appreciation of history generates a presumption in favor of anti-metaphysical naturalism. Williams rightly claims that "sophisticated and reflective observers have always had good reason to think that stories human beings tell themselves about the ethical tend to be optimistic, self-serving, superstitious, vengeful, or otherwise not what they seem to be."[16] Vico is, in fact, one such observer. The Tacitean side of his approach is never far to seek. But, like Pascal, he does not posit a necessary antithesis between an unblinking psychological realism and an affirmation of an ultimate end that includes but goes beyond self-preservation. On the contrary, he connects them. The ethical ideas of virtue, natural law, and humanity itself develop in spite of the conscious intentions of particular human beings. Vico understands this not as an exercise in massive self-delusion, but as genuine expansion of human vision of the good.

Vico provides an alternative, non-Nietzschean genealogy of morals that seeks to illuminate what the conceits of modernity hide. Against the pride of the moderns, he calls for humility, even if one can detect traces of modern pride in Vico himself. Where Nietzsche leaves us with "the eternal recurrence of the same," Vico rejects both fate and chance in favor of providence. Remarking on his fellow philologists, Nietzsche claims that "historical knowledge at present means: recognizing that all those who believe in a Providence have made things simple for themselves. There is no Providence."[17] Well before Nietzsche, Vico knows what "historical knowledge at present means." Yet he finds himself capable of affirming divine providence, without sacrificing his commitment to genuinely historical investigation. Are Nietzsche's cavalier dismissals of the tradition of thought represented by Vico justified? Does he provide the only tenable model of genealogy? Or, as becomes a positive spirit, can reading Vico enable us to replace the improbable with the more probable, possibly one error with another?

N O T E S

Preface

1. See Nietzsche, *On the Genealogy of Morals* Preface §4, pp. 17–18 (Colli-Montinari 5: 250–51).

2. Nietzsche, *On the Genealogy of Morals* Preface §4, p. 17 (Colli-Montinari 5: 250).

3. Nietzsche, *On the Genealogy of Morals* 1.2, p. 25 (Colli-Montinari 5: 259).

4. Nietzsche, *On the Genealogy of Morals* 1.2, p. 25 (Colli-Montinari 5: 259).

5. *Scienza nuova* §314 (Battistini 1: 537), §147 (1: 500).

6. Compare Nietzsche, *On the Genealogy of Morals* 1.5, p. 31 (Colli-Montinari 5: 264) and *Scienza nuova* §379 (Battistini 1: 573).

7. Nietzsche, *On the Genealogy of Morals* 1 (ending note), p. 55 (Colli-Montinari 5:289).

8. *Scienza nuova* §234 (Battistini 1: 518).

9. Bernard Williams, "Nietzsche's Minimalist Moral Psychology," in *Making Sense of Humanity,* pp. 75–76.

10. Alasdair MacIntyre, *First Principles, Final Ends and Contemporary Philosophical Issues,* p. 57.

11. *Scienza nuova* §1112 (Battistini 1: 971).

12. See Hans-Georg Gadamer, *Truth and Method,* p. 20.

13. This point is particularly well made in Jean-Luc Marion, *On Descartes' Metaphysical Prism,* pp. ix-xiv.

14. *Scienza nuova* §38 (Battistini 1: 443–44), "si dànno altri princìpi per dimostrate l'argomento che tratta sant'Agostino, *De virtute romanorum.*"

One. Ancients and Moderns

1. *De ratione* 1 (Cristofolini *OF* 793), "invidiam declinaverim, si me non tam nostra vel antiquorum incommoda reprehendere, quam utrius que aetatis commoda componere velle existimetis."

2. Gadamer, *Truth and Method,* pp. 20, 22.

3. *De ratione* 5 (Cristofolini *OF* 807).

4. *De ratione* 3 (Cristofolini *OF* 801), "tum de integro de iis quae edocti sunt suo ipsorum iudicio iudicent."

5. Ernesto Grassi, "Critical Philosophy or Topical Philosophy?" (reprinted in his *Rhetoric as Philosophy: The Humanist Tradition*, pp. 1–17) is the most visible specimen of this interpretation.

6. *De ratione* 3 (Cristofolini *OF* 801), "Quare utraque disserendi ratio viciosa: topicorum, quia saepe falsa arripiunt; criticorum, quia verisimilia quoque non assumunt."

7. For instance, in *De ratione* 3, "critica est ars verae orationis" and "critica verace, ita topica nos fieri copiosos" (Cristofolini *OF* 799). In *Prima risposta* (*OF* 135), Vico identifies his metaphysics with an "idea di vero," used to judge the other sciences and measure "i gradi della lor verità." In the *Seconda risposta* (*OF* 163), Vico does associate topics with "l'arte di apprender vero," but this is only after he has proclaimed that *topica ipsa critica erit*. He reiterates the association of truth with *critica*: "La topica ritruova ed ammassa; la critica dall'ammassato divide e rimuove: e perciò gl'ingegni topici sono più copiosi e men veri; i critici sono più veri, ma però asciutti" (*OF* 164). In the Proloquium of the *De uno*, he twice associates metaphysics with the *critica veri*. "Aeternam verorum scientiam, quam 'criticam veri' definiunt, metaphysica explicat" (Cristofolini *OG* 31.22). "Metaphysica autem est quae veri criticiam docet, nam docet veram Dei hominisque cognitionem" (*OG* 33.24). In the *Scienza nuova*, Vico speaks of the "new critical art" (§7, Battistini 1: 419) or the "metaphysical art of criticism" (§348, Battistini 1: 551) that his philosophy will use to examine philology. Montanari's description of *critica* as "la tecnica del confutare il senso comune" seems too extreme (*Vico e la politica dei moderni*, p. 69).

8. *Seconda risposta* (Cristofolini *OF* 164), "La topica ritruova ed ammassa; la critica dall'ammassato divide e rimuove: e perciò gl'ingegni topici sono più copiosi e men veri; i critici sono più veri, ma però asciutti."

9. *De antiquissima* 7.5 (Cristofolini *OF* 121), "neque enim inventio sine iudicio, neque iudicium sine inventione certum esse potest."

10. *De antiquissima* 7.5 (Cristofolini *OF* 121), "topica ipsa critica erit."

11. Although Vico tends to assimilate them, we might want to distinguish Bacon and Galileo. In *Novum Organum*, Book II, Aphorism 39 (*The Works of Francis Bacon*, vol. 4, ed. J. Spedding et al., p. 193), Bacon praises Galileo's discoveries, but proceeds in Aphorism 46 (*Works*, p. 212) to dismiss his theory of tides because it rests on the unproven assumption that the earth moves.

12. Isaiah Berlin, *Vico and Herder*, p. 9.

13. *De ratione* 2 (Cristofolini *OF* 795), "complua Ptolemaici de universo systematis vicia."

14. *De antiquissima* 7.5 (Cristofolini *OF* 125); *De mente heroica* (Battistini 1: 398). In the *Seconda risposta*, Vico praises Galileo's demonstrations that reduce

inequality to unity (*OF* 157) and implies that Descartes' success was partly due to his reading of Galileo (*OF* 167).

15. Eugenio Garin argues that by the time he had confronted his critics in 1711, Vico "was certainly working on the *Discorsi e dimostrazioni matematiche intorno a due nuove scienze.*" Garin contends that Vico consciously intended to contrast his own new science with that of Galileo ("Vico and the Heritage of Renaissance Thought," p. 102). Even if this is not quite the right description of Vico's relation to Galileo, it is a useful corrective to Ernan McMullin's assertion that Vico "was not familiar with the science of Galileo" ("Vico's Theory of Science," in Tagliacozzo, *Vico and Contemporary Thought*, p. 60).

16. *Seconda risposta* 4 (Cristofolini *OF* 163). For a catalogue of parallels between Herbert and Vico, see Nicola Badaloni, *Introduzione a Vico*, pp. 14–17.

17. *De ratione* 2 (Cristofolini *OF* 795).

18. *De ratione* 4 (Cristofolini *OF* 803). The importance of this quotation is suggested by the fact that it is the only passage from *De ratione* that Vico directly quotes in *De antiquissima* (Cristofolini *OF* 83).

19. *De ratione* 1 (Cristofolini *OF* 791), "in re literaria Verulamius egit, quales in rebus publicis maximorum potentes imperiorum, qui, summam in humanum genus potentiam adepti, ingentes suas opes in ipsam rerum naturam vexare, et sternere saxis maria, velificare montes, aliaque per naturam vetita irrito tamen conati sunt. Enimvero omne, quod homine scire datur, ut et ipse homo, finitum et imperfectum."

20. *De ratione* 4 (Cristofolini *OF* 803), "Demus igitur physicae operam, ut philosophi, nempe ut animum componamus: et in eo praestemus antiquis, quod illi haec studia excolebant, ut impie cum diis de felicitate contenderent."

21. *De ratione* 4 (Cristofolini *OF* 803), "nos autem, ut humanos spiritus deprimamus: iis quidem vestigemus verum, cuius sumus tantopere studiosi; sed, ubi non invenimus, hoc ipsum veri desiderium nos ad Deum Opt. Max., qui unus via et veritas est, manuducat." Vico's arguments for the contingency of nature, here and elsewhere, cannot be divorced from their roots in Christian theology. Michael Mooney oddly characterizes them as "Academic" and assumes that Vico "put[s] the Bishop of Hippo to secular purpose" (*Vico in the Tradition of Rhetoric*, p. 121 and p. 113). As a corrective, see Ferdinando L. Marcolungo, who concludes that "il richiamo di Vico alla topica, alla prudenza, alla fantasia, ossia a tutto quello che rientra nel senso comune, vuol essere anche un richiamo alla finitezza dell'uomo. Non si tratta di una posizione scettica, come qualcuno ha voluto interpretare, perché comunque la finitezza dell'uomo non si chiude in se stessa, ma si apre alla ricerca di una verità che la trascende" ("L'uomo e Dio nei primi scritti di Giambattista Vico," p. 91). Jacobelli-Isoldi finds in Vico's entire oeuvre "due motivi, quello della esaltazione e quello della mortificazione della natura umana" (*G.B. Vico: La vita e le opere*, p. 175), motives that may illuminate the nature of the reference to Pascal in the *Vita* (*OF* 16/ *Autobiography* 130).

22. *De ratione* 7 (Cristofolini *OF* 811), "non ex ista recta mentis regula, quae rigida est, hominum facta aestimari possunt; sed illa Lesbiorum flexili, quae non ad se corpora dirigit, sed se ad corpora inflectit, spectari debent." On the history of this *topos* from Aquinas through the humanists to Vico, see Giuseppe Giarrizzo, *Vico, la politica e la storia*, pp. 146–74.

23. *De ratione* 7 (Cristofolini *OF* 809), "Sed illud incommodum nostrae studiorum rationis maximum est, quod cum naturalibus doctrinis impenissime studeamus, moralem non tanti facimus. . . ."

24. *De ratione* 10 (Cristofolini *OF* 821), "Nam de iis rebus, quibus prudentia moderatur, artes, si multae, nullae; sin modicae, multae sunt."

25. *De ratione* 10 (Cristofolini *OF* 821), "quia prudentia ex rerum circumstantiis, quae infinitae sunt, sua capit consilia; quare omnis earum comprehensio, quam amplissima, nunquam est satis."

26. *De ratione* 7 (Cristofolini *OF* 811), "Et, quod ad prudentiam civilis vitae attinet, cum rerum humanarum dominae sint occasio et electio, quae incertissimae sunt, easque, ut plurimum, simulatio et dissimulatio, res fallacissimae ducant."

27. *De ratione* 3 (Cristofolini *OF* 797), "a verisimilibus gignitur sensus communis."

28. *De ratione* 10 (Cristofolini *OF* 821), "Deinde consuefaciunt auditores, ut communibus praeceptis adhaerescant: quo nihil in actu rerum inutilius experimur."

29. *De ratione* 7 (Cristofolini *OF* 811).

30. *De ratione* 7 (Cristofolini *OF* 811), "Proin stultus, qui nec ex genere, nec in specie vera norit, semper praesentem suae temeritatis fert poenam." The parallel passage in the *Vita* describes the *sapiens* as the embodiment of both Platonic "esoteric wisdom" and Tacitean "common wisdom." "And as Plato with his universal knowledge explores the parts of nobility (*le parti dell'onestà*) which constitute the man of intellectual wisdom, so Tacitus descends into all the counsels of utility (*tutti i consigli dell'utilità*) whereby, among the infinite irregular chances of malice and fortune, the man of practical wisdom brings good things to issue" (*OF* 20/*Autobiography* 138).

31. *De ratione* 7 (Cristofolini *OF* 811), "At sapientes, qui per agendorum obliqua et incerta ad aeternum verum collimant, quia recta non possunt, circumducunt iter; et consilia expediunt in temporis longitudinem, quantum natura fieri potest, profutura."

32. The phrase is used by Vico in *De ratione* 3 (Cristofolini *OF* 801).

33. *De ratione* 3 (Cristofolini *OF* 799), "At nostri critici, cum quid dubii iis oblatum est, illud respondent: — Ista de re sine cogitem. —"

34. *De ratione* 6 (Cristofolini *OF* 807–9). See *De antiquissima* 2 (Cristofolini *OF* 79), "In re medica, qui recta per theses pergunt, magis contendunt ne corrumpantur systemata, quam ut sanetur aegroti."

35. *De ratione* 3 (Cristofolini *OF* 797), "nam adolescentibus quam primum sensus communis est conformandus, ne in vita agenda aetate firmati in mira erumpant et insolentia."

36. *De ratione* 3 (Cristofolini *OF* 797), "sensus communis, ut omnis prudentiae, ita eloquentiae regula est."

37. *Vita* (Cristofolini *OF* 12/*Autobiography* 124), "portati a ben giudicare innanzi di ben apprendere, contro il corso natural dell'idee, che prima apprendono, poi giudicano, finalmente ragionano, ne diviene la gioventù arida e secca nello spiegarsi e, senza far mai nulla, vuol giudicar d'ogni cosa." Compare the end of *Scienza nuova* §159 (Battistini 1: 502).

38. The phrase belongs to Alasdair MacIntyre. See *After Virtue*, p. 216.

39. Descartes is no exception: his success in crafting works of philosophical persuasion owes much to his education in humanistic studies, as Vico implies at the end of the *Seconda risposta* (Cristofolini *OF* 166–67).

40. *De ratione* 7 (Cristofolini *OF* 811), "Docti vero imprudentes, qui ad peculiaria a vero ex genere recta pergunt, per anfractuosa vitae perrumpunt."

41. *De ratione* 7 (Cristofolini *OF* 811), "et suis consiliis frustrati, alienis decepti, quam saepissime abeunt."

42. *Orazioni* III (Visconti 130), "Stoicos, quam graviter et severe sapientis constantiam doceant." And see *De ratione* 9 (Cristofolini *OF* 821), where Vico identifies *constantia* as the supreme virtue of the martyrs. The contrast between the power of Rome and the virtue of the martyrs is repeated in the *Scienza nuova,* §1047 (Battistini 1: 934).

43. *De ratione* 8 (Cristofolini *OF* 819), "Rigor hic humanarum actionum, ut quis in omnibus et per omnia sibi constet, optime a Stoicis, quibus recentiores respondere videntur, docebatur."

44. This point is well made by Alasdair MacIntyre with respect to the virtue of "constancy" in Jane Austen. See MacIntyre, *After Virtue*, p. 242.

45. *De ratione* 10 (Cristofolini *OF* 821), "Quamobrem ut usui sint artes, quae prudentia constant, uti oratoria, poëtica, historica, deorum compitalium instar sint; et tantum demonstrent quo et qua sit eundem: nempe per philosophiam ad ipsius optimae contemplationem naturae."

46. *De antiquissima* 7.5 (Cristofolini *OF* 119), "si methodum geometricam in vitam agendam importes, 'nihilo plus agas, quam si des operam ut cum ratione insanias.'" The quotation is from Terence, *Eunuchus,* 62–63.

Two.   Eloquence and Prudence

1. *De ratione* 3 (Cristofolini *OF* 797), "sensus communis, ut omnis prudentiae, ita eloquentiae regula est." And see *De ratione* 3 (Cristofolini *OF* 801), "sensu communi ad prudentiam et eloquentiam invalescant. . . ."

2. *De ratione* 7 (Cristofolini *OF* 809–11), "Sed illud incommodum nostrae studiorum rationis maximum est, quod cum naturalibus doctrinis impensissime studeamus, moralem non tanti facimus, et eam potissimum partem, quae de humani animi ingenio eiusque passionibus ad vitam civilem et ad eloquentiam accommodate, de propriis virtutum ac viciorum notis, de bonis malisque artibus, de morum characteribus pro cuiusque aetate, sexu, condicione,

fortuna, gente, republica, et de illa decori arte omnium disserit: atque adeo amplissima praetantissimaque de republica doctrina nobis deserta fereme et iculta
iacet."

3. On the celerity of the good physician, see *De ratione* 6 (Cristofolini *OF*
807–9). For that of the orator, see *De ratione* 3 (*OF* 799).

4. *De ratione* 3 (Cristofolini *OF* 801), "Carneades autem utrumque com-
plectebatur oppositum, et uno die iustitiam esse, altero non esse, aequis rerum
momentis et incredibili disserendi vi, disputabat. Atque haec omnia inde orta,
quia verum unum, verisimilia multa, falsa infinita." In the *Scienza nuova,* Vico
will condemn the habit of arguing both sides of a case with equal facility as
"una falsa eloquenza" (§1102, Battistini 1: 966). As for the antecedents of Vico
on Carneades, see the *De oratore,* where Cicero describes the speech of Carneades
as "acerrimum et copiosissimum" (1.10). Quintilian recalls Carneades' ability
to argue *pro iustitia* on one day and *contra iustitia* on the next (*Institutio Oratoria* 12.2.35).

5. This point is well made in Vittorio Hösle, *Introduzione a Vico,* p. 44n69.

6. This was almost universally true until G. E. Moore's announcement in
chapter 1, section 3 of *Principia Ethica* that "scientific ethics" has nothing to do
with practice. A powerful—and implicitly Viconian—critique of such positions may be found in R. G. Collingwood's *Autobiography,* pp. 47–50.

7. *De ratione* 7 (Cristofolini *OF* 815), "Atque adeo animi perturbationes,
quae interioris hominis mala ab appetitu omnia, tamquam ab uno fonte, prove-
niunt, duae solae res ad bonos usus traducunt: philosophia, quae eas sapien-
tibus temperat, quo virtutes evadant; eloquentia, quae eas in vulgo incendit, ut
faciant officia virtutis."

8. *De ratione* 7 (Cristofolini *OF* 813), "mens quidem tenuibus istis veri
retibus capitur, sed animus non nisi his corpulentioribus machinis contorque-
tur et expugnatur."

9. *De ratione* 7 (Cristofolini *OF* 813–15), "per corporeas imagines est alli-
ciendus ut amet; nam ubi semel amat, facile docetur, ut credat, et ubi credit et
amat, est inflammandus, ut sua solita impotentia velit."

10. *De ratione* 7 (Cristofolini *OF* 815), "quae tri nisi qui fecerit, haud per-
suasionis opus effecerit."

11. The humanizing requirement applies not only to ethics, but even to
metaphysics. In the *Vita,* Vico rejects the metaphysics of Averroes on the
ground that it "left the Arabs no more humane or civilized than they had been
before" (Cristofolini *OF* 11/*Autobiography* 121). One can only wonder what he
would say about Strawson.

12. Its scope is universal. "For we must make no mistake about ourselves:
we are as much automaton as mind. As a result, demonstration is not the only
instrument for convincing us" (Pascal, *Pensées* 821).

13. *De ratione* 7 (Cristofolini *OF* 813), "Hunc animum sapienties sibi indu-
cunt voluntate, quae mentis placidissima pedissequa est; quare eos sat est,

doceas officium, ut faciant." The language that Vico uses here strongly recalls the description of prelapsarian humanity at *De uno* 18 (Cristofolini *OG* 49).

14. *De ratione* 15 (Cristofolini *OF* 853), "Nam quid aliud est eloquentia, nisi sapientia, quae ornate copioseque et ad sensum communem accommodate loquatur?" Compare *Vita* (*OF* 53/*Autobiography* 199), "Non ragionò mai delle cose dell'eloquenza se non in séguito della sapienza, dicendo che l'eloquenza altro non è che la sapienza che parla." In the *Vici vindiciae* (*OF* 347), Vico mocks critics who think that he "non esse philosophiae, sed philologiae, nempe eloquentiae professorem, quia cum vulgo putat eloquentiam a philosophia esse rem prorsus aliam." For the alliance of *eloquentia* and *sapientia* in Cicero, see *De inventione* 1.1. The theme is taken up by the Renaissance; a brief history can be found in Mooney, *Vico in the Tradition of Rhetoric,* pp. 42–47.

15. *De ratione* 3 (Cristofolini *OF* 799), "Utri credendum, Arnoldone, qui negat, an Ciceroni, qui se a topica potissimum eloquentem factum affirmat et profitetur, aliorium esto iudicium."

Three.   Critique of Descartes

1. An apparent exception to this claim would be Robert Crease, "Vico and the 'Cogito.'" The exception is merely apparent. Though insightful on Kant's relation to the *cogito,* Crease's essay contains but a single reference in passing to the first chapter of *De antiquissima.*

2. *De antiquissima* 1.3 (Cristofolini *OF* 71), "nostrae tempestatis dogmatici ante metaphysicam pro dubiis omnia vera habent."

3. *De antiquissima* 1.3 (Cristofolini *OF* 71), "non sunt quicquam certae de subiectis, de quibus agunt."

4. *De antiquissima* 1.3 (Cristofolini *OF* 71), "magnus eius meditator, qui eius sacris initiari velit." Here I have adopted Palmer's somewhat free rendering of this passage in *On the Most Ancient Wisdom of the Italians,* pp. 53–54.

5. *De antiquissima* 1.3 (Cristofolini *OF* 71), "finis, qui dogmaticos a scepticis distinet, erit primum verum, quod nos eius metaphysica reserat."

6. *De antiquissima* 1.3 (Cristofolini *OF* 71). That Vico intends a deliberate insult is obscured by renderings of *Renatus* by "Descartes." In the *Vita,* Vico will continue to employ this device, speaking of "Renato" rather than "Cartesio," a form he uses in that text only twice.

7. *De antiquissima* 1.3 (Cristofolini *OF* 73), "vulgarem cognitionem, quae indoctum quemvis cadat, ut Sosiam; non rarum verum et exquisitum, quod tanta maximi philosophi meditatione egeat ut inveniatur."

8. See Letter to Colvius (Adam-Tannery, *Oeuvres de Descartes,* vol. 3, p. 248; *The Philosophical Works of Descartes,* vol. 3, p. 159) and Letter to Mersenne (Adam-Tannery III, 261; *Philosophical Works,* vol. 3, p. 161).

9. *De antiquissima* 1.3 (Cristofolini *OF* 73), "quamquam conscius sit scepticus se cogitare, ignorat tamen cogitationis caussas, sive quo pacto cogitatio fiat."

10. *De antiquissima* 1.3 (Cristofolini *OF* 73), "scire enim est tenere genus seu formam, quo res fiat: conscientia autem est eorum, quorum genus seu formam demonstrare non possumus."

11. *De antiquissima* 1.3 (Cristofolini *OF* 73), "unde sentes illi illaeque spinae, in quas offendunt, et quibus mutuo compunguntur subtilissimi nostrae tempestatis metaphysici."

12. *De antiquissima* 1.3 (Cristofolini *OF* 73), "adacti ad occultam Dei legem tamquam ad machinam confugiunt, quod nervi mentem excitent, cum ab obiectis externis moventur; et mens intendat nervos, quando ei agere collibitum sit."

13. *De antiquissima* 1.3 (Cristofolini *OF* 73), "ignoratur genus, quo cogitatio fiat."

14. *De antiquissima* 1.3 (Cristofolini *OF* 73), "ne praeterquam quas ipsae res habent molestias, addat illas opinionis."

15. *De antiquissima* 1.3 (Cristofolini *OF* 73), "quis certus omnino esse potest quod sit, nisi esse suum ex re conficiat, de qua dubitare non possit."

16. *De antiquissima* 1.3 (Cristofolini *OF* 73), "si cogitatio esset caussa quod sim, cogitatio esset caussa corporis"; "sunt corpora, quae non cogitant."

17. *De antiquissima* 1.3 (Cristofolini *OF* 75), "cogitare non est caussa quod sim mens, sed signum; atqui techmerium caussa non est; techmeriorum enim certitudinem cordatus scepticus non negaverit, caussarum vero negaverit."

18. *De antiquissima* 1.3 (Cristofolini *OF* 75), "genera seu formas, quibus quaeque res fiant."

19. *De antiquissima* 1.4 (Cristofolini *OF* 75), "haec ab iis accepta contra ipsos sic regeras."

20. *De antiquissima* 1.4 (Cristofolini *OF* 75), "caussarum comprehensio, qua continentur omnia genera, seu omnes formae, quibus omnia effecta data sunt."

21. *De antiquissima* 1.4 (Cristofolini *OF* 75), "quod est Deus, et quidem Deus, quem Christiani profitemur."

22. *De antiquissima* 3 (Cristofolini *OF* 83), "geometrica ideo demonstramus, quia facimus; physica si demonstrare possemus, faceremus." Cf. *De ratione* 4 (*OF* 803).

23. *De antiquissima* 3 (Cristofolini *OF* 83), "nam tantundem esset, quantum Dei Deum se facere; et Deum negare, quem quaerunt."

24. *De antiquissima* 1.4 (Cristofolini *OF* 75), "nempe ea vera esse, humana, quorum nosmet nobis elementa fingamus, intra nos contineamus, in infinitum per postulata producamus; et, cum ea componimus, vera, quae componendo cognoscimus, faciamus; et ob haec omnia genus seu formam, qua faciumus, teneamus."

25. *Seconda risposta* (Cristofolini *OF* 166), "se talora alcuno se ne legge, si legge tradotto, perché si stimano oggi inutili gli studi delle lingue, sull'autorità di Renato."

26. *Seconda risposta* (Cristofolini *OF* 166), "si pensano, sì, nuovi metodi, ma non si trovano nouve cose; ma bensì queste si prendono dagli sperimentali e s'apparecchiano in nuovi metodi."

27. *Seconda risposta* (Cristofolini *OF* 167), "Ma che non regni altro che 'l proprio giudizio, non si disponga che con metodo geometrico, questo è pur troppo."

28. *Seconda risposta* (Cristofolini *OF* 167), "Renato egli ha fatto quel che sempre han soluto coloro che si son fatti tiranni, I quali son cresciuti in credito col parteggiare la libertà; ma, poiché si sono assicurati nella potenza, sono divenuti tiranni più gravi di quei che oppressero."

29. *Seconda risposta* (Cristofolini *OF* 167), "I giovani semplicetti volentieri cadono nell'ingano, perché la lunga fatica di moltissima lezione è molesta, ed è grande il piacer della mente d'apparar molto in brieve." Vico would repeat this charge nearly twenty years later in 1729, complaining to a correspondent that Descartes "has gathered a large number of followers because of that failing of our human nature that would like to acquire the knowledge of everything in the shortest possible time and with the minimum of effort, which is the reason why today there are no books produced other than the ones concerning new methods and compendia." See "Four Letters of Vico" (trans. Pinton), p. 51.

30. *Seconda risposta* (Cristofolini *OF* 167), "Renato avrassi stabilito tra loro il regno, e preso il frutto di quel consiglio di rea politica, che è di spegnere affatto coloro per li quali si è giunto al sommo della potenza."

31. *Seconda risposta* (Cristofolini *OF* 167), "ma esso, infatti, benché 'l dissimuli con grandissima arte in parole, fu versatissimo in ogni sorta di filosofie."

32. *Vita* (Cristofolini *OF* 6/Autobiography 113).

33. *Vita* (Cristofolini *OF* 6/Autobiography 113).

34. *Vita* (Cristofolini *OF* 15/Autobiography 129).

35. *Vita* (Cristofolini *OF* 20/Autobiography 138).

36. See Yvon Beleval, "Vico and Anti-Cartesianism," p. 78.

37. See Bergin and Fisch, *The Autobiography of Giambattista Vico*, p. 218n165.

38. This edition is mentioned by Jean-Luc Marion in his *Cartesian Questions*, p. 70. For the passage where Vico claims not to know French, see *Vita* (Cristofolini *OF* 17/Autobiography 134). One piece of evidence suggesting that in fact Vico knew some French is supplied later in the *Vita* itself, where Vico quotes a letter from Jean Le Clerc, the words of which are "puntualmente dal francese tradotte." See *Vita* (*OF* 34/Autobiography 164).

39. See Lachterman, *The Ethics of Geometry: A Genealogy of Modernity*, p. 124.

Four.   The Roots of Mathematics

1. Nietzsche, *Daybreak*, p. 1 (Colli-Montinari 3:11).

2. *Vita* (Cristofolini *OF* 20/Autobiography 138).

3. Berlin, *Vico and Herder*, p. 15. Jacobelli-Isoldi's assessment of Vico's philosophy of mathematics is more nuanced: she limits its "validità ad un piano di pura finzione, cioè ad un ambito strettamente umano" (*G.B. Vico: La vita e le opere*, p. 215).

4. *De antiquissima* 1.2 (Cristofolini *OF* 67), "per haec igitur, cum homo naturam rerum vestigabundus, tandem animadverteret se eam nullo assequi pacto, quia intra se elementa, ex quibus res compositae existant, non habet."

5. *De antiquissima* 1.2 (Cristofolini *OF* 67).

6. *De antiquissima* 1.2 (Cristofolini *OF* 67), "hoc sua mentis vicium in utiles vertit usus, et abstractione, quam dicunt, duo sibi confingit; puntum, quod designari, et unum, quod multiplicari posset."

7. *De antiquissima* 1.2 (Cristofolini *OF* 67), "punctum enim, si designes, punctum non est; unum, si multiplices, non est amplius unum."

8. *De antiquissima* 1.2 (Cristofolini *OF* 67), "ab his in infinitum usque procedere, ita ut lineas in innumerum ducere, unum per innumera multiplicare sibi liceret."

9. *De antiquissima* 1.2 (Cristofolini *OF* 67), "mundum quemdam formarum et numerum sibi condidit, quem intra se universum complecteretur."

10. *De antiquissima* 1.2 (Cristofolini *OF* 67), "producendo, vel decurtando, vel componendo lineas, addendo, minuendo, vel computando numeros infinita opera efficit, quia intra se infinita vera cognoscit." Lest one think that Vico is saying that humans have the capacity to create *real* infinities outside the mind, see the *Prima risposta* (*OF* 135), where Vico speaks of the "finto infinito" and "finta eternità" created by the mathematician.

11. *Prima risposta* (Cristofolini *OF* 135), "fanno il vero che insegnano; e l'uomo, contendendo dentro di sé un immaginato mondo di linee e di numeri, opera talmente in quello con l'astrazione, come Iddio nell'universo con la realtà."

12. *De antiquissima* 1.2 (Cristofolini *OF* 67), "Neque enim in solis problematibus, sed in theorematis ipsis, quae vulgo sola contemplatione contenta esse putantur, operatione opus est. Etenim, dum mens colligit eius veri elementa, quod contemplatur, fieri non potest quin faciat vera, quae cognoscit."

13. The label appears in the summary of *De antiquissima* 1.2 (Cristofolini *OF* 65). See also *Prima risposta* (*OF* 136), "che, per non essersi considerata la vera causa, comunemente sono stimate le matematiche essere scienze contemplative, né pruovar dalle cause; quando esse sole tra tutte sono le vere scienze operatrici e pruovano dalle cause, perché, di tutte le scienze umane, esse unicamente procedono a simiglianza della scienza divina."

14. *De antiquissima* 1.2 (Cristofolini *OF* 69), "eae certissimae sunt, quae originis vicium luunt, et operatione scientiae divinae similes evadunt, utpote in quibus verum et factum convertantur."

15. *Vici vindiciae* 16 (Cristofolini *OF* 353), "unde geometra in illo suo figurarum mundo est quidam deus, uti Deus optimus maximus in hoc mundo animorum et corporum est quidam geometra." Cf. *Seconda risposta* (Cristofolini

OF 157), "l'uomo opera nel mondo delle astrazioni come Iddio nel mondo delle cose reali."

16. *De antiquissima* 1.2 (Cristofolini *OF* 69), "human curiositas verum natura ei negatum vestigat."

17. *De antiquissima* 1.2 (Cristofolini *OF* 69).

18. See Antonio Corsano, *G.B. Vico,* pp. 108–27. Berlin also interprets Vico's mathematics along nominalist lines, characterizing it as the "manipulation of counters" (*Vico and Herder,* p. 21).

19. *De antiquissima* 1.2 (Cristofolini *OF* 65), "et a corpore excerpsit, seu, ut dicunt, abstraxit figuram, motum."

20. *De antiquissima* 1.2 (Cristofolini *OF* 65), "Etenim, illustris exempli caussa, hominem in corpus et animum, et animum in intellectum ac voluntatem dissecuit." Vico reiterates the view that *homo* is made of *animus* and *corpus* as the basis of his anthropology at *De uno* 10 (Cristofolini *OG* 45).

21. *De antiquissima* 1.2 (Cristofolini *OF* 65), "et ab his, uti ab omnibus aliis rebus, extulit ens et unum." On the abstractive character of *sum,* see *Scienza nuova* §693 (Battistini 1: 764).

22. *De antiquissima* 4.2 (Cristofolini *OF* 91). Although "Zeno" (a conflation of the Eleatic and Stoic, common in his day) is cited here and in the *Vita* (cf. *OF* 7 on "i punti di Zenone"), he probably borrowed the term, if not the concept, from Leibniz. In the *New System of Nature,* Leibniz speaks of both "mathematical points" and "metaphysical points." Illuminating commentary on Vico's metaphysical points and possible connections to Leibniz may be found in Flint, *Vico,* pp. 122–28, and Lachterman, "Mathematics and Nominalism in the *Liber Metaphysicus,*" pp. 71–75.

23. *De antiquissima* 4.2 (Cristofolini *OF* 87), "per malignum aditum puncti." Cf. *Seconda risposta* (*OF* 157), "il punto geometrica sia una simiglianza del metafisico."

24. *De antiquissima* 4.2 (Cristofolini *OF* 93), "geometria a metaphysica suum verum accipit, et acceptum in ipsam metaphysicam refundit." The fullest discussion of the issues may be found in David Lachterman, "Mathematics and Nominalism in Vico's *Liber Metaphysicus.*" Lachterman attends closely to textual details in sustaining his central thesis that "the unqualifiedly nominalist interpretation of Vico enunciated, if not always defended, by Croce, Berlin, Fisch, Pompa, et. al., faces serious and, in my judgement, insuperable objections" (p. 52). Palmer's citation of the locus from *De antiquissima* does not call Lachterman's interpretation into question, as she thinks, but actually confirms it. Moreover, her charge that the locus has "escaped the attention" of Lachterman is unfounded. Lachterman explicitly considers and rejects Croce's view that Vico's conception of the relationship between metaphysical and geometrical points is a "vicious circle." See Palmer, Introduction to *On the Most Ancient Wisdom of the Italians,* pp. 26–28, and Lachterman, "Mathematics and Nominalism in Vico's *Liber Metaphysicus,*" p. 68.

25. *De antiquissima* 4.2 (Cristofolini *OF* 87), "omnis veri fons et unde in alias scientias omnes derivatur."

26. Descartes, *Regulae ad directionem ingenii,* ed. Giovanni Crapulli (The Hague: Martinus Nijhoff, 1966), p. 2.

27. *Prima risposta* (Cristofolini *OF* 142), "conoscere chiara e distintamente è vizio anziché virtù dell'intendimento umano."

28. *De antiquissima* 2 (Cristofolini *OF* 77), "docent genera seu modus, quibus res fiunt"; and "homo intra se habet elementa, quae docet."

29. *De antiquissima* 2 (Cristofolini *OF* 77), "analysis, quamquam certum suum det opus, opera tamen incerta est; quia ab infinito rem repetit, et inde descendit ad minima; atqui in infinito reperire omnia datur; at qua via reperire possis non datur."

30. *De ratione* 5 (Cristofolini *OF* 807).

31. *Vita* (Cristofolini *OF* 13/*Autobiography* 125).

32. Elio Gianturco, in Vico's *On the Study Methods of Our Time,* p. 27n21.

33. Milbank, *The Religious Dimension,* vol. 1, p. 161.

34. *Vici vindiciae* 16 (Cristofolini *OF* 353).

35. Milbank, *The Religious Dimension,* vol. 1, p. 161.

Five.   *Verum-Factum*

1. *De antiquissima* 1.1 (Cristofolini *OF* 63).

2. *De antiquissima* 1.1 (Cristofolini *OF* 63), "Latinis 'verum' et 'factum' reciprocantur, seu, ut Scholarum vulgus loquitur, convertuntur."

3. *De antiquissima* Proemium (Cristofolini *OF* 57), "locutionibus satis doctis"; "ab alia docta natione."

4. This phrase, used at the end of the Proemium (Cristofolini *OF* 59), is included in the work's full title: *De antiquissima Italorum sapientia ex linguae latinae originibus eruenda.*

5. *De antiquissima* Proemium (Cristofolini *OF* 59), "ex philosophia, quam ipsi docti fuerant et excolebant."

6. *De antiquissima* Proemium (Cristofolini *OF* 59), "nos vero, nullius sectae addicti." Cf. *Vita* (*OF* 17/*Autobiography* 133).

7. In the *Prima risposta* (Cristofolini *OF* 135), Vico acknowledges that "le origini delle voci volgari latine mi han messo avanti questo disegno, sopra il quale ho così meditato." Etymologies suggest a design or blueprint for meditation, not a straitjacket.

8. *De antiquissima* 1.1 (Cristofolini *OF* 63).

9. *De antiquissima* 1.1 (Cristofolini *OF* 63), "uti verba idearum, ita ideae symbola et notae sunt rerum: quare quemadmodum legere eius est, qui colligit elementa scribendi, ex quibus verba componuntur; ita intelligere sit colligere omnia elementa rei, ex quibus perfectissima exprimatur idea." Vico's language here both points forward to modern "expressivism" and recalls the Thomist doctrine of the *verbum mentis.*

10. Galileo, *The Assayer,* pp. 237–38. Hobbes, *Leviathan,* Introduction, in *The English Works of Thomas Hobbes,* ed. W. Molesworth, vol. 3, p. xi.

11. *De antiquissima* 1.1 (Cristofolini *OF* 63), "ac proinde in Deo esse primum verum, quia Deus primus Factor."

12. *De antiquissima* 1.1 (Cristofolini *OF* 63), "Deus omnia elementa rerum legit, cum extima, tum intima, quia continet et disponit."

13. *De antiquissima* 1.1 (Cristofolini *OF* 63), "unde mentis humanae cogitatio, divinae aute intelligentia sit propria."

14. *De antiquissima* 1.1 (Cristofolini *OF* 63), "mens autem humana, quia terminata est, et extra res ceteras omnes, quae ipsa non sunt, rerum duntaxat extrema coactum eat, nunquam omnia colligat."

15. *De antiquissima* 1.1 (Cristofolini *OF* 63), "particeps sit rationis, non compos."

16. *De antiquissima* 1.1 (Cristofolini *OF* 63), "verum divinum est imago rerum solida, tamquam plasma; humanum monogramma, seu imago plana, tamquam pictura."

17. *De antiquissima* 2 (Cristofolini *OF* 81), "homo enim neque nihil est, neque omnia."

18. *De antiquissima* 1.1 (Cristofolini *OF* 65), "Deum ethnici philosophi coluerunt, qui semper ad extra, quod nostra theologia negat, sit operatus." In a sense, Vico would agree with Proposition 18 of Book 1 of Spinoza's *Ethics:* "God is the immanent, not the transitive, cause of all things."

19. In replying to his critics, Vico makes it clear that the distinction between uncreated truth and created truth corresponds to the distinction between divine making *ad intra* and *ad extra:* "in Dio il vero si converta *ad intra* col generato, *ad extra* col fatto" (*Prima risposta* [Cristofolini *OF* 135]).

20. *De antiquissima* 1.1 (Cristofolini *OF* 65), "Quemadmodum Sacrae paginae, elegantia vere divina, Dei Sapientiam, quae in se omnium rerum ideas continet et idearum omnium proinde elementa, 'Verbum' appellarunt."

21. As Severino comments, "la distinzione di *verum* e *genitum* consente a Vico di evitare anche il pericolo del panteismo perchè il ver divino si converte per lui nel fatto solo attraverso la mediazione del *genitum,* di quel Verbo cioè che generato *ab aeterno* dal Padre, gli rende possibilile una scelta assolutamente libera." See Giulio Severino, *Principi e modificazioni della mente in Vico,* pp. 14–15.

22. *De antiquissima* 1.2 (Cristofolini *OF* 65), "principio habemus, quod cum in Deo exacte verum sit, omnino verum profiteri debemus, quod nobis est a Deo revelatum."

23. *De antiquissima* 1.2 (Cristofolini *OF* 65), "genus, quo modo verum sit."

24. *Scienza nuova prima* §41 (Battistini 1: 1001), "colla divisione, procedendo dalla cognizione delle parti, per via indi della composizione, pervenire alla cognizione del tutto che vuol sapersi."

25. *De antiquissima* 1.2 (Cristofolini *OF* 65), "Deus scit omnia, quia in se continet elementa, ex quibus omnia componit; homo autem studet, dividendo, ea scire."

26. *De antiquissima* 1.2 (Cristofolini *OF* 67), "idem verbum 'minuere' et diminutionem et divisionem, significat; quasi quae dividimus non sint amplius quae erant composita, sed deminuta, mutata, corrupta."

Six.   The Intention and Form of the *Diritto universale*

1. Nietzsche, *On the Genealogy of Morals* 1.2, p. 25 (Colli-Montinari 5: 2).

2. See Nietzsche, *History in the Service and Disservice of Life* §3, in *Unmodern Observations,* p. 102 (Colli-Montinari 1: 269).

3. On the relations between Nietzsche and Burckhardt, see Erich Heller, *The Disinherited Mind,* pp. 66–88.

4. Strauss, *Natural Right and History,* p. 13.

5. See the "Preface to the 7th Impression (1971)" of Strauss, *Natural Right and History,* p. vii. To concur with Strauss on this point does not, of course, imply any connection between the present interpretation and the "Straussian" readings offered by Vaughn, Morrison, or Bedani.

6. In the only English-language exposition of Vico that we have from the nineteenth century, Robert Flint characterizes Vico as "the founder of the historical school and method" (*Vico,* p. 155) and finds the "distinctive honour of Vico as a writer on jurisprudence" to consist in his status as "the first to expound and apply in an explicit, self-consistent, and systematic manner, the principles of the historical method" (p. 164). This may be hyperbolic, since one can always point to other thinkers who anticipate Vico on particular points, but it at least approaches the truth.

7. Grotius, *De iure belli ac pacis,* Prolegomena (§58).

8. *De uno* Proloquium (Cristofolini *OG* 31.20).

9. *Vita* (Cristofolini *OF* 28/*Autobiography* 155), "Ma Ugon Grozio pone in sistema di un diritto universale tutta la filosofia e la filologia in entrambe le parti di questa ultima, sì della storia delle cose o favolosa o certa, sì della storia delle tre lingue, ebrea, greca e latina, che sono le tre lingue dotte antiche che ci son pervenute per mano della cristiana religione."

10. For this characterization of Grotius, see *Scienza nuova prima* §15 (Battistini 2: 987) and *Scienza nuova* §§394, 493 (Battistini 1: 581, 637).

11. *De uno* Caput Ultimum (Cristofolini *OG* 341).

12. *De uno* 9 (Cristofolini *OG* 45).

13. See *De uno* Proloquium (Cristofolini *OG* 31.21) and *De constantia* 1.2 (*OG* 355).

14. Lachterman, "Vico and Marx: Notes on a Precursory Reading," p. 46.

15. See *De uno* Proloquium (Cristofolini *OG* 35.28) and the *Vita*'s summary of an address given in 1719 that describes the structure of the *Diritto universale* (*OF* 29/*Autobiography* 156).

16. *Sinopsi* (Cristofolini *OG* 5).

17. *De constantia* 2.8 (Cristofolini *OG* 427.4), "ad verum geometricum propius accedere." Compare the claim in the penultimate chapter of the *De uno*

that the "religio christiana est humanitus planissime demonstrata" (*De uno* 221 [*OG* 341]).

18. In his article on "Vico and Spinoza," Morrison attempts a comparative study of the *Scienza nuova* and the *Theological-Political Treatise*. It seems, however, that the *Ethics* would be of equal importance in a full assessment of the Vico-Spinoza relationship.

19. The first mention of Le Clerc's letter comes early in the *Vita* (Cristofolini *OF* 13/*Autobiography* 126). If we can trust Vico's reproduction of his letter, Le Clerc says that the work is "ordita con 'metodo mattematico,' che 'da pochi princìpi tragge infinità di conseguenze" (see *OF* 34/*Autobiography* 164).

20. *Notae in Librum Priorem* (Cristofolini *OG* 741.4), "Et Deum esse primum verum tum in essendo, ut dicunt, tum in cognoscendo." *Notae* (*OG* 741.5), "Itaque primum verum metaphysicum et primum verum logicum unum idemque esse."

21. Compare *Scienza nuova* §238 (Battistini 1: 519) and Spinoza, *Ethics* 2.7.

22. See Leibniz, *New Essays on Human Understanding,* particularly pp. 50, 89–101, 370–71.

23. For an indication of Vico's high estimation of Leibniz, see the reference at *Scienza nuova* §347 (Battistini 1: 551).

24. Lilla, *G.B. Vico,* p. 70.

25. Kelley, *The Human Measure,* p. 236.

26. Kelley, *The Human Measure,* p. 238.

27. *Vita* (Cristofolini *OF* 28, *Autobiography,* p. 155), "intorno alle leggi, egli co' suoi canoni non s'innalzò troppo all'universo delle città ed alla scorsa di tutti i tempi nè alla distesa di tutte le nazioni."

28. *Vita* (Cristofolini *OF* 28/*Autobiography* 155), "Ma Ugon Grozio pone in sistema di un diritto universale tutta la filosofia e la filologia."

29. *De uno* Proloquium (Cristofolini *OG* 39.38). Vico's critics immediately recognized his encyclopaedic ambitions, as the *Vita* itself suggests by quoting those who considered the argument, particularly in the third part, more magnificent than effectual, saying that Pico della Mirandola had not assumed such a burden when he proposed to sustain *conclusiones de moni scibili* (*OF* 29–30/*Autobiography* 156–57).

30. On the transition from ancient to modern notions of encyclopaedia, see Donald R. Kelley, "History and the Encyclopedia," p. 14. Kelley notes the importance of Jacob Brucker in this respect, suggesting a link between Brucker's coinage of the term "history of ideas" and Vico's decision to take the *storia delle idee umana* as an aspect of the final *Scienza nuova*. Brucker is mentioned at *Scienza nuova* §347 (Battistini 1: 551), where Vico criticizes him for beginning "quando i filosofi cominciaron a riflettere sopra l'umane idee." One must acknowledge that Vico also draws upon Renaissance notions of encyclopaedia; see Giuseppe Mazzotta, *The New Map of the World,* pp. 95–112 and also Mazzotta, "Vico's Encyclopedia." It remains, however (as the passages from the *Vita* plainly suggest) that Vico does not hesitate to align himself with modern encyclopaedic programs, even if he gives them his own peculiar inflection.

31. See Mazzotta, *The New Map of the World,* pp. 251–55.

32. The point can be overstated. Caponigri takes Vico to be "committed without qualification to the classical enterprise of the natural law" (*Time and Idea,* p. 36). Surely the historicization of the natural law in the *Diritto,* which Caponigri himself takes account of, counts as a "qualification" of the classical doctrine.

33. On the problems that attend any reading of Augustine as possessing the modern historical consciousness in this sense, see Ernest Fortin, "Augustine's *City of God* and the Modern Historical Consciousness," especially the reflections at pp. 327–28 and his conclusion at p. 343.

Seven.   Justice and Equity

1. See *Meno* 79b and *Nicomachean Ethics* 1130a.

2. *De uno* 43 (Cristofolini *OG* 57), "vis veri, seu ratio humana, virtus est quantum cupiditate pugnat; eadem ipsa est iustitia quantum utilitates dirigit et exaequat." Croce remarks that the unity of virtue and justice "implies that Vico does not distinguish, at least in the systematic exposition of the *Diritto universale,* between law and morality" (*The Philosophy of Giambattista Vico,* pp. 96–97).

3. *De uno* 43 (Cristofolini *OG* 57), "Quae est unum universi iuris principium unusque finis."

4. *De uno* 44 (Cristofolini *OG* 57).

5. *De uno* 44 (Cristofolini *OG* 57.1), "Communis corporum mensura seu regula est commensus."

6. *De uno* 44 (Cristofolini *OG* 59.2), "Haec autem fluxarum utilitatum aequalitas aeterna inter omnes constat."

7. *De uno* 44 (Cristofolini *OG* 59.2), "unum sit genus assenionis."

8. *De uno* Proloquium (Cristofolini *OG* 37.36), "Nam qui officio faciendo non assentitur, is, perturbatione aliqua animi, id perspicue faciendum non cernit: quare, ubi perturbatio sedata sit, et animus ea sit defaecatus, hominem poenitet prave facti. Quod quia in geometricis rebus, exempli gratia, non evenit, quia linearum nulla sunt studia sive affectus nulli, quibus perturbari homines possint, iccirco in iis ac in vitae officiis faciendius diversum assensionis genus esse videtur."

9. *De uno* 44 (Cristofolini *OG* 57–59.1), "At quod est aequum dum metiris, idem est iustum quum eligis." See also *Sinopsi* (*OG* 6), "Quindi mostra esser giusto in natura, perchè quello ch'è eguale mentre il misuri, è giusto quando l'eleggi."

10. *De uno* 45 (Cristofolini *OG* 59). In *Scienza nuova* §135 and §309 (Battistini 1: 497, 535) Vico identifies the claims that *ius* is natural and humans are naturally social.

11. *De uno* 45 (Cristofolini *OG* 59.1), "homo, quem vidimus per communes veri aeterni notionescum ceteris hominibus communicare, a Deo vi fundendi sermonis praeditus."

12. *De uno* 45 (Cristofolini *OG* 59.2), "Atqui homo non solum ratione et sermone, sed vultu quoque a brutis animantibus differt (bestiae enim faciem habent, vultum non habent).

13. *De uno* 45 (Cristofolini *OG* 59.2), "prior humanitatis pars est, nempe hominem hominis misereri; quam excipit posterior illa, hominem homini opem ferre."

14. *De uno* 45 (Cristofolini *OG* 59.2), "societas est utilitatum communio."

15. Compare Gadamer, *Truth and Method,* p. xxxii. "The judge's decision, which has a practical effect on life, aims at being correct and never an arbitrary application of the law; hence it must rely on a 'correct' interpretation, which necessarily includes the mediation between history and the present in the act of understanding itself." See also *Truth and Method,* pp. 328–29.

16. *De uno* 46 (Cristofolini *OG* 61).

17. *De uno* 46 (Cristofolini *OG* 61.1), "Fluxa aeternum non possunt gignere, nec corpora quid supra corpus."

18. *De uno* 46 (Cristofolini *OG* 61.1), "per quam homines, natura sociales et originis vitio divisi, infirmi et indigi ad colendam societatem, sive adeo ad celebrandam suam socialem naturam raperentur."

19. *De uno* 46 (Cristofolini *OG* 61.3), "Quamobrem concludendum, uti corpus non est caussa, sed occasio ut in hominum mente excietur idea veri, ita utilitas corporis non est caussa, sed occasio ut excitetur in anmo voluntas iusti." Compare *Sinopsi* (*OG* 6), "l'utilità è occasione per la quale si desti nella mente dell'uomo l'idea dell'ugualità, che è la cagione eterna del giusto."

20. Compare *De uno* 50 (Cristofolini *OG* 65), "De duplici rerum societate naturali: altera veri, altera aequi boni," and *De uno* 54 (*OG* 69), "Societas veri in societate aequi boni inest et vicissim."

21. *De uno* 51 (Cristofolini *OG* 65.2), where the Ciceronian phrase "intima philosophia" (*De legibus* 1.5) is identified with "naturae humane cognitio," as distinct from the "cognatio naturae," which is grounded in humanity's blood ties and common parentage.

22. *De uno* 53 (Cristofolini *OG* 69).

23. *De uno* 54 (Cristofolini *OG* 69), "Et veri et aequi boni societas ex divinae proprietate originis ita est comparata, ut utraque in altera contineatur."

24. *De uno* 64 (Cristofolini *OG* 81.2). These terms, as Vico himself tells us in a footnote to *De uno* 62 (*OG* 75) are Grotius's translations from the Greek. Vico uses these terms throughout in the Latin *De uno,* but does not hesitate elsewhere to speak of "le due giustizie commutativa e distributiva" (*Sinopsi* [*OG* 6]).

25. *De uno* 64 (Cristofolini *OG* 81).

26. *De uno* 64 (Cristofolini *OG* 81).

27. Milbank, *The Religious Dimension,* vol. 2, p. 128.

28. *De uno* 70 (Cristofolini *OG* 89), "unum verum, una aeterna ratio, quae id dictat; unum verum bonum; una aeterna electio, quae id iubet; una aeterna iustitia, unus Deus."

Eight. Natural Law

1. *Sinopsi* (Cristofolini *OG* 5–6), "E così dalle tre parti della virtù fa nascere tre ius o ragioni: dominio, libertà, tutela." On the suitability of "ragione" as a translation of "ius," see *De uno* 77 (*OG* 99.4).

2. *De uno* 71 (Cristofolini *OG* 89), "prudens utilitatum destinatio, hoc est, destinatio facta ratione, non cupiditate, suadente, gignit dominium"; "temperatus utilium usus gignit libertatem, quae in aequabili rerum usu consistit." *Sinopsi* (*OG* 6), "dalla temperanza, o moderato arbitrio di sé e delle sue cose, la libertà."

3. *De uno* 71 (Cristofolini *OG* 89), "vis fortitudine recta gignit inculpatam tutelam." *Sinopsi* (*OG* 6), "dalla fortezza, o forza moderata, la tutela."

4. *De uno* 10 (Cristofolini *OG* 45), "nosse, velle, posse finitum, quod tendit ad infinitum." The phrase is also used at the beginning of the *Sinopsi* (*OG* 5).

5. Milbank, *The Religious Dimension,* vol. 2, p. 149 and p. 146.

6. *De uno* 72 (Cristofolini *OG* 91), "Dominium est ius disponendi de re ut velis; libertas est ius vivendi ut velis; tutela est ius tuendi te et tua, si velis."

7. On the history of the notion of "active rights," see Richard Tuck, *Natural Rights Theories,* pp. 5–6.

8. *De uno* 73 (Cristofolini *OG* 91).

9. *De uno* 73 (Cristofolini *OG* 91), "Namque avari, luxuriosi natura sunt mancipia, non domini; immodice liberi seu licentiosi sunt natura servi, non liberi; qui iniurias tuentur, non sunt natura fortes, sed violenti vel temerarii."

10. *De uno* 74 (Cristofolini *OG* 91), "Dominium, libertas, tutela sunt homini ingenita et per occasiones nata."

11. *De uno* 74 (Cristofolini *OG* 91), "in specie libertas iuris ante bella erat quidem, sed, servitute per bellicas captivitates introducta, agnita est et nomen accepit."

12. *De uno* 74 (Cristofolini *OG* 91), "Sic dominia rerum soli per divisionem agrorum agnita sunt: quare ab iurisconsulto dominia divisione, non introducta, sed 'distincta' esse dicuntur."

13. *De uno* 74 (Cristofolini *OG* 91), "ex potentia, statim nascendo, exist tutela sui, quae eminet in pueritia et geritur sensuum iudicio et auctoritate, quos pueri habent acerrimos."

14. *De uno* 74 (Cristofolini *OG* 91).

15. *De uno* 74 (Cristofolini *OG* 91), "Adcrescente aetate, ex voluntate existit libertas quae eminet in adolescentia et solutis animi affectibus agitatur."

16. *De uno* 74 (Cristofolini *OG* 91).

17. *De uno* 74 (Cristofolini *OG* 91), "Tandem, per aetatem explicata cognitione, confirmatur in homine ratio, quae sensuum tutelae et affectuum libertati tanquam domina moderatur."

18. *De uno* 75 (Cristofolini *OG* 91.1), "Itaque tutela sensuum et affectuum libertas sane sunt ius naturale, quod antiqui interpretes appellant 'prius,' et stoicis dicuntur 'prima naturae.'"

19. *De uno* 75 (Cristofolini *OG* 91–93.1), "dominium rationis, affectuum aequalitas, tutela consilii est ius naturale eorundem antiquorum interpretum 'secundarium,' quod dicunt, et 'naturae consequentia' stoicorum." In the *Sinopsi* (*OG* 6) and at *De uno* 77 (*OG* 97.4), Vico uses the labels "ius naturale prius" and "ius naturale posterius," the usage to be followed here.

20. *De uno* 75 (Cristofolini *OG* 93.2), "Deus Optimus Maximus, infinita sua potentia, sapientia et bonitate, creavit ad sui similitudinem hominem, et potentia dedit ei esse, sapientia nosse, bonitate velle, quo vult suum esse suumque nosse, sive adeo suae naturae perfectionem."

21. *De uno* 75 (Cristofolini *OG* 93.3), "duae iuris naturalis partes: alter, qua homo suum vult esse; altera, qua suum vult nosse."

22. This is confirmed at *De uno* 216 (Cristofolini *OG* 331), "the *ius civile commune* was, as it were, the bud through which the *ius gentium maiorum* flowered into the *ius gentium minorum*."

23. See *De uno* 75 (Cristofolini *OG* 93.1), "Quae duo quia Hugo Grotius bina falso putaverit . . . res digna est quam ex iisdem nostris principiis paullo altius repetamus."

24. *De uno* 75 (Cristofolini *OG* 93.4), "vita hominis cum brutis communis."

25. *De uno* 75 (Cristofolini *OG* 93.4), "immo praesentibus sensuum notis, voluptate et dolore, vitae utilia sequi, declinare noxia, ut suum sibi esse conservet: quod, si prohibeatur utilibus, urgeatur in noxia nec aliter illa assequi, haec declinare possit, vim vi propulset."

26. See *Sinopsi* (Cristofolini *OG* 7), *De uno* 100 (*OG* 111–15). One looks in vain for his consideration of the *lex hatris*.

27. *De uno* 75 (Cristofolini *OG* 95.7), "ex hoc igitur iure descendit ut ob nostri corporis tutelam vim et iniuriam propulsemus, et maris et foeminae coniunctio, liberorum procreatio, educatio."

28. *De uno* 75 (Cristofolini *OG* 95.6), "nos in nostra *Metaphysica* rebus inanimis et brutis omnem conatum abnegavimus."

29. On the "seeds of eternal truth," see the definition of the *vis veri* at *De uno* 34 (Cristofolini *OG* 53) and *De constantia* 1.1 (*OG* 353.1).

30. *De uno* 75 (Cristofolini *OG* 95.8), "qua homo vult suum nosse, quae est vita hominis propria, et nihil aliud est quam nosse." See *De constantia* 1.12 (*OG* 373.3), which subdivides the human life into the "vitae hominis divina" (contemplation) and the "vitae hominis humana" (action tied to contemplation).

31. *De uno* 75 (Cristofolini *OG* 95.8), "non vivitur ex vero et ratione, non vivitur socialiter."

32. *De uno* 75 (Cristofolini *OG* 95.10), "Cumque vita hominis longe praetantior sit vita bruti, proinde haec pars posterior iuris naturalis priori dominatur."

33. *De uno* 75 (Cristofolini *OG* 95.10), "Navigare est necesse, vivere non est necesse."

34. *De uno* 75 (Cristofolini *OG* 95.10), "Recta agere est necesse, vivere non est necesse."

35. *De uno* 75 (Cristofolini *OG* 95.10), "uti ad tuendam hanc brutam vitam ab Omnipotentia vi corporis praediti sumus, ita ad tuendam vitam nostram rationalem a divina Sapientia vi veri praediti sumus, ex qua virtus existit, ut supra diximus, et est appellata."

36. *De uno* 77 (Cristofolini *OG* 97.4), "uti ius naturale prius, seu prima naturae, sunt omnis iuris voluntarii materies, ita ius naturale posterius, seu naturae consequentia, sunt omnis iuris voluntarii forma, quae si prorsus absit, iura voluntaria nulla sunt."

37. Vico quotes Ulpian's definition at *De uno* Proloquium (Cristofolini *OG* 27.11), "quod neque in totum a iure naturali vel genitum recedit, nec per omnia ei servit, sed partim addit, partim detrahit." Vico also quotes the definition at *De uno* 77 (*OG* 97–99.4), but omits the identification of *ius naturale* and *ius gentium*.

38. On the "topical" or "inter-translatable" character of the *ius gentium* in Vico, see Milbank, *The Religious Dimension*, vol. 2, p. 145.

39. This is suggested by Gaius' definition of *ius civile*, which Vico also likes to quote. The definition is cited in the *Sinopsi* (Cristofolini *OG* 9), and at *De uno* 136 (*OG* 163.1), "omnes populi, qui legibus et moribus reguntur, partim suo proprio, partim communi omnium hominium iure utuntur." Milbank concludes that "it is difficult to see how *ius civile* is other than a further development of the *ius gentium*," and draws attention to the fact that Vico also calls it the *ius gentium posterius* (*The Religious Dimension*, vol. 2, p. 145). On the importance of Gaius for Vico's thought, see Donald R. Kelley, "Vico and Gaianism: Perspective on a Paradigm."

40. See Milbank, *The Religious Dimension*, vol. 2, p. 145.

41. *De uno* 77 (Cristofolini *OG* 97.2), "iuris naturalis pars altera non permittit, sed aut vetat aut praecipit."

42. *Sinopsi* (Cristofolini *OG* 6), "dà le giuste misure alla libertà, al dominio, alla tutela, e gli dà forma eterna di giusto."

43. Milbank, *The Religious Dimension*, vol. 2, p. 145.

44. *De uno* 77 (Cristofolini *OG* 93.3), "ex hoc iure naturali posteriore immutabile prius est, quia naturae licita vetari lege possunt, sed lege fieri non potest ut per naturam non liceant."

45. *Sinopsi* (Cristofolini *OG* 6).

46. *De uno* 136 (Cristofolini *OG* 163), "de iure naturali gentium et iure naturali philosophorum" (chapter title). See also *De uno* 218 (*OG* 337.1).

47. *De uno* 136 (Cristofolini *OG* 163.1), "Quod ius communibus gentium moribus explicatum est ius naturale iurisconsultorum, a iure naturali philosophorum longe diversum."

48. *De uno* 136 (Cristofolini *OG* 163.2), "ius populorum seu gentium commune proprius accessit ad ius naturale." Lilla also notes the importance of this passage, but oddly abbreviates the Latin to "ius civile accessit ius naturale" (*G.B. Vico*, p. 94).

49. Additional evidence suggesting that Vico does not "unconsciously" make this equation, as Fassò arbitrarily supposes (see "The Problem of Law and

the Historical Origin of the *New Science,*" p. 13), is the fact that in 1744 he still speaks of "tre spezie di giurisprudenze ovvero sapienze." See *Scienza nuova* §937 (Battistini 1: 868).

50. *Vita* (Cristofolini *OF* 81/*Autobiography* 116), "massime generali di giusto"; "l'interpreti eruditi, che poi avverti ed estimò essere puri storici del diritto civile romano."

Nine.   *Verum-Certum*

1. *De uno* 82 (Cristofolini *OG* 101.1), "Verum autem est proprium ac perpetuum adiunctum iuris necessarii."

2. *De uno* 83 (Cristofolini *OG* 101.2), "Durum est, sed scriptum est."

3. Pascal, *Pensées* 103.

4. *De uno* Proloquium (Cristofolini *OG* 23.2, 25.6).

5. *De uno* 81 (Cristofolini *OG* 99), "Mens legis est voluntas legislatoris: ratio legis est conformatio legis ad factum."

6. *De uno* 81 (Cristofolini *OG* 99).

7. *De uno* Proloquium (Cristofolini *OG* 23.2, 25.6).

8. Gadamer, *Truth and Method,* p. xxxii.

9. *De uno* 82 (Cristofolini *OG* 101).

10. *De uno* 82 (Cristofolini *OG* 101.2), "ut certo teneant ea ex parte verum auctoritate, quod hominum pudore tenere non possunt."

11. *De uno* 77 (Cristofolini *OG* 97.4), "ius naturale posterius, seu naturae consequentia, sunt omnis iuris voluntarii forma, quae si prorsus absit, iura voluntaria nulla sunt."

12. *De uno* 83 (Cristofolini *OG* 101.1), "certum ab auctoritate esse, uti verum a ratione, et auctoritatem cum ratione omnino pugnare non posse; nam ita non leges essent, sed monstra legum."

13. *De uno* 83 (Cristofolini *OG* 101.2), "auctoritas pars rationis."

14. *De uno* 83 (Cristofolini *OG* 101.1), "non omnium eorum, quae a maioribus nostris constituta sunt, rationem reddi posse."

15. *De uno* 83 (Cristofolini *OG* 101.2), "Requiras igitur ab auctoritate rationem civilem, hoc est communem utilitatem, quam legibus omnibus aliquam subesse necesse est."

16. *De uno* 83 (Cristofolini *OG* 101.3), "ratio civilis cum dictet publicam utilitatem, hoc ipso pars rationis naturalis est."

17. *De uno*, Proloquium (Cristofolini *OG* 25.7), "iuris interpretandi ars."

18. *De uno* 85 (Cristofolini *OG* 103.3), "Omnis interpretatio ex aequo bono est ex universaliori ratione."

19. Gadamer, *Truth and Method,* p. 328.

20. *De uno* 85 (Cristofolini *OG* 103.4), "Privilegia enim sunt iuris civilis quidem restrictiones, sed explicationes iuris naturalis: non enim sine aliquo merito irrogantur, ut quis iure ceteris aequo eximatur et solvatur legibus quae omnes tenent."

21. *De uno* 85 (Cristofolini *OG* 103.5), "Restrictiones iuris civilis sunt ampliationes iuris naturalis, et vicissim."

22. *De uno* 85 (Cristofolini *OG* 105.7), "patrimonium, haereditas, respublica sunt fictiones, quantum iis personas quasdam indicimus; sed, uti rationes universae, sunt rerum genera et, quia genera, maxime vera."

23. Fassò denies this view, arguing that the *verum-factum* principle is entirely absent from the *Diritto universale* ("The Problem of Law and the Historical Origin of the *New Science*," p. 11). Against this, Milbank contends that "there is no call for Fassò to distinguish the *verum-certum* from the *verum-factum* schema, and to claim that the former is more decisive for the later Vico, since *certum* (in the context of law) is merely *factum* under the aspect of its sheer positive givenness, rather than its genetic derivation or critical comprehension" (*The Religious Dimension*, vol. 2, p. 3). One might add that in several places, the *Diritto* itself alludes to the metaphysics of *De antiquissima;* see *De uno* Proloquium (Cristofolini *OG* 35.30), *De uno* 75 (*OG* 95.6), *De constantia* 1.17 (*OG* 380.2). Nonetheless, there may be slightly more to Fassò's view than Milbank allows. See the nuanced commentary of Botturi on the whole issue in *La sapienza della storia,* pp. 209–19.

Ten. *Constantia* and Christian Prudence

1. Pascal, *Pensées* 118.

2. *Vita* (Cristofolini *OF* 10/*Autobiography* 119), "la dottrina di sant'Agostino posta in mezzo, come a due estremi, tra la calvinistica e la pelagiana e alle altre sentenze che o all'una di queste due o all'altra si avvicinano."

3. Much work on the relation between Augustine and Vico remains to be done. See Ada Lamacchia: "Vico e Agostino: La Presenza del *De civitate dei* nella *Scienza nuova.*"

4. *De uno* 100 (Cristofolini *OG* 111–13).

5. *De uno* 100 (Cristofolini *OG* 113.6), "ius privatae violentiae, quo homines exleges quidque sua manu capiebant, usu capiebant, vi tuebantur, suum usum seu possessionem rapiebant, et sic vi sua recipiebant."

6. *De uno* 104 (Cristofolini *OG* 121.11), "ex deorum falsa religione videas has imperfectas virtutes inter eos ortas."

7. *De uno* 117 (Cristofolini *OG* 139.4).

8. *De uno* 117 (Cristofolini *OG* 139.4).

9. *De uno* 125 (Cristofolini *OG* 147), "a veritate violentiae"; "ad veri pudorem."

10. *De uno* 124 (Cristofolini *OG* 145.1). The *imitationes violentiae* are attested by what Vico proceeds to call (citing Justinian) the *fabulae iuris antiqui* (*OG* 145.2). Links between the lingering violence of pagan right and its "fabulous" origins will be suggested by the *Scienza nuova* as well.

11. *De uno* 36 (Cristofolini *OG* 53), "ab hac vi veri, quae est humana ratio, virtus existit et appellatur."

12. *Sinopsi* (Cristofolini *OG* 5), "la ragione umana abbracciata dalla volontà sia virtù in quanto combatte la cupidità."

13. *De uno* 38 (Cristofolini *OG* 55.2), "Vis veri, quae cum cupiditate pugnat et eius genitrice, *philautia*, est virtus ethica christiana, qua homo sui delicias in sui contemptum abiectionemque convertit, vocaturque 'humilitas,' omnium christianarum virtutum fundamentum." Cf. Augustine, *De civitate Dei* 14.28.

14. *Sinopsi* (Cristofolini *OG* 5), "il fondamento essere l'umiltà dello spirito umano, la forma la carità, e perciò l'autore e 'l fine Dio." *De constantia* 1.11 (*OG* 371.2), "Quare spiritus humilitas omnium christianarum virtutum subiectum est." And see *Notae in Librum Alterum* 3 (*OG* 757), where Vico assigns the theological virtues of faith, hope, charity to *nosse, velle,* and *posse* respectively, and repeats the identification of the subject of the virtues with humility of the soul, by which it "amorem sui in sui contemptu convertit." Vico's language here strongly recalls Augustine's distinction between the two kinds of love in *De civitate Dei* 14.28.

15. *De constantia* 1.11 (Cristofolini *OG* 371), "solam divinam gratiam veram praestare virtutem posse" (title of a chapter in which divine grace is identified as the "victrix cupiditatis humanae").

16. *De uno* 219 (Cristofolini *OG* 339), "ius naturale primum lege iustae, ut ita dicam, libidinis iustaeque violentiae ortum, deinde quibusdam iustae violentiae fabulis inductum, tandem ratione aperta et generosa veritate perfectum extaret."

17. *De uno* 220 (Cristofolini *OG* 339), "per has omnes, inquam, fabulas iuris, veritas naturae intecta prodiret tandem in usus christianae religionis."

18. *De uno* 221 (Cristofolini *OG* 341), "ut, a tanta rerum consensione, sapientem, ut in omnibus constet, oporteat esse christianum. Quod erir perpetuum libri secundi argumentum."

19. *De constantia* 1.9 (Cristofolini *OG* 371), "falsa humanae miseriae persuasio."

20. *De constantia* 1.12 (Cristofolini *OG* 373.1).

21. *De constantia* 1.12 (Cristofolini *OG* 373.2), "praecipuum, immo summum, philosophiae fructum esse unionem mentis cum Deo."

22. *De constantia* 1.12 (Cristofolini *OG* 373.3).

23. *De constantia* 1.12 (Cristofolini *OG* 373.4).

24. See *Vita* (Cristofolini *OF* 11/*Autobiography* 122); *De constantia* 1.4 (Cristofolini *OG* 356.4); *Scienza nuova* §131 (Battistini 1: 496), and its ancestor in *De uno* 152 (Cristofolini *OG* 201.6).

25. *De constantia* 1.13 (Cristofolini *OG* 373.2), "vivere convenienter natruae rationali, iis celebre illud est 'sequi Deum.'"

26. *De constantia* 1.13 (Cristofolini *OG* 373.3).

27. *De uno* 77 (Cristofolini *OG* 97.4). See also *Sinopsi* (Cristofolini *OG* 6).

28. *De constantia* 1.13 (Cristofolini *OG* 13.3), "Haecque ipsis sunt 'nature,' quae dicunt 'consequentia,' quae nos demonstravimus eadem omnio esse ac ius naturale posterius antiquorum iuris interpretum, seu naturalem ratione."

29. *De constantia* 1.13 (Cristofolini *OG* 375.5), "apatheia, sive affectuum vacuitas"; "irritum humanae fragilitatis votum."

30. *De constantia* 1.14 (Cristofolini *OG* 375), "Epicuri in morali doctrina lapsus" (chapter title).

31. *De constantia* 1.14 (Cristofolini *OG* 375.1).

32. *De constantia* 1.14 (Cristofolini *OG* 375.2).

33. *De constantia* 1.14 (Cristofolini *OG* 375.1), "praescribit eo pulcherrimo morum canone, ut sapiens ex voluptatibus eas sequatur quae minium doloris, ex doloribus eos qui plurimum secum afferunt voluptatis."

34. *De constantia* 1.14 (Cristofolini *OG* 375.2), "Epicurus Epicuro convincitur."

35. *De constantia* 1.14 (Cristofolini *OG* 375), "Epicuri prava positio, methodus recta."

36. *De constantia* 1.17 (Cristofolini *OG* 381.2).

37. *De constantia* 1.15 (Cristofolini *OG* 377), "Aristotelis de finibus dogmata corriguntur" (chapter title).

38. *De constantia* 1.15 (Cristofolini *OG* 377.1), "Aristoteles falsus per eas ipsas sane aureas quas de contemplativae vitae felicitate sententias in *Libris ethicis* profert."

39. *De constantia* 1.15 (Cristofolini *OG* 377.2).

40. *De constantia* 1.15 (Cristofolini *OG* 377.2).

41. *De constantia* 1.12 (Cristofolini *OG* 373.3), "operatio cum virtute, non finis, sed medium est ad felicitatem, ut eius frequent exercitatione cupiditatem restinguamus."

42. *De constantia* 1.15 (Cristofolini *OG* 377.3), "in hac vita non detur."

43. *De constantia* 1.15 (Cristofolini *OG* 377.3), "Nam, si verum unum, verum bonum unum quoque esse necese est; et, si verum unum aeternum, una spectanda est aeterna felicitas." The use of the ambiguous *spectanda* in this context is almost certainly deliberate.

44. *De constantia* 1.15 (Cristofolini *OG* 377.4).

45. *De constantia* 1.15 (Cristofolini *OG* 377.4), "post hanc vitam."

46. *De constantia* 1.15 (Cristofolini *OG* 377–79.4–5).

47. *De constantia* 1.15 (Cristofolini *OG* 377.4), "nedum singuli ac secreti, nedum unius civitatis cives, sed universum genus humanum."

48. *De constantia* 1.15 (Cristofolini *OG* 377.5), "Boni metaphysici praxim una charitas christiana docet."

49. *De constantia* 1.15 (Cristofolini *OG* 377–79.5), "sapientia christiana"; "unum finem"; "longe omni ethnica eminentiorem." Vico's use of "eminence" in this context may be intended to recall *De civitate Dei* 2.29.

50. See Aristotle, *Nicomachean Ethics* 1.2 (1094b5–10); *Politics* 1.1 (1252a1–6).

51. *De constantia* 1.15 (Cristofolini *OG* 379.6), "bonum diffundit in genus humanum universum."

52. See Milbank, *The Religious Dimension,* vol. 2, pp. 113, 172, 269, 272.

53. Lilla, *G.B. Vico,* p. 209.

54. One should not overlook the importance of *De civitate Dei* 5.18 for a more subtle interpretation of Augustine's thought than readings which attribute to him an utterly satanic view of Rome. Although he occasionally calls Rome "the city of the devil" (e.g., at 17.20), Augustine is also capable of regarding aspects of Roman culture as exemplary for Christians. "If we do not display, in the service of the most glorious City of God, the qualities of which the Romans, after their fashion, gave us something of a model, in their pursuit of the glory of their earthly city, then we ought to feel the prick of shame" (5.18, Bettenson translation). I am indebted to conversations with John von Heyking on this topic.

55. *Scienza nuova* §1047 (Battistini 1: 934).

56. Here Lilla's argument is more sound. His description of Vico's project as "a deeply un-Augustinian science of natural religion" contains a substantial amount of truth (*G.B. Vico,* p. 145). He comments that "whereas God's providence remains hidden for Augustine, it is evident and comprehensible for both Eusebius and Orosius" (p. 151). In assimilating Vico to the "Eusebian historical tradition," however, he fails to take adequate account of Vico's critique of Rome. Given his general emphasis upon the opening chapters of the *De uno* and the *De constantia philosophiae,* it is odd that he should entirely neglect Vico's use of the Augustinian contrast between pagan and Christian virtue.

57. *Scienza nuova* §38 (Battistini 1: 443–44), "si dànno altri princìpi per dimostrate l'argomento che tratta sant'Agostino, *De virtute romanorum.*"

58. *Vita* (Cristofolini *OF* 50/*Autobiography* 194).

Eleven.   Vico, Geneaology, History

1. Nietzsche, *Daybreak* 1.95, p. 93 (Colli-Montinari 3:86).

2. See Milbank, *The Religious Dimension,* vol. 2, p. 269.

3. See *Scienza nuova* §§385–399 (Battistini 1: 576–84).

4. Mazzotta, *The New Map of the World,* p. 218.

5. Mazzotta, *The New Map of the World,* p. 221.

6. *Scienza nuova* §391 (Battistini 1: 579).

7. See *Scienza nuova* §392 (Battistini 1: 580), "Quarto aspetto è una critica filosofica, la qual nasce dalla istoria dell'idee anzidetta; e tal critica giudicherà il vero sopra gli autori delle nazioni medesime."

8. *Scienza nuova* §392 (Battistini 1: 580), "Tal critica filosofica, quindi incominciando da Giove, ne darà una teogonia naturale, o sia generazione degli dèi fatta naturalmente nelle menti degli autori della gentilità, che furona per natura poeti teologi."

9. Milbank, *The Religious Dimension,* vol. 2, p. 270.

10. Foucault stresses this point about Nietzsche's genealogy. For a reading of Vico that emphasizes a "continous origination" of culture (to which my own analysis of this issue is indebted) see Milbank, *The Religious Dimension,* vol. 2, p. 14.

11. *De antiquissima* 7.4 (Cristofolini *OF* 117), "'ingenium' facultas est in unum dissita, diversa coniungendi"; *De antiquissima* 7.5 (*OF* 123), "quo homo est capax contemplandi ac facendi similia."

12. Michel Foucault, "Nietzsche, la généalogie, l'histoire," p. 136 (*The Foucault Reader,* p. 77). The juxtaposed quotations are from Nietzsche's *Gay Science* 7 and *Human, All Too Human* 3. Also compare Foucault's avowal that a moral genealogy "will cultivate the details and accidents that accompany every beginning; it will be scrupulously attentive to their petty malice; it will await their emergence, once unmasked, as the face of the other" ("Nietzsche, la généalogie, l'histoire," p. 40; *The Foucault Reader,* p. 80).

13. See Collingwood, *The Idea of History,* p. 69.

14. Mannheim, *Essays on the Sociology of Knowledge,* quoted in Ian Hacking, *The Social Construction of What?* p. 20.

15. Nietzsche, *On the Genealogy of Morals* 1.17, p. 55 (Colli-Montinari 5:289).

16. *Scienza nuova* §354 (Battistini 1: 554), "narrano le storie delle cose ch'esse voci significano, incominciando dalla propietà delle lor origini e prosieguendone i naturali progressi de' lor trasporti secondo l'ordine dell'idee, sul quale dee procedere la storia delle lingue."

17. *Scienza nuova* §234 (Battistini 1: 518), "andarono con pari passi a spedirsi e l'idee e le lingue."

18. *Scienza nuova* §151 (Battistini 1: 500), "i testimoni più gravi degli antichi costumi de' popoli, che si celebrarono nel tempo ch'essi si formaron le lingue."

19. *Scienza nuova prima* §387 (Battistini 2: 1164), "stesse umane necessità o utilità comuni a tutte"; "secondo la diversità de' loro siti, cieli e quindi nature e costumi."

20. See Montanari, *Vico e la politica dei moderni,* p. 158.

21. Mazzotta, *The New Map of the World,* p. 210.

Twelve.   Unmasking the Philosophers and Philologists

1. *Vita* (Cristofolini *OF* 35/*Autobiography* 166), "tal maniera negativa di dimonstrare quanto fa di strepito nella fantasia tanto è insuave all'intendimento, poiché con essa nulla più si spiega la mente umana."

2. See *De constantia* 1.4 (Cristofolini *OG* 361.9), *Scienza nuova* §§391, 711 (Battistini 1: 579, 773).

3. *Scienza nuova prima* §9 (Battistini 2: 983–84).

4. *Scienza nuova prima* §10 (Battistini 2: 984).

5. Lilla, *G.B. Vico*, p. 164. The defenses of Rome against Athens and Homer against Socrates, cited as evidence of Vico's alleged intention to defend primitivism against philosophy, are less straightforward than Lilla supposes, unless one assumes a very simple model of the relations between common and esoteric wisdom.

6. Nietzsche, *Mixed Opinions and Maxims* §157, printed in an appendix to *On the Genealogy of Morals*, p. 176.

7. *Scienza nuova prima* §11 (Battistini 2: 985), "una certa *acme,* o sia uno stato di perfezione"; "misurare i gradi e gli estremi, per li quali e dentro i quali, come ogni altra cosa mortale, deve essa umanità delle nazioni correre e terminare."

8. *Scienza nuova prima* §11 (Battistini 2: 985), "la sapienza riposta de' filosofi dasse la mano e reggesse la sapienza volgare delle nazioni, e, 'n cotal guisa, vi convenissero gli più riputati delle accademie con tutti i sapienti delle repubbliche."

9. *Scienza nuova prima* §12 (Battistini 2: 986).

10. *Scienza nuova prima* §12 (Battistini 2: 986), "annientano l'umanità con volerla affatto insensata alle passioni, e riducono alla disperazione gli uomini di poter praticare la loro virtù con quella loro massima assai più dura che ferro: che i peccati sien tutti eguali e che tanto si pecchi con battere uno schiavo un poco più del di lui merito quanto <con> uccidere il padre."

11. *Scienza nuova prima* §12 (Battistini 2: 986), "Tanto le sètte di questi filosofi son comportevoli con la giurisprudenza romana, che una ne divelle la massima, un'altra ne rinnega la pratica più importante dei di lei princìpi!" Compare the exclamation at the end of *Scienza nuova* §335 (Battistini 1: 544).

12. *Scienza nuova prima* §13 (Battistini 2: 986), "Solo il divino Platone egli meditò in una sapienza riposta che regolasse l'uomo a seconda delle massime che egli ha apprese dalla sapienza volgare della religione e delle leggi."

13. Lilla, *G.B. Vico,* p. 228.

14. *Scienza nuova prima* §13 (Battistini 2: 986), "dover di filosofo si debba vivere in conformità delle leggi, ove anche all'eccesso divengan rigide con una qualche ragione." It is difficult to establish textually that Vico professes little admiration for Socrates. See the tribute to Socrates at the beginning of the *De constantia* (*De constantia* 1.1 [Cristofolini OG 353.1]) and the numerous loci in the final *Scienza nuova* where Vico contrasts the "cattivo Aristofane" with "il buonissimo Socrate" (§808 in Battistini 1: 822; see also §§906 and 911 in Battistini 1: 850 and 852). There is also Vico's last public statement, *Le accademie e i rapporti tra la filosofia e l'eloquenza,* where he comments that "l'Accademia fondata da Socrate era un luogo dov'egli con eleganza, con copia, con ornamenti ragionava di tutte le parti dell'umano e divin sapere" (Battistini 1: 405).

15. *Scienza nuova prima* §13 (Battistini 2: 986), "Però esso Platone perdè di veduta la provvedenza quando, per un errore comune delle menti umane, che

misurano da sè le nature non ben conosciute di altrui, innalzò le barbare e rozze origini dell'umanità gentilesca allo stato perfetto delle sue altissime divine cognizioni riposte (il quale, tutto a rovescio, doveva dalle sue 'idee' a quelle scendere e profondare)."

16. *Scienza nuova prima* §13 (Battistini 2: 986), "erudito errore"; "una repubblica ideale ed uno pur ideal giusto"; "storcere e disusare."

17. *Scienza nuova prima* §§13, 269 (Battistini 2: 987, 1111).

18. *Scienza nuova* §§394, 493 (Battistini 1: 581, 637).

19. *Scienza nuova prima* §16 (Battistini 2: 987). The "notorious *etiamsi*" refers to the famous passage in the Prolegomena of the *De iure belli ac pacis* in which Grotius declares that his theory of natural law would be true "even if (*etiamsi*) we should concede that which cannot be conceded without the utmost wickedeness, that there is no God, or that the affairs of men are of no concern to him" (Prolegomena, §11).

20. *Scienza nuova prima* §16 (Battistini 2: 988), "semplicioni solitari, venuti poi alla vita socievole, dettata loro dall'utilità. Che è, in fatti, l'ipotesi di Epicuro." Compare *Scienza nuova* §395 (Battistini 1: 581).

21. *Scienza nuova prima* §18 (Battistini 2: 988), "dà un'ipotesi affatto epicurea ovvero obbesiana (che in ciò è una cosa stessa)." Compare *Scienza nuova* §397 (Battistini 1: 582).

22. *Scienza nuova prima* §17 (Battistini 2: 988). Compare *Scienza nuova* §396 (Battistini 1: 581).

23. *Scienza nuova prima* §19 (Battistini 2: 988), "Quindi, perchè niuno degli tre, nello stabilire i suoi princìpi, guardò la provvedenza, perciò e niuno degli tre scuoprì le vere e finora nascoste origini di niuna di tutte le parti che compongono tutta l'iconomia del diritto natural delle genti, che sono religioni, lingue, costumanze, leggi, società, governi, commerzi, ordini, imperi, domìni, giudìci, pene, guerra, pace, rese, schiavitù, alleanze."

24. *Scienza nuova prima* §20 (Battistini 2: 989), "un diritto naturale uscito con essi costumi delle nazioni."

25. *Scienza nuova prima* §37 (Battistini 2: 998), "la propietà delle nazioni nei loro incominciamenti selvagge e ritirate." Compare *Scienza nuova* §303 (Battistini 1: 533–34).

26. See *Scienza nuova prima* §§14, 25 (Battistini 2: 987, 992).

27. *Scienza nuova prima* §23 (Battistini 2: 990), "ci è mancata finora una scienza la quale fosse, insieme, istoria e filosofia dell'umanità."

28. *Scienza nuova prima* §23 (Battistini 2: 990), "natura umana, dalla quale eran provenute le religioni e le leggi, in mezzo alle quali provennero essi filosofi."

29. *Scienza nuova prima* §27 (Battistini 2: 993), "uomini bestioni vi fussero per un certo senso umano convenuti."

30. *Scienza nuova prima* §27 (Battistini 2: 993), "essa natura de' princìpi, che in tutte le cose sono semplici e rozzi."

31. *Scienza nuova prima* §32 (Battistini 2: 996), "Ma niuna cosa è che s'involva in tante dubbiezze ed oscurità quanto l'origine delle lingue ed il principio della propagazione delle nazioni."

32. *Scienza nuova prima* §40 (Battistini 2: 1000), "senza lingua e non con altre idee che di soddisfare alla fame, alla sete e al fomento della libidine, giunsero a stordire ogni senso di umanità."

33. *Scienza nuova* §120 (Battistini 1: 494), "L'uomo, per l'indiffinita natura della mente umana, ove questa si rovesci nell'ignoranza, egli fa sé regola dell'universo." Compare *Scienza nuova prima* §111 (Battistini 2: 1040).

34. *Scienza nuova* §§122, 123 (Battistini 1: 494–95), "È altra propietà della mente umana ch'ove gli uomini delle cose lontane e non conosciute non possono fare niuna idea, le stimano dalle cose loro conosciute e presenti"; "picciole, rozze, oscurissime." Compare *Scienza nuova prima* §254 (Battistini 2: 1105).

35. *Scienza nuova* §124 (Battistini 1: 495), "boria delle nazioni"; "boria de' dotti." The *borie* are to some extent similar to Bacon's *idola,* but there are important differences between them. As Verene writes, "Vico's first four axioms are not a portrait of simple ignorance, but a portrait of how ignorance is turned into arrogance" (*Vico's Science of Imagination,* p. 134).

36. *Scienza nuova* §125 (Battistini 1: 495), "abbiano avuto tal boria: d'aver esse prima di tutte l'altre ritruovati i comodi dela vita umana e conservar le memorie delle loro cose fin dal principio del mondo."

37. *Scienza nuova* §127 (Battistini 1: 495), "la boria de' dotti, i quali ciò ch'essi sanno, vogliono che sia antico quanto che 'l mondo."

38. *Scienza nuova* §129 (Battistini 1: 496), "La filosofia, per giovar al gener umano, dee sollevar e reggere l'uomo caduto e debole, non convellergli la natura né abbandonarlo nella sua corrozione."

39. *Scienza nuova* §130 (Battistini 1: 496), "Questa Degnità allontana dalla scuola di questa Scienza gli stoici, i quali vogliono l'ammortimento de' sensi, e gli epicurei, che ne fanno regola."

40. *Scienza nuova* §130 (Battistini 1: 496), "entrambi niegano la provvedenza, quelli faccendosi strascinare dal fato, questi abbandonandosi al caso." Compare Vico's sense of the basic convergence of two schools that are superficially opposed with Sidgwick's assertion that "the antithetical relation of Stoicism to Epicureanism is simple, permanent, and easily apprehended" (*Outlines of the History of Ethics,* p. xx).

41. *Scienza nuova* §130 (Battistini 1: 496), "oppinando che muoiano l'anime umane coi corpi, i quali entrambi si dovrebbero dire 'filosofi monastici o solitari.'"

42. *Scienza nuova* §130 (Battistini 1: 496), "i filosofi politici, e principalmente i platonici, i quali convengono con tutti i legislatori in questi tre principali punti: che si dia provvedenza divina, che si debbano moderare l'umane passioni e farne umane virtù, e che l'anime umane sien immortali."

43. *Scienza nuova* §131 (Battistini 1: 496), "La filosofia considera l'uomo quale dev'essere, e sì non può fruttare ch'a pochissimi, che vogliono vivere nella repubblica di Platone, non rovesciarsi nella feccia di Romolo."

44. *Scienza nuova* §138 (Battistini 1: 498), "La filosofia contempla la ragione, onde viene la scienza del vero; la filologia osserva l'autorità dell'umano arbitrio, onde viene la coscienza del certo."

45. *Scienza nuova* §140 (Battistini 1: 498), "dimonstra aver mancato per metà così i filosofi che non accertarono le loro ragioni con l'autorità de' filologi, come i filologi che non curarono d'avverare le loro autorità con la ragion de' filosofi; lo che se avessero fatto, sarebbero stati più utili alle repubbliche e ci avrebbero prevenuto nel meditar questa Scienza."

Thirteen.   Knowledge as Archaeology

1. *Scienza nuova* §357 (Battistini 1: 554), "i grandi frantumi dell'antichità, inutili finor alla scienza perché erano giaciuti squallidi, tronchi e slogati, arrecano de' grandi lumi, tersi, composti ed allogati ne' luoghi loro." Compare *Scienza nuova prima* §23 (Battistini 2: 990–91), where Vico's remedy for the ills of contemporary philology is phrased in similar language.

2. *Scienza nuova prima* §40 (Battistini 2: 1000), "ridurci in uno stato di una somma ignoranza di tutta l'umana e divina erudizione, come se per questa ricerca non vi fussero mai stati per noi né filosifi né filologi." The parallel to the *indifferenza attiva* of the wise man is evoked even more vividly in an appendix to the *Scienza nuova* at §1132 (Nicolini 4.2: 173).

3. *Scienza nuova* §330 (Battistini 1: 541), "per questa ricerca, si dee far conto come se non vi fussero libri nel mondo."

4. *Scienza nuova* §331 (Battistini 1: 541–42), "Ma, in tal densa notte di tenebre ond'è coverta la prima da noi lontanissima antichità, apparisce questo lume eterno, che non tramonta, di questa verità, la quale non si può a patto alcuno chiamar in dubbio; che questo mondo civile egli certamente è stato fatto dagli uomini, onde se ne possono, perché se ne debbono, ritruovare i princìpi dentro le modificazioni della nostra medesima mente umana. Lo che, a chiunque vi rifletta, dee recar maraviglia come tutti i filosofi seriosamente si studiarono di conseguire la scienza di questo mondo naturale, del quale, perché Iddio egli il fece, esso solo ne ha la scienza; e traccurarono di meditare su questo mondo delle nazioni, o sia mondo civile, del quale, perché l'avevano fatto gli uomini, ne potevano conseguire la scienza gli uomini."

5. *Scienza nuova* §349 (Battistini 1: 552), "Anzi ci avvanziamo ad affermare ch'in tanto chi medita questa Scienza egli narri a se stesso questa storia ideal eterna, in quanto—esssendo questo mondo di nazioni stato certamente fatto dagli uomini (ch'è 'l primo principio indubitato che se n'è posto qui sopra), e perciò dovendosene ritruovare la guisa dentro le modificazioni della nostra medesima mente umana—egli, in quella pruova 'dovette, deve, dovrà,'

esso stesso sel faccia; perché, ove avvenga che chi fa le cose esso stesso le narri, ivi non può essere più certa l'istoria. Così questa Scienza procede appunto come la geometria, che, mentre sopra i suoi elementi il costruisce o'l contempla, essa stessa si faccia il mondo delle grandezze; ma con tanto più di realità quanta più ne hanno gli ordini d'intorno alle faccende degli uomini, che non ne hanno punti, linee, superficie e figure. E questo istesso è argomento che tali pruove sieno d'una spezie divina e che debbano, o leggitore, arrecarti un divin piacere, perocché in Dio il conoscer e 'l fare è una medesima cosa."

6. *Scienza nuova* §2 (Battistini 1: 415), "mondo civile"; "il mondo delle menti umane, ch'è 'l mondo metafisico."

7. *Vita* (Cristofolini *OF* 14/*Autobiography* 127), "nella nostra mente sono certe eterne verità che non possiamo sconoscere o riniegare, e in conseguenza non sono da noi." Clearly Bedani is right to suggest that Vico does not argue that "man makes history," *if* "history" is identified with the ultimate causes of the *mondo civile* (see *Vico Revisited*, pp. 193–95). Nonetheless, Bedani's conclusion that humans in no sense make their own history seems too extreme, in light of Vico's emphasis on *both* the directive role of providence and the creative *ingenium* of human beings. The tension here bears an analogy to that between divine grace and human agency, as felt by participants on both sides of the controversy *de auxiliis*. Bedani seems not to find the tension in Vico, perhaps because of his belief that (*sic*) "the Catholic doctrine of grace is straightforward enough" (p. 149). More adequate is Verene's formulation, which admirably refrains from denying the tension: "History is seen not as made by men but as enacted by them through the eternal pattern of providence" (*Vico's Science of Imagination*, p. 121). Cf. Rigol, *Poiesis y verdad en Giambattista Vico,* "La realización de la historia depende de la razón práctica de los hombres y de la actuación de la Providencia" (p. 89).

8. *De uno* 53 (Cristofolini *OG* 69).

9. *Scienza nuova* §357 (Battistini 1: 554), "i grandi frantumi dell'antichità, inutili finor alla scienza perché erano giaciuti squallidi, tronchi e slogati, arrecano de' grandi lumi, tersi, composti ed allogati ne' luoghi loro." Compare *Scienza nuova prima* §23 (Battistini 2: 990–91), where Vico's remedy for the ills of contemporary philology is phrased in similar language.

10. See the appendix to the *Scienza nuova* (§1133), where Vico claims both that he proceeds in accordance with a strict geometric method and that his conclusions are a source of wonder.

11. *Scienza nuova* §2 (Battistini 1: 416), "una teologia civile ragionata della provvedenza divina." See also *Scienza nuova* §§342, 385 (Battistini 1: 548, 576).

12. *Scienza nuova* §2 (Battistini 1: 415), "il mondo delle menti umane, ch'è 'l mondo metafisico"; "mondo degli animi umani, ch'è 'l mondo civile, o sia il mondo delle nazioni."

13. Perhaps the most lucid presentation of the "three worlds" is at *Scienza nuova* §42 (Battistini 1: 446).

14. *Scienza nuova prima* §40 (Battistini 2: 1000–1001), "la teorica universalissima della divina filosofia"; "la universalissima pratica"; "la metafisica dell'umana mente"; "condurla a Dio com'eterna verità"; "innalzando"; "contemplare il senso comune del genere umano come una certa mente umana delle nazioni, per condurla a Dio come eterna provvedenza."

15. See *Scienza nuova prima* §40 (Battistini 2: 1000).

16. See *Scienza nuova* §§34, 338, 378, 700 (Battistini 1: 440, 547, 572, 767); *Scienza nuova prima* §§42, 261 (Battistini 2: 1003, 1107). On the point that we cannot literally re-enter the world of the first human beings, the textual evidence is clear. This is not to deny, of course, the importance of overcoming anachronism through the type of "empathy" proper to any good historian. In this more modest sense, which prohibits the facile assimilation of imagistic modes of apprehension to conceptual modes of thought, *fantasia* may well be the "master key" of the new science. Verene's book is certainly the clearest and best argued statement in favor of the centrality of *memoria* and *fantasia* to Vico's project. The most pointed criticisms of Verene's reading are to be had in Milbank, *The Religious Dimension,* vol. 2, pp. 183–84; Bedani, *Vico Revisited,* pp. 188–91; Pompa, *Vico: A Study of the 'New Science',* pp. 230–36.

17. These are clearly not identical to the Elements of the science. In "The Idea of the Work," Vico speaks of the civil elements as the actual *facta* that constitute human beginnings (see *Scienza nuova* §§2, 40 [Battistini 1: 415, 444]). The Elements of the science, by contrast, are available only to the modern reflective mind. They include philosophical, theological, psychological, and anthropological data that by necessity were unavailable to the first humans.

18. *Scienza nuova* §41 (Battistini 1: 446), "Le tenebre nel fondo della dipintura sono la materia di questa Scienza, incerta, informe, oscura, che si propone nella Tavola cronologica e nelle a lei scritte Annotazioni."

19. *Scienza nuova prima* §41 (Battistini 2: 1001), "colla divisione, procedendo dalla cognizione delle parti, per via indi della composizione, pervenire alla cognizione del tutto che vuol sapersi."

20. *Scienza nuova* §163 (Battistini 1: 504), "il metodo di filosofare più accertato di Francesco Bacone signore di Verlumio." Cf. *Scienza nuova* §359 and §499 (Battistini 1: 554 and 640).

21. *Vita* (Cristofolini *OF* 50/*Autobiography* 194), "dalla mente di Platone e altri chiari filosofi tentava di scendere nelle menti balorde e scempie degli autori della gentilità."

22. See Morrison, "Vico's Doctrine of the Natural Law of the Gentes," p. 51.

23. *Scienza nuova* §119 (Battistini 1: 494), "le quali, come per lo corpo animato il sangue, così deono per entro scorrervi ed animarla in tutto ciò che questa Scienza ragiona della comune natura delle nazioni."

24. *Scienza nuova prima* §40 (Battistini 2: 1000), "per sì fatto immenso oceano di dubbiezze, appare questa sola picciola terra dove si possa fermare il piede." *Scienza nuova* §331 (Battistini 1: 541), "in tal densa notte di tenebre

ond'è coverta la prima da noi lontanissima antichità, apparisce questo lume eterno, che non tramonta, di questa verità, la quale non si può a patto alcuno chiamar in dubbio."

25. *Scienza nuova* §331 (Battistini 1: 541–42), "questo mondo civile egli certamente è stato fatto dagli uomini, onde se ne possono, perché se ne debbono, ritruovare i princìpi dentro le modificazioni della nostra medesima mente umana."

26. I deliberately omit the alleged imperative to "enter into" the imaginations of the first peoples. For writers such as Isaiah Berlin, the discovery of the "reconstructive imagination" is at the heart of Vico's method and constitutes his crowning achievement. Berlin writes that "we must do what we can to 'enter into' these vast imaginations" and cites paragraph 378 of the *Scienza nuova*. The sense of the passage, however, is exactly contrary to Berlin's exhortation, for it suggests that men are "naturalmente niegato di poter entrare nella vasta immaginativa di que' primi uomini" (*Scienza nuova* §378 [Battistini 1: 572]). Berlin's omission of the first four words in his citation of the Italian is revelatory. Cf. *Vico and Herder,* p. 44.

27. *Scienza nuova* §394 (Battistini 1: 581), "incominciandola dalla metà in giù, cioè dagli ultimi tempi delle nazioni ingentilite."

28. *Scienza nuova* §347 (Battistini 1: 551), "quando i filosofi cominciaron a riflettere sopra l'umane idee"; "d'allora ch'i primi uomini cominciarono a umanamente pensare."

29. *Scienza nuova* §347 (Battistini 1: 551), "si conduce fin all'ultime controversie che ne hanno avuto i due primi ingegni di questa età, il Leibnizo e 'l Newtone."

30. *Scienza nuova* §346 (Battistini 1: 550–51). See Milbank, *The Religious Dimension,* vol. 2, pp. 18–19.

31. Cf. MacIntyre, *After Virtue,* p. 216 and Berlin, *Vico and Herder,* pp. 38 and 70.

32. *Scienza nuova* §147 (Battistini 1: 500), "Natura di cose altro non è che nascimento di esse in certi tempi e con certe guise." Cf. the earlier identification of *natura* and *nascendi* in *De uno* 74 and 144 (Cristofolini *OG* 91 and 177).

33. *Scienza nuova* §148 (Battistini 1: 500), "Le propietà inseparabili da' subbietti devon essere produtte dalla modificazione o guisa con che le cose son nate; per lo che esse ci posson avverare tale e non altra essere la natura o nascimento di esse cose."

34. *Scienza nuova* §333 (Battistini 1: 542), "tutte le nazioni così barbare come umane, quantunque, per immensi spazi di luoghi e tempi tra loro lontane, divisamente fondate."

35. See Leibniz, *Discourse on Metaphysics* §5.

36. *Scienza nuova* §343 (Battistini 1: 549), "vi debbe spiegar i suoi ordini per vie tanto facili quanto sono i naturali costumi umani."

37. *Scienza nuova* §343 (Battistini 1: 549), "ha per consigliera la sapienza infinita."

38. *Scienza nuova* §343 (Battistini 1: 549), "ha per suo fine la sua stessa immensa bontà, quanto vi ordina debb'esser indiritto a un bene sempre superiore a quello che si han proposta essi uomini."

39. See *Vico and Herder,* p. 81, where Berlin rightly argues that Vico is and must be more empirical than, say, Leibniz. The ideal eternal history, however *a priori* it may appear, is known through the deciphering of actual histories. Yet it is something more than an empirically derived statement of the past *wie eigentlich es gewesen.* Cf. Verene's comment that the *storia ideale eterna* "is an ideal truth, but not an a priori or fictional one" (*Vico's Science of Imagination,* p. 125).

40. See *Scienza nuova* §221 (Battistini 1: 516), where Vico contends that later humans who still fear divine punishment attribute their customs to the gods, thereby distorting the original sense of the myths.

41. Vico specifically criticizes Iamblichus for reading neoplatonism into Egyptian myths. See *Scienza nuova* §412 (Battistini 1: 592–93).

42. The Bergin and Fisch translation confuses things by making Vico say both that the history of human ideas is the "second" aspect of his science (§347) and that it is the "third" aspect (§§386, 391). Vico himself is not inconsistent; §347 says only that "per quest'altro principale suo aspetto, questa Scienza è una storia dell'umane idee" (Battistini 1: 551).

43. *Scienza nuova* §238 (Battistini 1: 519), "L'ordine dell'idee dee procedere secondo l'ordine delle cose."

44. Here Lilla seems to equivocate. At one point, he assumes that the "order of ideas" is only the "window" through which the human scientist must discern things, and implies that what most interests Vico is the "order of things." But then, more in line with the texts, he acknowledges that for Vico "man's 'ideas' are the metaphysical cause of the 'things' he makes in time." Lilla assumes that Vico is interested in "metaphysical" causes primarily for the sake of knowing their "political" effects. But Vico's self-understanding is quite different. He thinks of his science as philosophy, as the search for causes, with a genuine but secondary interest in effects. "Ideas" are more than a key that can be thrown away after the order of things is unlocked. Compare *Scienza nuova prima* §44 (Battistini 2: 1007) with *G.B. Vico,* pp. 128–32.

45. *Scienza nuova prima* §268 (Battistini 2: 1110), "la serie dell'idee comuni dintorno le umane necessità o utilità."

46. *Scienza nuova* §149 (Battistini 1: 500), "pubblici motivi di vero." *Scienza nuova* §356 (Battistini 1: 554), "un pubblico fondamento di vero."

47. *Vita* (Cristofolini *OF* 50/*Autobiography* 194), "divisamente dagli uni e dagli altri ragionò del metodo con cui si conducessero le materie di questa Scienza, le quali, con altro metodo, dovevano fil filo uscire da entrambi i detti princìpi: onde vi avvennero molti errori nell'ordine."

48. Collingwood, *Principles of Art,* p. 249.

49. See Gadamer, *Truth and Method,* pp. 474 ff.

50. *Scienza nuova* §§494, 433 (Battistini 1: 638, 603–4).

51. *Scienza nuova* §401 (Battistini 1: 585), "tal prima lingua ne' primi tempi mutoli delle nazioni, come si è detto nelle *Degnità,* dovette cominciare con cenni o atti o corpi ch'avessero naturali rapporti all'idee."

52. *Scienza nuova* §403 (Battistini 1: 587), "i propi parlari delle favole (ché tanto suona tal voce)."

53. On the tendency of Vico's later writings to construe *factum* as *signum,* see Milbank, *The Religious Dimension,* vol. 2, p. 5.

54. *Scienza nuova* §151 (Battistini 1: 500), "I parlari volgari debbon esser i testimoni più gravi degli antichi costumi de' popoli, che si celebrarono nel tempo ch'essi si formaron le lingue."

55. *Scienza nuova* §352 (Battistini 1: 553), "diritte, facili e naturali."

56. On this crucial point, see Botturi, *La sapienza della storia,* pp. 223–24.

57. *Scienza nuova* §346 (Battistini 1: 551), "le quali non posson altronde esser nate che da tali e non altri nascimenti, in tali tempi, luoghi e con tali guise, o sia da tali nature." Compare *Scienza nuova* §348 (Battistini 1: 552).

58. See Milbank, *The Religious Dimension,* vol. 2, p. 233.

59. *Scienza nuova* §345 (Battistini 1: 550), "la loro catena eterna delle cagioni"; "ella penda dall'onnipotente, saggia e benigna volontà dell'Ottimo Massimo Dio." Compare *Scienza nuova* §387 (Battistini 1: 577).

60. *Scienza nuova* §345 (Battistini 1: 550), "pruoverà un divin piacere, in questo coropo mortale, di contemplare nelle divine idee questo mondo di nazioni per tutta la distesa de' loro luoghi, tempi e varietà."

61. *Scienza nuova* §346 (Battistini 1: 550), "sublimi pruove teologiche naturali."

62. See *Scienza nuova prima* §§11, 398 (Battistini 2: 985, 1171) and *Scienza nuova* §§14, 129, 363 (Battistini 1: 425, 496, 560).

63. *Scienza nuova seconda* §1136 (Nicolini 4.2: 174), "contiene tutte discoverte in gran parti diverse, e molte dello 'n tutto contrarie, all'oppenione che, delle cose le quali qui si ragionano, si è avuto finora."

64. *Scienza nuova seconda* §1137 (Nicolini 4.2: 174), "ti priego a volertici avvezzare, con leggere almeno tre volte quest'opera." *Scienza nuova seconda* §1135 (Nicolini 4.2: 174), "i quali odono una o due corde più sonore del gravicembalo con dispiacenza, perché non odono le altre con le quali, toccate dalla mano maestra di musica, fanno dolce e grata armonia."

65. *Scienza nuova* §330 (Battistini 1: 541).

66. See *Scienza nuova prima* §9 (Battistini 2: 983–84).

Fourteen.   Pagan Consciousness in the Age of the Gods

1. *Scienza nuova* §314 (Battistini 1: 537), "Le dottrine debbono cominciare da quando cominciano le materie che trattano."

2. *Scienza nuova* §333 (Battistini 1: 542–43), "abbiamo presi questi tre costumi eterni ed universali per tre primi princìpi di questa Scienza."

3. *Scienza nuova* §334 (Battistini 1: 543), "[ebrei e cristiani] credono nella divinità d'una mente infinita libera"; "[i gentili] credono di più dèi, immaginati composti di corpo e di mente libera." For the increased "interiority" of Hebrew and Christian belief, see *Scienza nuova* §350 (1: 553) and §396 (1: 582).

4. *Scienza nuova* §52 (Battistini 1:461), "due grandi verità filologiche"; "non meno maravigliosi delle loro piramidi."

5. *Scienza nuova* §174 (Battistini 1: 507), "mentova una lingua più antica della sua, che certamente fu lingua eroica, e la chiama 'lingua degli dèi." More detail is given at *Scienza nuova* §437 (Battistini 1: 607).

6. *Scienza nuova* §175 (Battistini 1: 507), "Varrone ebbe la diligenza di raccogliere trentamilia nomi di dèi."

7. *Scienza nuova* §175 (Battistini 1: 507), "i quali nomi si rapportavano ad altrettante bisogne della vita o naturale o morale o iconomica o finalmente civile de' primi tempi."

8. *Scienza nuova* §7 (Battistini 1: 419), "istorie de' tempi che gli uomini della più rozza umanità gentilesca credettero tutte le cose necessarie o utili al gener umano essere deitadi."

9. *Scienza nuova* §31 (Battistini 1: 438), "l'età degli dèi, nella quale gli uomini gentili credettero vivere sotto divini governi, e ogni cosa essere lor comandata con gli auspìci e con gli oracoli, che sono le più vecchie cose della storia profana."

10. *Scienza nuova* §382 (Battistini 1: 575), "a 'quali due princìpi va di séguito quello de' sagrifizi, ch'essi facevano per 'proccurare' o sia ben intender gli auspìci." See also *Scienza nuova prima* §111 (Battistini 2: 1040).

11. *Scienza nuova* §149 (Battistini 1: 500), "pubblici motivi di vero." *Scienza nuova* §150 (1: 500), "Questo sarà altro grande lavoro di questa Scienza: di ritruovarne i motivi del vero, il quale, col volger degli anni e col cangiare delle lingue e costumi, ci pervenne ricoverto di falso." See *Scienza nuova* §356 (1: 554).

12. *Scienza nuova* §7 (Battistini 1: 419), "vere e severe istorie de' costumi delle antichissime genti di Grecia."

13. *Scienza nuova* §401 (Battistini 1: 585). See also *Scienza nuova* §403 (1: 587) and §814 (1: 825).

14. *Scienza nuova prima* §266 (Battistini 2: 1109), "perchè non si può dare dell'idee false, perocché il falsa consiste nella sconcia combinazione delle idee, così non si può dare tradizione, quantunque favolosa, che non abbia da prima avuta alcun motivo di vero."

15. *Scienza nuova prima* §9 (Battistini 2: 983), "Sì fatta vana scienza, dalla quale dovette incominciare la sapienza volgare di tutte le nazioni gentili, nasconde però due gran princìpi di vero: uno, che vi sia provvendenza divina che governi le cose umane; l'altro, che negli uomini sia libertà d'arbitrio, per lo quale, se vogliono e vi si adoperano, possono schivare ciò che, senza provvederlo, altramenti loro apparterebbe."

16. *Scienza nuova* §385 (Battistini 1: 576), "dentro i nembi di quelle prime tempeste e al barlume di que' lampi, videro questa gran verità: che la provvedenza divina sovraintenda alla salvezza di tutto il gener umano."

17. *Scienza nuova* §191 (Battistini 1: 510), "le false religioni non nacquero da impostura d'altrui, ma da propia credulità."

18. Nietzsche, *On the Genealogy of Morals* 1.6, p. 33 (Colli-Montinari 5: 266).

19. *Scienza nuova* §178 (Battistini 1: 507).

20. Milbank, *The Religious Dimension,* vol. 2, p. 47.

21. Compare Milbank, *The Religious Dimension,* vol. 2, p. 47.

22. *Scienza nuova* §490 (Battistini 1: 636), "vero di metafisica ragionata d'intorno all'ubiquità di Dio, ch'era stato appreso con falso senso di metafisica poetica: *Iovis omnia plena.*" *Scienza nuova* §591 (1: 703), "in que' tempi che le nazioni erano stordite e stupide." *Scienza nuova* §385 (1: 576), "la falsa divinità di Giove."

23. *Scienza nuova prima* §9 (Battistini 2: 983), "l'idolatria, or sia culto di deitadi fantasticate sulla falsa credulità d'esser corpi forniti diforze superiori alla natura, che soccorrano gli uomini ne' loro estremi malori." See also *Scienza nuova prima* §11 (Battistini 2: 1040).

24. *Scienza nuova* §916 (Battistini 1: 859), "una natura poetica o sia creatrice, lecito ci sia dire divina, la qual a' corpi diede l'essere di sostanze animate di dèi, e gliele diede dalla sua idea."

25. *Scienza nuova* §916 (Battistini 1: 859), "per forte inganno di fantasia, la qual è robustissima ne' debolissimi di raziocinio." In general, and contrary to readings that take him to exalt imagination over reason, Vico consistently associates imagination with falsehood and error. This association is manifest not only throughout the *Scienza nuova,* but also in his correspondence — see, for example, the letter to Estevan, where he complains that "the majority are all memory and fantasy, for which reason they have spoken evil of the *Scienza nuova* because the *Scienza nuova* has turned upside down everything they erroneously remembered and had imagined about the principles of all divine and human erudition." See "Four Letters of Vico" (trans. Pinton), pp. 48–49. Croce takes this letter to be revelatory of Vico's general character; see *The Philosophy of Giambattista Vico,* p. 263.

26. *Scienza nuova* §916 (Battistini 1: 916), "altronde era fiera ed immane; ma, per quello stesso errore di fantasia, eglino temevano spaventosamente gli dèi ch'essi stessi si avevano finti."

27. *Scienza nuova* §377 (Battistini 1: 571), "spaventati ed attoniti dal grand'effetto di che non sapevano la cagione, alzarono gli occhi ed avvertirono il cielo."

28. *Scienza nuova* §376 (Battistini 1: 570–71), "perturbava all'eccesso essi medesimi che fingendo le si criavano, onde furon detti 'poeti,' che lo stesso in greco suona che 'criatori.'"

29. *Scienza nuova* §406 (Battistini 1: 589).

30. *Scienza nuova* §405 (Battistini 1: 589).

31. *Scienza nuova* §376 (Battistini 1: 570), "dalla lor idea criavan essi le cose." Compare *Scienza nuova prima* §257 (Battistini 2: 1106), "dall'idea del poeta dà tutto l'essere alle cose che non lo hanno."

32. See Lachterman, "Vico and Marx: Notes on a Precursory Reading," p. 56.

33. *Scienza nuova* §377 (Battistini 1: 571), "d'uomini tutti robuste forze di corpo, che, urlando, brotolando, spiegavano le loro violentissime passioni."

34. *Scienza nuova* §377 (Battistini 1: 571), "la natura della mente umana porta ch'ella attribuisca all'effetto la sua natura."

35. *Scienza nuova* §377 (Battistini 1: 571), "si finsero il cielo esser un gran corpo animato, che per tal aspetto chiamarono Giove, il primo dio delle genti dette 'maggiori,' che col fischio de' fulmini e col fragore de' tuoni volesse dir loro qualche cosa."

36. Compare the language of *Scienza nuova* §§13, 376, 377 (Battistini 1: 423, 570, 571) with *De antiquissima* 1.2. Hobbes may be an influence here; he too speaks of men "feigning" gods in the twelfth chapter of *Leviathan.*

37. *Scienza nuova* §376 (Battistini 1: 570), "perocché Iddio, nel suo purissimo intendimento, conosce e, conoscendole, cria le cose; essi, per la loro robusta ignoranza, il facevano in forza d'una corpolentissima fantasia."

38. *Scienza nuova* §379 (Battistini 1: 572–73), "sì popolare, perturbante ed insegnativa, ch'essi stessi, che sel finsero, sel credettero e con ispaventose religioni, le quali appresso si mostreranno, il temettero, il riverirono e l'osservarono."

39. *Scienza nuova* §383 (Battistini 1: 575), "egli è impossibile ch'i corpi sieno menti (e fu creduto che 'l cielo tonante si fusse Giove)."

40. *Scienza nuova* §382 (Battistini 1: 575), "il timore fu quello che finse gli dèi nel mondo; ma, come si avvisò nelle *Degnità,* non fatto da altri ad altri uomini, ma da essi a se stessi."

41. *Scienza nuova* §379 (Battistini 1: 573).

42. *Scienza nuova* §376 (Battistini 1: 571), "d'insegnar il volgo a virtuosamente operare, com'essi l'insegnarono a se medesimi."

43. *Scienza nuova* §379 (Battistini 1: 573–74), "E da questo primo gran beneficio fatto al gener umano vennegli il titolo di 'sotere' o di 'salvadore,' perché non gli fulminò (ch'è il primo degli tre princìpi ch'abbiamo preso di questa Scienza); e vennegli quel di 'statore' o di 'fermatore,' perché fermò que' pochi giganti dal loro ferino divagamento, onde poi divennero i principi delle genti."

44. *Scienza nuova* §1099 (Battistini 1: 963), "le repubbliche erculee, nelle quali pii, sappienti, casti, forti e magnanimi debellasser superbi e difendessero deboli, ch'è la forma eccellente de' civili governi."

45. *Scienza nuova* §517 (Battistini 1: 652).

46. *Scienza nuova* §518 (Battistini 1: 654), "fanatismo di superstizione."

47. *Scienza nuova prima* §9 (Battistini 1: 983), "l'idolatria nata ad un parto con la divinazione, o sia vana scienza dell'avvenire, a certi avvisi sensibili, creduti esser mandati agli uomini dagli dèi."

48. For the division of the sons of Noah into "Eastern" and "Western," see *Scienza nuova* §62 (Battistini 1: 466).

49. *Scienza nuova* §62 (Battistini 1: 466), "una spezie di divinazione più dilicata dall'osservare i moti de' pianeti e gli aspetti degli astri."

50. *Scienza nuova* §250 (Battistini 1: 521), "i padri nello stato delle famiglie dovetter esser i sappienti in divinità d'auspìci." For a compressed listing of *tutti i primi elementi di questo mondo di nazioni*, see *Scienza nuova* §40 (Battistini 1: 444).

51. *Scienza nuova* §381 (Battistini 1: 574), "ovvero sappienti che s'intendevano del parlar degli dèi conceputo con gli auspìci di Giove."

52. *Scienza nuova* §938 (Battistini 1: 868), "talché di questa prima giurisprudenza fu il primo e propio «*interpretari*», detto quasi «*interpatrari*», cioè «entrare in essi padri», quali furono dapprima detti gli dèi." See also the parallel passage at §448 (1: 617), which additionally suggests a link between the *patrare* of the fathers and the divine *facere*.

53. *Scienza nuova prima* §61 (Battistini 2: 1017), "prima e principale delle quali tutte certamente sono le nozze."

54. *Scienza nuova* §503 (Battistini 1: 644), "la pietà volgarmente è la madre di tutte le morali, iconomiche e civili virtù."

55. *Scienza nuova* §504 (Battistini 1: 644), "Cominciò, qual dee, la moral virtù dal conato."

56. *Scienza nuova* §504 (Battistini 1: 644), "la virtù dell'animo, contenendo la loro libidine bestiale di esercitarla in faccia al cielo, di cui avevano uno spavento grandissimo."

57. *Scienza nuova* §504 (Battistini 1: 645), "si usarono con esse la venere umana al coverto, nascostamente, cioè a dire con pudicizia; e sì incominciarono a sentir pudore, che Socrate diceva esser il 'colore della virtù.'"

58. In his account of "the creation of the gods and moral virtue" (*Vico Revisited*, pp. 81–85), Bedani dwells on "fear" but fails to mention *pudore*. The intended effect is to lend plausibility to Bedani's "naturalistic" reading; the actual effect is to underscore the distance between text and commentator.

59. *Scienza nuova* §120 (Battistini 1: 494), "L'uomo, per l'indiffinita natura della mente umana, ove questa si rovesci nell'ignoranza, egli fa sé regola dell'universo."

60. *Scienza nuova* §505 (Battistini 1: 645), "carnali congiugnimenti pudichi fatti col timore di qualche divinità."

61. *Scienza nuova* §§506–508 (Battistini 1: 645–47).

62. *Scienza nuova* §509 (Battistin 1: 647).

63. *Scienza nuova* §510 (Battistini 1: 647), "di prendersi le spose con una certa finta forza, dalla forza vera con la quale i giganti strascinarono le prime donne dentro le loro grotte."

64. See Lilla, *G.B. Vico*, p. 172.

65. *Scienza nuova* §511 (Battistini 1: 647).

66. *Scienza nuova* §513 (Battistini 1: 648), "dispotica signoria."

67. *Scienza nuova* §§516, 14, 1099 (Battistini 1: 651, 424–25, 963).

68. *Scienza nuova* §§516, 398, 14 (Battistini 1: 651, 582, 424).

69. *Scienza nuova* §516 (Battistini 1: 651), "contenti d'una sola donna per tutta la loro vita."

70. *Scienza nuova* §514 (Battistini 1: 649), "la pietà co' matrimoni è la scuola dove s'imparano i primi rudimenti di tutte le grandi virtù." Marriage is also the origin of friendship and the "three final goods" of the noble, the useful, and the pleasant. See *Scienza nuova* §554 (Battistini 1: 678).

71. Vico conjectures that the first peoples used "twelve" to signify any large number. See *Scienza nuova* §642 (Battistini 1: 738).

72. *Scienza nuova* §514 (Battistini 1: 649).

73. *Scienza nuova* §515 (Battistini 1: 650–51).

74. For the attribution of the notion to Aristotle, see *Scienza nuova* §§1042, 1101 (Battistini 1: 928, 965).

75. *Scienza nuova* §1098 (Battistini 1: 962), "con certe mogli fecero certi figliuoli e ne divennero certi padri." At *Scienza nuova* §321 (Battistini 1: 539), Vico says that *certum* means "particolarizzato" or, in the language of the Schools, "individuato" and notes that in overelegant Latin, *certum* and *commune* are contraries.

76. *Scienza nuova* §554 (Battistini 1: 678), "la vera amicizia naturale egli è matrimonio, nella quale naturalmente si comunicano tutti e tre i fini de' beni, cioè l'onesto, l'utile e'l dilettevole."

77. Cf. Nietzsche, *Mixed Opinions and Maxims* §137, printed in an appendix to *On the Genealogy of Morals,* p. 175.

78. *Scienza nuova* §179 (Battistini 1: 508), "la cristiana religione, la quale inverso tutto il gener umano, nonché la giustizia, comanda la carità."

Fifteen.   The Hebrew Difference

1. See, for example, Karl Löwith, *Meaning in History,* p. 130.

2. Mazzotta, *The New Map of the World,* p. 240. Mazzotta well catches the genealogical dimension of this aspect of Vico's authorship when he speaks of his "archaeology of culture [that] will demolish the illusion of the primacy of the gentiles over the Jews" (p. 240).

3. *De antiquissima* 1.2 (Cristofolini *OF* 65).

4. See the heading of *Scienza nuova prima* §25 (Battistini 2: 992), which reads "oltre quella delle fede, umana necessità è di ripetere i princìpi di questa scienza dalla storia sacra." Cf. *De constantia* 2.7 (Cristofolini *OG* 425.3), "certa origo et successio historiae universae ab historia sacra repetenda" and *Vita* (*OF* 35/*Autobiography* 166): "Imperciocché egli appruova una indispensabile necessità, anche umana, di ripetere le prime origini di tal Scienza da' principi della storia sacra."

5. *Vita* (Cristofolini *OF* 38/*Autobiography* 173).

6. *Scienza nuova* §165 (Battistini 1: 504), "le più antiche profane che ci son pervenute." Cf. *De constantia* 2.8 (Cristofolini *OG* 425.2), which claims that "[sacra historia] omnibus profanis esse antiquiorem."

7. *Scienza nuova* §165 (Battistini 1: 504), "narra tanto spiegatamente e per lungo trattto di più di ottocento anni lo stato di natura sotto de' patriarchi, o sia lo stato delle famiglie"; "del quale stato la storia profana ce ne ha o nulla o poco e assai confusamente narrato."

8. *Scienza nuova* §166 (Battistini 1: 505), "gli ebrei han conservato tanto spiegatamente le loro memorie fin dal principio del mondo." Cf. *Scienza nuova* §54 (1: 462).

9. Caponigri recognizes this point: "the normative principle of the 'New Science' is sacred history" (*Time and Idea,* p. 29).

10. *Scienza nuova* §51 (Battistini 1: 460), "per assistere con ragioni anco umane a tutto il credibile cristiano, il quale tutto incomincia da ciò: che 'l primo popolo del mondo fu egli l'ebreo, di cui fu principe Adamo, il quale fu criato dal vero Dio con la criazione del mondo." Mazzotta notes the importance of this locus in *The New Map of the World,* p. 240.

11. *Scienza nuova prima* §25 (Battistini 2: 992), "ella, più spiegatamente che non fanno tutte le gentilesche, ne narra sul principio del mondo uno stato di natura, o sia il tempo delle famiglie, le quali i padri reggevano sotto il governo di Dio, che da Filone elegantemente si chiama *theocratia.*"

12. *Scienza nuova prima* §25 (Battistini 2: 992), "per le due schiavitù tra loro sofferte, con molto più di gravità che non fa quella de' greci, ci narra le cose antiche degli egizi e degli assiri."

13. *De constantia* 1.4 (Cristofolini *OG* 357.3), "Ada integer mente pura contemplabatur Deum, puro animo diligebat."

14. *De constantia* 1.4 (Cristofolini *OG* 357.4). On Vico's use of Varro (as mediated by Augustine), compare *De constantia* 1.4 (*OG* 357.2–3) with *De uno* Proloquium (*OG* 33.24)

15. *De constantia* 1.4 (Cristofolini *OG* 359.8), "eius [honoris] discrimen inter hebraeos et gentes." Also see *De uno* 156 (*OG* 211.6), where Vico mentions the *discrimen,* but promises that "latius libro secundo explicabimus."

16. *De constantia* 1.4 (Cristofolini *OG* 360.8), "mentis castitate magis quam corporis, vero Deo sacra faciebant"; "solo puro corpore diis exhibitus honor."

17. *De constantia* 1.4 (Cristofolini *OG* 361.9), "contemplatio mater divinationis."

18. *De constantia* 1.4 (Cristofolini *OG* 361.9), "Hinc populus hebraeus, qui verum Deum colebat, nulla divinatione fundatus, quae est praecipua ratio cur a gentibus segregaretur, quibus, simul cum idolatria, gemina divinatio orta est." Verene thinks that Vico "makes no special use of idolatry as a principle to distinguish the Hebrews from the gentiles" ("On Translating Vico: The Penguin Classics Edition of the *New Science*," p. 104). Whether or not Vico's use of the principle qualifies as "special," we do not know. Certainly it

is pervasive, present in both sections of the *De constantia* and in all versions of the *Scienza nuova*.

19. *De constantia* 1.4 (Cristofolini *OG* 361.10), "Atqui Dei cultus ex veri aeterni cognitione cum mente pura in homine integro aeternus fuisset, nam semper uniformis fuisset. Hinc, homine per peccatum cognitione veri ex mente pura in vitae agendis mulctato, substitutum est vero certum."

20. *De constantia* 1.4 (Cristofolini *OG* 361.10), "et legibus certi dii, certae cerimoniae, certae formulae verborum institutae, ut religiones, quantum in humanis liceret, aeternae essent."

21. *Scienza nuova* §137 (Battistini 1: 498), "gli uomini che non sanno il vero delle cose proccurano d'attenersi al certo, perché, non potendo soddisfare l'intelletto con la scienza, almeno la volontà riposi sulla coscienza."

22. *De constantia* 1.4 (Cristofolini *OG* 361.10), "apud vulgus respondent rebus divinis quas philosophi rationibus docent, et sunt prima et aeterna vera quae metaphysica statuit."

23. *De constantia* 1.4 (Cristofolini *OG* 361.10), "Quare, de quibus metaphysica agit sunt populis religiones fundatae: vera hebraeis, qui unum increatum mundi Creatorem sub nulla imagine; falsae gentibus, quae mundum, mundique animam, eiusque animae mentem, seu vim motricem mundo coaevam, necessario agentem et in partibus mundi divisam, — ut, exempli gratia, vim motricem aëris Iovem, maris Neptunum—sub idolis sunt veneratae."

24. *De constantia* 1.4 (Cristofolini *OG* 361–62.10).

25. *De constantia* 1.4 (Cristofolini *OG* 363.11), "religio deistarum falsa demonstratur."

26. See *Scienza nuova* §129 (Battistini 1: 496).

27. See *De constantia* 1.4 (Cristofolini *OG* 363.13).

28. *Scienza nuova* §948 (Battistini 1: 873), "agli ebrei prima e poi a' cristiani, per interni parlari, alle menti, perché voci d'un Dio tutto mente; ma con parlari esterni, così da' profeti, come da Gesù Cristo agli appostoli, e da questi palesati alla Chiesa."

29. *Scienza nuova* §948 (Battistini 1: 873), "a' gentili, per gli auspìci, per gli oracoli ed altri segni corporei creduti divini avvisi, perché creduti venire dagli dèi, ch'essi gentili credevano esser composti di corpo."

30. *Scienza nuova* §1047 (Battistini 1: 934), "nascere nuovo ordine d'umanità tralle nazioni, acciocché secondo il natural corso delle medesime cose umane ella fermamente fussesi stabilita."

31. *Scienza nuova* §366 (Battistini 1: 562), "spezie la nostra teologia cristiana, mescolata di civile e di naturale e di altissima teologia rivelata."

32. For a representative example of this view, see Karl Löwith, *Meaning in History*, p. 129.

33. A letter from Anton Francesco Marmi to Muratori in October 1723 reports that Vico had been working on a book with this title. See Manuela Sanna, "Le epistole vichiane e la nascita dell'idea di *Scienza Nuova*," p. 122.

34. Mazzotta, *The New Map of the World,* pp. 234–35.

35. *Scienza nuova* §370 (Battistini 1: 565), "di giganti così fatti fu sparsa la terra dopo il diluvio." On the twelve gods of the natural theogony, see *Scienza nuova* §§69, 317, 392, 734 (Battistini 1: 469, 537–38, 580, 786–87).

36. See Paolo Rossi, *The Dark Abyss of Time,* p. 133 and pp. 176–79.

37. *Scienza nuova* §369 (Battistini 1: 564), "dissolver i matrimoni e disperdere le famiglie coi concubiti incerti; e, con un ferino error divagando per la gran selva della terra."

38. *Scienza nuova* §369 (Battistini 1: 564–65), "crescere senza udir voce umana nonché apprender uman costume"; "senza alcuno timore di dèi, di padri, di maestri, il qual assidera il pìu rigoglioso dell'età fanciullesca."

39. *Scienza nuova* §369 (Battistini 1: 565), "nudi rotolare dentro le fecce loro proprie"; "i sali nitri in maggior copia s'insinuavano ne' loro corpi."

40. The contrast is indicated most concisely at *Scienza nuova* §172 (Battistini 1: 506). See also *Scienza nuova* §§13, 167–68 (Battistini 1: 424, 505).

41. Mazzotta, *The New Map of the World,* p. 244.

42. *Scienza nuova* §167 (Battistini 1: 505), "la religion ebraica fu fondata dal vero Dio sul divieto della divinazione, sulla quale sursero tutte le nazioni gentili."

43. For the connection between *divinazione* and "scienza del bene e del male," see *Scienza nuova* §365 (Battistini 1: 561).

44. *Scienza nuova* §481 (Battistini 1: 630), "Ma gli ebrei adoravano il vero Altissimo, ch'è sopra il cielo, nel chiuso del tabernacolo; e Mosè, per dovunque stendeva il popolo di Dio le conquiste, ordinava che fussero bruciati i boschi sagri che dice Tacito, dentro i quali si chiudessero i 'luci.'"

45. See *Scienza nuova* §482 (Battistini 1: 631).

46. *Scienza nuova* §60 (Battistini 2: 1016), "né, per volger d'anni e nazioni, nonché costumi, moltiplicò giammai la divinità."

47. *Scienza nuova* §172 (Battistini 1:506), "la ferina educazione di quelli e dall'umana di questi"; *Scienza nuova* §313 (1: 536–37), "le genti n'ebbero i soli ordinari aiuti dalla provvedenza; gli ebrei n'ebbero anco aiuti estraordinari dal vero Dio." See also *Scienza nuova prima* §49 (Battistini 2: 1010).

48. On the *mystae,* see *Scienza nuova* §381 (Battistini 1: 574) and §938 (1: 868).

49. Milbank, *The Religious Dimension,* vol. 2, pp. 70–71.

50. *Scienza nuova prima* §62 (Battistini 2: 1017), "questo debbe essere stato il primo antichissimo diritto naturale delle genti nello stato delle famiglie, il quale deve essere stato comune a' gentili con gli ebrei; e molto più osservato dagli ebrei che d' gentili."

51. See *De constantia* 2.11 (Cristofolini *OG* 449.18) and 2.13 (*OG* 475.14). Milbank ascribes to Vico the view that "Moses was not a metaphysician," citing *Scienza nuova prima* §28 (Battistini 2: 994). In holding that Moses "non fece niun uso della sapienza riposta de' sacerdoti di Egitto," Vico strongly suggests that Moses was a poet and not a philosopher. (See *The Religious*

Dimension, vol. 2, p. 81.) In 1721, however, Vico still seems to think of Moses as a philosopher.

52. *Scienza nuova* §465 (Battistini 1: 625).

53. *Scienza nuova prima* §264 (Battistini 2: 1108), "la lingua ebrea, benché si tutta poetica, sicché vince di sublimità quella del medesimo Omero, come il riconoscono pure i filologi."

54. Milbank, *The Religious Dimension,* vol. 2, p. 76.

55. Milbank, *The Religious Dimension,* vol. 2, p. 78. A summary of Milbank's reading of Vico on the Hebrews can also be had in his *The Word Made Strange,* pp. 72–73.

56. See Milbank, *The Religious Dimension,* vol. 2, pp. 78–79 and *De constantia* 2.21 (Cristofolini OG 569.11).

57. Milbank, *The Religious Dimension,* vol. 2, pp. 81–82. For Vico's use of Exodus 3:14, see *Scienza nuova prima* §28 (Battistini 2: 994) and *De constantia* 1.3 (Cristofolini OG 355).

58. Milbank, *The Religious Dimension,* vol. 2, p. 81. (Emphasis in original.)

59. Milbank, *The Religious Dimension,* vol. 2, pp. 83–85. Cf. *De constantia* 2.10 (Cristofolini OG 445.4), which finds that Abraham establishes a "paternum imperium, ab illo gentium diversum, quo vitae et necis ius, non patris, sed Dei erat, ut Isaaci historia testatur."

60. Milbank, *The Religious Dimension,* vol. 2, p. 81.

61. Milbank, *The Religious Dimension,* vol. 2, p. 70.

62. Milbank, *The Religious Dimension,* vol. 2, p. 93.

Sixteen.   From Achilles to Socrates

1. *Scienza nuova* §629 (Battistini 1: 727), "scorse l'età degli dèi, perché dovette durar ancora quella maniera religiosa di pensare che gli dèi facessero tutto ciò che facevan essi uomini." Bedani mentions neither this passage nor *Scienza nuova* §412 (Battistini 1: 592–93) when he argues that Vico intends a rigorous distinction between the two ages (*Vico Revisited,* p. 62).

2. *Scienza nuova* §923 (Battistini 1: 862), "'l diritto di Achille, che pone tutta la ragione nella punta dell'asta."

3. *Scienza nuova* §1098 (Battistini 1: 961), "uno stato di repubbliche, per così dire, monastiche."

4. *Scienza nuova* §965 (Battistini 1: 884).

5. On the identity of *sagra* and *segreta,* see *Scienza nuova* §§95, 586, 953, 999 (Battistini 1: 481, 699, 877, 904).

6. *Scienza nuova* §1100 (Battistini 1: 963), "abusando delle leggi della protezione, di quelli facevan aspro governo"; "essendo usciti dall'ordine naturale, ch'è quello della giustizia."

7. *Scienza nuova* §20 (Battistini 1: 429), "ristucchi di dover servire sempre a' signori." *Scienza nuova* §597 (Battistini 1: 707), "le prime plebi dell'eroiche città."

8. *Scienza nuova* §584 (Battistini 1: 697), "più di tutti feroce e di spirito più presente." See also *Scienza nuova* §264 (Battistini 1: 524).

9. *Scienza nuova* §584 (Battistini 1: 697), "senza umano scorgimento o consiglio, si truovaron aver uniti i loro privati a ciascun loro comune, il quale si disse 'patria,' che, sottointesovi 'res,' vuol dir 'interesse di padri,' e i nobili se ne dissero 'patricii': onde dovettero i soli nobili esser i cittadini delle prime patrie."

10. *Scienza nuova* §584 (Battistini 1: 697). The same axiom is quoted in *De uno* 46 (Cristofolini *OG* 61.2) and *De constantia* 2.21 (*OG* 597.63).

11. *Scienza nuova* §585 (Battistini 1: 699), "non nacquero né da froda né da forza d'un solo." See also *Scienza nuova* §§1011–13 (Battistini 1: 912–13).

12. *Scienza nuova* §629 (Battistini 1: 729), "fuori d'ogni loro proposito, convennero in un bene universale civile, che si chiama 'republica.'"

13. *Scienza nuova* §585 (Battistini 1: 689–99). Compare *Scienza nuova* §261 (Battistini 1: 523): "È propietà de' forti gli acquisti fatti con virtù non rillasciare per infingardaggine, ma, o per necessità o per utilità, rimetterne a poco a poco e quanto meno essi possono."

14. *Scienza nuova* §984 (Battistini 1: 894), "perpetua corporale possessione."

15. See *De uno* Sinopsi (Cristofolini *OG* 7) and Montanari, *Vico e la politica dei moderni,* pp. 164–75.

16. *Scienza nuova* §597 (Battistini 1: 707), "ch'andando il dominio di séguito alla potestà, ed avendo i famoli la vita precaria da essi eroi, i quali l'avevano loro salvata ne' lor asili, diritto era e ragione ch'avessero un dominio similmente precario, il qual essi godessero fintanto ch'agli eroi fusse piaciuto di mantenergli nel possesso de' campi ch'avevano lor assegnati."

17. *Scienza nuova* §275 (Battistini 1: 526), "Le repubbliche arisocratiche conservano le ricchezze dentro l'ordine de' nobili, perché conferiscono alla potenza di esso ordine."

18. *Scienza nuova* §95 (Battistini 1: 481), "loro medesime plebi, ond'ella ha avuto appo tutte il nome di 'sagra,' ch'è tanto dire quanto 'segreta.'"

19. *Scienza nuova* §953 (Battistini 1: 877), "l'anima con cui vivono le repubbliche aristocratiche."

20. *Scienza nuova* §917 (Battistini 1: 859), "figliuoli di Giove, siccome quelli ch'erano stati generati con gli auspìci di Giove."

21. Cf. Berlin, *Vico and Herder,* p. 89.

22. *Scienza nuova* §410 (Battistini 1: 592), "i mostri poetici." *Scienza nuova* §566 (Battistini 1: 688), "uomini d'aspetto e brutte bestie di costumi." Berlin is right to suggest that the inferior status of the plebs is "founded upon the metaphysical assumption of the inherent inequality" of heroic and plebeian natures (*Vico and Herder,* p. 62). I would add that the metaphysical assumption itself is linguistically enabled and conditioned.

23. *Scienza nuova* §209 (Battistini 1: 514), "i caratteri poetici, che sono generi o universali fantastici, da ridurvi come a certi modelli, o pure ritratti ideali, tutte le spezie particolari a ciascun suo genere simiglianti." On the close

relations between the terms *caratteri poetici, generi fantastici,* and *universali fantastici,* see Verene, *Vico's Science of Imagination,* pp. 65–66.

24. See *Scienza nuova* §532 (Battistini 1: 665), where Vico speaks of "la maniera di pensare de' primi popoli per caratteri poetici," in correction of Livy. See also *Scienza nuova* §416 (Battistini 1: 594–95), quoted in full below, and Verene, *Vico's Science of Imagination,* p. 74, where Vico is distinguished from any kind of euhemerism.

25. *Scienza nuova* §410 (Battistini 1: 591), "provennero per necessità di tal prima natura umana, qual abbiamo dimostrato nelle *Degnità* che non potevan astrarre le forme o le propietà da' subbietti."

26. See *Scienza nuova* §405 (Battistini 1: 589).

27. *Scienza nuova* §647 (Battistini 1: 740), "fierezza di pene eroiche." See also *Scienza nuova* §1021 (Battistini 1: 918).

28. *Scienza nuova* §649 (Battistini 1: 741), "si truova aver abbracciato le canne"; "la leggerezza"; "la vanità de' matrimoni naturali."

29. *Scienza nuova* §649 (Battistini 1: 741), "i centauri, cioè a dire i plebei, i quali sono i mostri di discordanti nature che dice Livio."

30. *Scienza nuova* §649 (Battistini 1: 741), "i patrizi romani appruovano a' lor plebei ciascun di loro esser mostro, perché essi 'agitabant connubia more ferarum.'"

31. *Scienza nuova* §654 (Battistini 1: 742–43).

32. *Scienza nuova* §655 (Battistini 1: 743), "il minotauro, mostro di due nature diverse."

33. *Scienza nuova* §410 (Battistini 1: 592), "nati da donna onesta senza la solennità delle nozze."

34. *Scienza nuova* §566 (Battistini 1: 688), "i parti brutti e deformi"; "gittavano dal monte Taigeta."

35. See *Scienza nuova* §§989, 1061, 1076 (Battistini 1: 898, 941, 948).

36. *Scienza nuova* §568 (Battistini 1: 689).

37. *Scienza nuova* §579 (Battistini 1: 693), "precipitato dal cielo e restonne zoppo."

38. *Scienza nuova* §580 (Battistini 1: 694), "che non può afferrare le poma che s'alzano né toccare l'acqua che bassasi." See also *Scienza nuova* §583 (Battistini 1: 696).

39. *Scienza nuova* §580 (Battistini 1: 694), "perché tutto ciò che tocca è oro, si muore di fame." See also *Scienza nuova* §649 (Battistini 1: 741).

40. *Scienza nuova* §580 (Battistini 1: 694) , "contende con Apollo nel canto, e, vinto, è da quello ucciso." See also *Scienza nuova* §647 (Battistini 1: 740).

41. *Scienza nuova* §661 (Battistini 1: 746), "tennero esse plebi in ossequio de' lor ordini eroici."

42. See *Scienza nuova* §401 (Battistini 1: 585).

43. See *Scienza nuova* §§461–68, 930 (Battistini 1: 622–25, 864).

44. *Scienza nuova* §499 (Battistini 1: 640), "ridusse la plebe romana sollevata all'ubbidienza."

45. For a stimulating but flawed account of the tropes and their role in historical change, see Hayden White, "The Tropics of History: The Deep Structure of the *New Science*."

46. Bedani takes Vico to argue, inconsistently, that irony is not possible in the heroic age, and that irony emerges with the creation of "Aesop" in that age. What Vico actually says, however, is that irony is not possible for the heroic fathers. He does not deny—indeed, he is committed to—the assumption that the seeds of the later age have to somehow be present in the earlier. Bedani's reading seems inspired less by the textual evidence than by the motive to find Vico applying the "predicament of those who cannot express their true opinions" to himself. See *Vico Revisited*, p. 31.

47. *Scienza nuova* §425 (Battistini 1: 598), "Nunc fabularum cur sit inventum genus, /Brevi docebo. Servitus obnoxia, /Quia, quae volebat, non audebat dicere, /Affectus proprios in fabellos transtulit. /Aesopi illius semita feci viam." I quote from the English translation in Bergin and Fisch, *The New Science of Giambattista Vico*, p. 136.

48. *Scienza nuova* §425 (Battistini 1: 598), "la bellezza civile era stimata dal nascere da' matrimoni solenni."

49. *Scienza nuova* §426 (Battistini 1: 599), "avvisi"; "utili al viver civile libero . . . dettati dalla ragion naturale."

50. *Scienza nuova* §426 (Battistini 1: 599), "le favole d'intorno alla morale filosofia."

51. See *Scienza nuova* §§579–81 (Battistini 1: 693–84).

52. *Scienza nuova* §414 (Battistini 1: 593), "dovett'esser alcuno uomo sappiente di sapienza volgare, il quale fusse capoparte di plebe ne' primi tempi ch'Athene era repubblica aristocratica."

53. *Scienza nuova* §416 (Battistini 1: 594–95), "Quindi Solone fu fatto autore di quel celebre motto 'Nosce te ipsum,' il quale, per la grande civile utilità ch'aveva arrecato al popolo ateniese, fu inscritto per tutti i luoghi pubblici di quella città; e poi gli addottrinati il vollero detto per un grande avviso, quanto infatti lo è, d'intorno alle metafisiche ed alle morali cose, e funne tenuto Solone per sappiente di sapienza riposta e fatto principe de' sette saggi di Grecia. In cotal guisa, perché da tal riflessione incominiciarono in Atene tutti gli ordini e tutte le leggi che formano una repubblica democratica, perciò, per questa maniera di pensare per caratteri poetici e' primi popoli, tali ordini e tali leggi, come dagli egizi tutti i ritruovati utili alla vita umana civile a Mercurio Trimegisto, furon tutti dagli ateniesi richiamati a Solone."

54. *Scienza nuova* §443 (Battistini 1: 612), "siccome la lingua eroica ovvero poetica si fondò dagli eroi, così le lingue volgari sono state introdutte dal volgo, che noi dentro ritruoveremo essere state le plebi de' popoli eroici."

55. See *Scienza nuova* §§931–32 (Battistini 1: 864–65).

56. *Scienza nuova* §935 (Battistini 1: 865), "si compongono di parole, che sono quasi generi de' particolari co' quali avevan innanzi parlato le lingue eroiche."

57. *Scienza nuova* §460 (Battistini 1: 621), "universali ragionati o filosofici"; "nacquero per mezzo di essi parlari prosaici."

58. *Scienza nuova* §612 (Battistini 1: 718), "la legge in una pubblica tavola, con la quale determinatosi il gius incerto, manifestatosi il gius nascosto."

59. *Scienza nuova* §936 (Battistini 1: 866), "Per cotal signoria e di lingue e di littere debbon i popoli liberi esser signori delle lor leggi, perché dànno alle leggi que' sensi ne' quali vi traggono ad osservale i potenti, che, come nelle *Degnità* fu avvisato, non le vorrebbono."

60. On the natural conservatism of the nobles, see *Scienza nuova* §§261, 609 (Battistini 1: 523, 716).

61. *Scienza nuova* §424 (Battistini 1: 598), "padre di tutte le sètte de' filosofi."

62. *Scienza nuova* §424 (Battistini 1: 598), "la dialettica con l'induzione." *Scienza nuova* §1001 (Battistini 1: 905), "La plebe romana, a guisa dell'ateniese, tuttodì, comandava delle leggi singolari, perché d'universali ella non è capace."

63. *Scienza nuova* §460 (Battistini 1: 622), "co' quali generi volgari, e di voci e di lettere, s'andarono a fare più spedite le menti de' popoli ed a formarsi astrattive, onde poi vi poterono provenir i filosofi, i quali formaron i generi intelligibili."

64. See *Scienza nuova* §§363, 779 (Battistini 1: 560, 808).

65. *Scienza nuova* §1040 (Battistini 1: 927), "certamente furono prima le leggi, dopo i filosofi."

66. *Scienza nuova* §1040 (Battistini 1: 927–28), "egli è necessario che Socrate, dall'osservare ch'i cittadini ateniesi nel comandare le leggi si andavan ad unire in un'idea conforme d'un'ugual utilità partitamente comune a tutti, cominciò ad abbozzare i generi intelligibili, ovvero gli universali astratti, con l'induzione, ch'è una raccolta di uniformi particolari, che vanno a comporre un genere di ciò nello che quei particolari sono uniformi tra loro."

67. *Scienza nuova* §666 (Battistini 1: 750), "giustizia ragionata con massime di morale socratica."

68. See *Scienza nuova* §§1041, 1042 (Battistini 1: 928–29).

69. *Scienza nuova* §1043 (Battistini 1: 929), "se vi fussero al mondo filosofi, non farebber uopo religioni"; "se non vi fussero state religioni, e quindi repubbliche, non sarebber affatto al mondo filosofi, e che se le cose umane non avesse così condotto la provvedenza divina, non si avrebbe niuna idea né di scienza né virtù."

70. See *Scienza nuova* §617 (Battistini 1: 720).

71. *Scienza nuova* §661 (Battistini 1: 746), "a' plebei romani la forza degli dèi negli auspìci, de' quali i nobili dicevano aver la scienza, gli mantiene nell'ubbidienza de' nobili."

72. See *Scienza nuova* §§1033–36 (Battistini 1: 924–26) and especially §1037 (Battistini 1: 926), where Vico quotes Justinian on the *antiqui iuris fabulas*.

73. See *Scienza nuova* §987 (Battistini 1: 896–97).

74. See *Scienza nuova* §592 (Battistini 1: 704).

75. *Scienza nuova* §662 (Battistini 1: 747), "una perpetua mitologia istorica di tante, sì varie e diverse favole greche."

76. See *Scienza nuova* §§1038–39 (Battistini 1: 926–27).

77. *Scienza nuova* §501 (Battistini 1: 642).

Seventeen.   Modern Nihilism and the Barbarism of Reflection

1. *Scienza nuova* §241 (Battistini 1: 519–20), "Gli uomini prima sentono il necessario, dipoi badano all'utile, appresso avvertiscono il comodo, più innanzi si dilettano del piacere, quindi si dissolvono nel lusso, e finalmente impazzano in istrappazzar le sostanze."

2. *Scienza nuova* §242 (Battistini 1: 520), "La natura de' popoli prima è cruda, dipoi severa, quindi benigna, appresso dilicata, finalmente dissoluta."

3. *Scienza nuova* §243 (Battistini 1: 520), "Nel gener umano prima surgono immani e goffi, qual'i Polifemi; poi magnanimi ed orgogliosi, quali gli Achilli; quindi valorosi e giusti, quali gli Aristidi, gli Scipioni affricani; più a noi gli appariscenti con grand'immagini di virtù che s'accompagnano con grandi vizi, ch'appo il volgo fanno strepito di vera gloria, quali gli Alessandri e i Cesari; più oltre i tristi riflessivi, qual'i Tiberi; finalmente i furiosi dissoluti e sfacciati, qual'i Caligoli, i Neroni, i Domiziani."

4. See *Scienza nuova* §191 (Battistini 1: 510).

5. See, for example, *Scienza nuova* §§940, 946, 951 (Battistini 1: 869, 871–72, 875).

6. *Scienza nuova* §1106 (Battistini 1: 967), "i popoli marciscano in quell'ultimo civil malore."

7. *Scienza nuova* §1105 (Battistini 1: 967), "de' quali uno è che chi non può governarsi da sé, si lasci governare da altri che 'l possa"; "che governino il mondo sempre quelli che sono per natura migliori."

8. *Scienza nuova* §1106 (Battistini 1: 967), "la provvedenza a questo estremo lor male adopera questo estremo rimedio."

9. *Scienza nuova* §1106 (Battistini 1: 967), "poiché tai popoli a guisa di bestie si erano accostumati di non ad altro pensare ch'alle particolari propie utilità di ciascuno ed avevano data nell'ultimo della dilicatezza o, per me' dir, dell'orgoglio, ch'a guisa di fiere, nell'essere disgustate d'un pelo, si risentono e s'infieriscono, e sì, nella loro maggiore celebrità o folla de' corpi, vissero come bestie immani in una somma solitudine d'animi e di voleri, non potendovi appena due convenire, seguendo ogniun de' due il suo proprio piacere o capriccio, — per tutto ciò, con ostinatissime fazioni e disperate guerre civili, vadano a fare selve delle città, e delle selve covili d'uomini."

10. *Scienza nuova* §1106 (Battistini 1: 967), "fiere più immani con la barbarie della riflessione che non era stata la prima barbarie del senso."

11. *Scienza nuova* §1106 (Battistini 1: 968), "primiera semplicità del primo mondo de' popoli, sieno religiosi, veraci e fidi."

12. *Scienza nuova* §1106 (Battistini 1: 968), "ritorni tra essi la pietà, la fede, la verità, che sono i naturali fondamenti della giustizia e sono grazie e bellezze dell'ordine eterno di Dio."

13. See "Only a God Can Save Us: *Der Spiegel's* Interview with Martin Heidegger," p. 277.

14. Readings of the *Pratica* can be found in Pons, "Prudence and Providence"; Milbank, *The Religious Dimension*, vol. 2, pp. 261–64; and Erny, *Theorie und System der Neuen Wissenschaft von Giambattista Vico*, pp. 173–89.

15. *Pratica della Scienza nuova* §1406 (Nicolini 4.2: 268), "Ma tutta quest'-opera è stata finora ragionata come una mera scienza contemplativa d'intorno alla comune nature delle nazioni. Però sembra, per quest'istesso, mancare di soccorrere alla prudenza umana, ond'ella s'adoperi perché le nazioni, le quali vanno a cadere, o non rovinino affatto o non s'affrettino alla loro roina; e 'n conseguenza mancare nella pratica, qual dee essere di tutte le scienze che si ravvolgono d'intorno a materie le quali dipendono dall'umano arbitrio, che tutte si chiamano 'attive.'"

16. *Pratica della Scienza nuova* §1406 (Nicolini 4.2: 268), "buoni ordini e legge ed esempli richiamar i popoli alla loro *acme*, o sia stato perfetto."

17. *Pratica della Scienza nuova* §1406 (Nicolini 4:2: 268), "La pratica, la qual ne possiamo dar noi da filosofi, ella si può chiudere dentro dell'accademie."

18. *Pratica della Scienza nuova* §1406 (Nicolini 4.2: 274), "l'accademie colle loro sètte de' filosofi non secondino la corrottella della setta di questi tempi, ma quelli tre princípi sopra i quali si è questa Scienza fondata—cioè: che si dia provvedenza divina; che, perché si possano, si debbano moderare l'u-mane passioni; e che l'anime nostre sien immortali." Cf. the nearly identical language at *Scienza nuova* §§130, 360 (Battistini 1: 496, 554–55).

19. *Pratica della Scienza nuova* §1406 (Nicolini 4.2: 268), "non parlan d'al-tro che d'onestá e di guistizia."

20. *Pratica della Scienza nuova* §1407 (Nicolini 4.2: 269), "la natura del mondo civile, ch' è'l mondo il qual è stato fatti dagli uomini, abbia tal materia e tal forma quali essi uomini hanno."

21. *Pratica della Scienza nuova* §1411 (Nicolini 4.2: 271), "salve, fioriscono e son felici, quando il corpo vi serva e la mente vi comandi"; "bivo di Ercole"; "via del piacere con viltá, disprezzo e schiavitú"; "quella della virtú con onore, gloria e felicitá."

22. *Scienza nuova* §1097 (Battistini 1: 961), "Platone, il quale fa una quarta spezie di repubblica, nella quale gli uomini onesti e dabbene fussero supremi signori."

23. *Scienza nuova* §1102 (Battistini 1: 966), "nascendo quindi una falsa eloquenza, apparecchiata egualmente a sostener nelle cause entrambe le parti opposte."

24. See *Scienza nuova* §1101 (Battistini 1: 965).

25. *Scienza nuova* §14 (Battistini 1: 425), "altri princìpi alla moral filosofia, onde la sapienza riposta de' filosofi debba cospirare con la sapienza volgare de' legislatori."

26. *Seconda risposta* 4 (*OF* 166), "Sorse la setta stoica, e, ambiziosa, volle confonder gli ordini e occupare il luogo de' matematici con quel fastoso placito: '*Sapientem nihil opinari*'; e la repubblica non fruttò alcuna altra cosa migliore. Anzi nacque un ordine, tutto opposto, degli scettici, inutilissimi all'umana società; e n'ebbero dagli stoici lo scandalo, perché quelli, vedendo questi asseverare per vere le cose dubbie, si misero a dubitare di tutto. La repubblica, spenta d' barbari, dopo lunghi secoli sugli stessi ordini si rimise, che 'l censo de' filosofi fosse il probabile, de' matematici il vero."

27. *Vita* (Cristofolini *OF* 11/*Autobiography* 122), "una morale di solitari: degli epicurei, perché di sfaccendati chiusi ne' loro orticelli, degli stoici, perché di meditanti che studiavano non sentir passione."

28. *Vita* (Cristofolini *OF* 38/*Autobiography* 172–73), "de' cui princìpi non vi è cosa più contraria a quelli, non che di essa giurisprudenza, di tutta la civiltà." See also *Scienza nuova prima* §12 (Battistini 2: 985–86).

29. See Milbank, *The Religious Dimension*, vol. 2, p. 54.

30. See *De ratione* 5 (Cristofolini *OF* 807) and the passage in the *Vita* on the "oracolo dell'analitica" (*OF* 13/*Autobiography* 125).

31. *De antiquissima* 2 (Cristofolini *OF* 79), "Loqui universalibus verbis infantium est aut barbarorum."

32. *Scienza nuova* §38 (Battistini 1: 443–44), "si dànno altri princìpi per dimostrate l'argomento che tratta sant'Agostino, *De virtute romanorum.*"

33. *Scienza nuova* §1047 (Battistini 1: 934), "virtù de' martiri incontro la potenza romana." The derivation of *contemplatio* from *templa coeli* may be found in *Scienza nuova* §711 (Battistini 1: 773).

34. *Scienza nuova* §529 (Battistini 1: 662), "sparsero i sepolcri di tanta religione, o sia divino spavento, che 'religiosa loca' per eccellenza restaron detti a' latini i luoghi ove fussero de' sepolcri. E quivi cominciò l'universale credenza, che noi pruovammo sopra ne' *Princìpi* (de' quali questo era il terzo che noi abbiamo preso di questa Scienza), cioè dell'immortalità dell'anime umane."

35. For the most concise statement of these equivalences, see *Scienza nuova* §360 (Battistini 1: 554–55).

36. *Scienza nuova* §391 (Battistini 1: 579), "nella scienza augurale si disse da' romani 'contemplari' l'osservare le parti del cielo donde venissero gli augùri o si osservassero gli auspìci, le quali regioni, descritte dagli àuguri co' loro litui, si dicevano 'templa coeli,' onde dovettero venir a' greci i primi *theoremata* e *mathemata*, 'divine o sublimi cose da contemplarsi', che terminarono nelle cose astratte metafisiche e mattematiche." See also *Scienza nuova* §711 (1: 773).

37. *Scienza nuova* §391 (Battistini 1: 579). See also §508 (Battistini 1: 647).

38. *Scienza nuova* §585 (Battistini 1: 698), "dove poi gli stoici ficcarono il loro dogma di Giove soggetto al fato."

39. Milbank, *The Religious Dimension*, vol. 2, p. 50.

40. *Scienza nuova* §585 (Battistini 1: 698), "ma Giove e gli altri dèi tennero consiglio d'intorno a tai cose degli uomini, e sì le determinarono con libera volontà."

41. *Scienza nuova* §335 (Battistini 1: 544), "gli stoici, che danno Dio in infinito corpo infinita mente soggetta al fato (che sarebbero per tal parte gli spinosisti)."

42. *Scienza nuova* §345 (Battistini 1: 550), "e gli stoici che la loro catena eterna delle cagioni, con la qual vogliono avvinto il mondo, ella penda dall'onnipotente, saggia e benigna volontà dell'Ottimo Massimo Dio."

43. *Scienza nuova* §335 (Battistini 1: 544), "gli epicurei, che non danno altro che corpo e, col corpo, il caso."

44. *Vita* (Cristofolini *OF* 13/*Autobiography* 126), "ch'è una filosofia da soddisfare le menti corte de' fanciulli e le deboli delle donnicciuole."

45. *Vita* (Cristofolini *OF* 13/*Autobiography* 126), "si era cominciata a coltivare la filosofia d'Epicuro sopra Pier Gassendi."

46. *Scienza nuova* §1102 (Battistini 1: 966), "Ma—corrompendosi ancora gli Stati popolari, e quindi ancor le filosofie (le quali cadendo nello scetticismo, si diedero gli stolti dotti a calonniare la verità)."

47. *Scienza nuova* §129 (Battistini 1: 496), "reggere l'uomo caduto e debole, non convellergli la natura né abbandonarlo nella sua corrozione."

48. *Scienza nuova* §779 (Battistini 1: 808), "com'in embrioni o matrici, si è discoverto essere stato abbozzato tutto il sapere riposto."

49. *Scienza nuova* §779 (Battistini 1: 808), "dentro di quelle [le favole] per sensi umani essere stati dalle nazioni rozzamente descritti i princìpi di questo mondo di scienze, il quale poi con raziocinî e con massime ci è stato schiarito dalla particolare riflessione de' dotti."

50. *Scienza nuova* §179 (Battistini 1: 507–8), "d'accrescere la greca filosofia di questa gran parte, della quale certamente aveva mancato"; "di considerar l'uomo in tutta la società del gener umano."

51. *Scienza nuova* §179 (Battistini 1: 507), "con quanto magnanimo sforzo, con altrettanto infelice evento."

52. See *Vita* (Cristofolini *OF* 11/*Autobiography* 122); *De constantia* 1.4 (Cristofolini *OG* 356.4); *Scienza nuova* §131 (Battistini 1: 496), and its ancestor in *De uno* 152 (Cristofolini *OG* 201.6).

53. For acute commentary on the genealogy of these categories, see Jordan, *On the Alleged Aristotelianism of Thomas Aquinas*, pp. 1–8.

54. See the third set of "Corrections, Meliorations and Additions" to the 1730 edition of the *Scienza nuova*, most easily found in the *Opere* (Nicolini 5: 377).

55. *Scienza nuova* §1112 (Battistini 1: 971).

Conclusion

1. See Michel Foucault, *The Archaeology of Knowledge*, p. 158. Here Foucault acknowledges that what he calls "Vico's history" might be among a set of

counterexamples to the analyses found in *The Order of Things*. He even admits that those aware of such counterexamples might have a "quite legitimate impatience" with Foucault's silence concerning them. Despite this concession, however, Foucault strikes a defiant pose: "I not only admit that my analysis is limited; I want it so; I have made it so. . . . What, for them, is a lacuna, an omission, an error is, for me, a deliberate, methodical exclusion."

2. Nietzsche, *On the Genealogy of Morals* 1.9, p. 36 (Colli-Montinari 5: 284).

3. Philippa Foot, *Virtues and Vices*, p. 92.

4. Philippa Foot, *Virtues and Vices*, p. 93.

5. MacIntyre, *Three Rival Versions of Moral Enquiry*, p. 207.

6. MacIntyre, *Three Rival Versions of Moral Enquiry*, p. 209.

7. Berkowitz, *Nietzsche: The Ethics of an Immoralist*, p. 80.

8. MacIntyre, "Imaginative Universals and Historical Falsification," p. 23.

9. MacIntyre, "Imaginative Universals and Historical Falsification," p. 23.

10. Berkowitz, *Nietzsche: The Ethics of an Immoralist*, pp. 68–69.

11. Discussion of this topic requires a thorough assessment of Nietzsche's corpus. We would concur with Berkowitz's judgment that "the doctrines of will to power and eternal return do not escape the nihilism they are meant to overcome." See Berkowitz, *Nietzsche: The Ethics of an Immoralist*, p. 291n3.

12. Williams, *Ethics and the Limits of Philosophy*, p. 199.

13. "The only possible criticism of a philosophy, the only criticism that proves anything at all, is trying to see if one can live by it," Nietzsche writes in "Schopenhauer as Educator" (*Unmodern Observations*, p. 220). One wonders if Nietzsche passed his own test.

14. For the suggestion that the later thought of Foucault unconvincingly attempts something like the latter, see John Milbank, *Theology and Social Theory*, p. 315.

15. Here I am following the contours of a lecture given by Bernard Williams at the University of Notre Dame on April 21, 1995. Williams proceeded to characterize reductivist hostility to truth as the "no bullshit bullshit."

16. Williams, "Replies," p. 204.

17. Nietzsche, *We Philologists* 4.16 (*Unmodern Observations*, p. 349).

B I B L I O G R A P H Y

Editions of Vico

Epistole, con Aggiunte le Epistole dei Suoi Corrispondenti. Edited by Manuela Sanna. Morano: Naples, 1993.

Opere di Giambattista Vico (cited as *Opere*). Edited by Benedetto Croce, Giovanni Gentile, and Fausto Nicolini, 8 vols. Bari: Laterza, 1911–1941.

Opere filosofiche (cited as *OF*). Edited by Paolo Cristofolini. Firenze: Sansoni, 1971.

Opere giuridiche (cited as *OG*). Edited by Paolo Cristofolini. Firenze: Sansoni, 1974.

Opere (cited as "Battistini" with volume number). Edited by Andrea Battistini. 2 vols. Milano: Mondadori, 1990.

Orazioni Inaugurali, I–VI. Edited by Gian Galeazzo Visconti. Bologna: Il Mulino, 1982.

Vico in English Translation

Autobiography of Giambattista Vico. Translation of *Vita di Giambattista Vico scritta da se medesimo* (1725–1731) by Max Harold Fisch and Thomas Goddard Bergin. Ithaca, N.Y.: Cornell University Press, 1944.

"Four Letters of Giambattista Vico on the *First New Science*." Translations by Giorgio A. Pinton in *New Vico Studies* 16 (1998): 31–58.

The New Science of Giambattista Vico. Translation of *Princìpi di scienza nuova d'intorno alla comune nature delle nazioni, in questa terza impressione dal medesimo autore in un gran numero di luoghi corretta, schiarita, e notabilmente accresciuta* (1744) by Thomas G. Bergin and Max H. Fisch. Rev. ed. Ithaca, N.Y.: Cornell University Press, 1984.

On the Heroic Mind. Translation of *De mente heroica* (1732) by Elizabeth Sewell and A.C. Sirignano. In *Vico and Contemporary Thought*, edited by Giorgio Tagliacozzo et al., pp. 228–45. Atlantic Highlands, N.J.: Humanities Press, 1979.

On Humanistic Education: Six Inaugural Orations 1699–1707. Translation of
   Le Orazioni Inaugurali (1699–1707) by Giorgio A. Pinton and Arthur W.
   Shippee. Ithaca, N.Y.: Cornell University Press, 1993.
On the Most Ancient Wisdom of the Italians. Translation of *De antiquissima Italo-
   rum sapientia* (1710), with *Prima* and *Seconda risposte* (1711–12) by Lucia M.
   Palmer. Ithaca, N.Y.: Cornell University Press, 1988.
On the Study Methods of our Time. Translation of *De nostri temporis studiorum
   ratione* (1709) by Elio Gianturco. Indianapolis, Ind.: Library of Liberal Arts,
   1965. Reprinted with a preface by Donald Phillip Verene. Ithaca, N.Y.:
   Cornell University Press, 1990.
Vico: Selected Writings. Edited and translated by Leon Pompa. Cambridge: Cambridge University Press, 1982.

Works on Vico

The listing below is not a comprehensive guide to scholarship on Vico. It
includes only the works actually cited in the body of the text or the end-
notes.

Badaloni, Nicola. *Introduzione a Vico.* Bari: Laterza, 1984.
Bedani, Gino. *Vico Revisted: Orthodoxy, Naturalism and Science in the Scienza
   Nuova.* Oxford and New York: St. Martin's Press, 1989.
Beleval, Yvon. "Vico and Anti-Cartesianism." In *Giambattista Vico: An Interna-
   tional Symposium,* edited by Giorgio Tagliacozzo and Hayden V. White,
   pp. 77–91. Baltimore: The Johns Hopkins University Press, 1969.
Berlin, Isaiah. *Vico and Herder.* London: The Hogarth Press, 1976.
Botturi, Francesco. *La sapienza della storia: Giambattista Vico e la filosfia pratica.*
   Milano: Università Cattolica del Sacro Cuore, 1991.
Caponigri, A. Robert. *Time and Idea: The Theory of History in Giambattista Vico.*
   Notre Dame: University of Notre Dame Press, 1968.
Corsano, Antonio. *Giambattista Vico.* Bari: Laterza, 1956.
Crease, Robert. "Vico and the 'Cogito.'" In *Vico: Past and Present,* edited by
   Giorgio Tagliacozzo, vol. 1, pp. 171–80. Atlantic Highlands, N.J.: Hu-
   manities Press, 1981.
Croce, Benedetto. *The Philosophy of Giambattista Vico.* Translated by R.G.
   Collingwood. New York: Russell & Russell, 1964.
Erny, Nicola. *Theorie und System der Neuen Wissenschaft von Giambattista Vico.*
   Würzburg: Königshausen & Neumann, 1994.
Fassò, Guido. "The Problem of Law and the Historical Origin of the *New Sci-
   ence.*" In *Giambattista Vico's Science of Humanity,* edited by Giorgio Taglia-
   cozzo and Donald Phillip Verene, pp. 3–14. Baltimore: The Johns Hop-
   kins University Press, 1976.
Flint, Robert. *Vico.* Edinburgh and London: W. Blackwood and Sons, 1884.

Garin, Eugenio. "Vico and the Heritage of Renaissance Thought." In *Vico: Past and Present,* edited by Giorgio Tagliacozzo, vol. 1, pp. 99–116. Atlantic Highlands, N.J.: Humanities Press, 1981.

Giarrizzo, Giuseppe. *Vico, la politica e la storia.* Napoli: Guida, 1981.

Grassi, Ernesto. *Rhetoric as Philosophy: The Humanist Tradition.* University Park, Penn.: Pennsylvania State University Press, 1980.

Hösle, Vittorio. *Introduzione a Vico: La scienza del mondo intersoggettivo.* Milano: Guerni e Associati, 1997.

Jacobelli-Isoldi, Angela. *G.B. Vico: La vita e le opere.* Bologna: Capelli, 1960.

Kelley, Donald R. "History and the Encyclopedia." In *The Shapes of Knowledge from the Renaissance to the Enlightenment,* edited by D.R. Kelley and R.H. Popkin, pp. 7–22. Dordrecht: Kluwer Academic Publishers, 1991.

———. *The Human Measure: Social Thought in the Western Legal Tradition.* Cambridge, Mass.: Harvard University Press, 1990.

———. "Vico and Gaianism: Perspective on a Paradigm," in *Vico: Past and Present,* edited by Giorgio Tagliacozzo, vol. 1, pp. 66–72. Atlantic Highlands, N.J.: Humanities Press, 1981.

Lachterman, David. "Mathematics and Nominalism in Vico's *Liber Metaphysicus.*" In *Sachkommentar zu G. Vico's Liber Metaphysicus,* edited by Stephan Otto and Helmut Viechtbauer, pp. 47–85. Munich: Wilhelm Fink Verlag, 1985.

———. "Vico and Marx: Notes on a Precursory Reading." In *Vico and Marx,* edited by Giorgio Tagliacozzo, pp. 38–61. Atlantic Highlands, N.J.: Humanities Press, 1983.

Lamacchia, Ada. "Vico e Agostino: La Presenza del *De civitate dei* nella *Scienza nuova.*" In *Giambattista Vico: Poesia, Logica, Religione,* edited by G. Santinello, pp. 270–319. Brescia: Morcelliana, 1986.

Lilla, Mark. *G.B. Vico: The Making of an Anti-Modern.* Cambridge, Mass.: Harvard University Press, 1993.

Löwith, Karl. *Meaning in History.* Chicago: University of Chicago Press, 1949.

Marcolungo, Ferdinando L.. "L'uomo e Dio nei primi scritti di Giambattista Vico." In *Metafisica e teologia civile in Giambattista Vico,* edited by Ada Lamacchia, pp. 81–102. Bari: Levante, 1992.

Mazzotta, Giuseppe. *The New Map of the World: The Poetic Philosophy of Giambattista Vico.* Princeton: Princeton University Press, 1999.

———. "Vico's Encyclopedia," *Yale Journal of Criticism* 1 (1988): 65–79.

Milbank, John. *The Religious Dimension in the Thought of Giambattista Vico.* Vols. 1 and 2. Lewiston, N.Y.: The Edwin Mellen Press, 1991.

———. *The Word Made Strange.* Oxford: Blackwell, 1997.

Montanari, Marcello. *Vico e la politica dei moderni.* Bari: Palomar Athenaeum, 1995.

Mooney, Michael. *Vico in the Tradition of Rhetoric.* Princeton, N.J.: Princeton University Press, 1985.

Morrison, James. "Vico's Doctrine of the Natural Law of the Gentes." *Journal of the History of Philosophy* 16 (1978): 47–60.

———. "Vico and Spinoza." *Journal of the History of Ideas* 41 (1980): 49–68.

Pompa, Leon. *Vico: A Study of the 'New Science.'* 2d. ed. Cambridge: Cambridge University Press, 1985.

Pons, Alain. "Prudence and Providence: The *Practica della Scienza Nuova* and the Problem of Theory of Practice in Vico." In *Giambattista Vico's Science of Humanity,* edited by Giorgio Tagliacozzo and Donald Phillip Verene, pp. 431–48. Baltimore: The Johns Hopkins University Press, 1976.

Rigol, Montserrat Negre. *Poiesis y verdad en Giambattistia Vico.* Sevilla: Publicaciones de la Universidad de Sevilla, 1986.

Rossi, Paolo. *The Dark Abyss of Time: The History of the Earth and the History of Nations from Hooke to Vico.* Chicago: University of Chicago Press, 1984.

Sanna, Manuela. "Le epistole vichiane e la nascita dell'idea di *Scienza Nuova.*" *Bollettino del Centro di Studi Vichiani* 24–25 (1994–95): 119–129.

Santinello, G., ed. *Giambattista Vico: Poesia, Logica, Religione.* Brescia: Morcelliana, 1986.

Severino, Giulo. *Principi e modificazioni della mente in Vico.* Genova: Il Melangolo, 1981.

Tagliacozzo, Giorgio, ed. *Vico and Marx: Affinities and Contrasts.* Atlantic Highlands, N.J.: Humanities Press, 1983.

———, ed. *Vico: Past and Present.* 2 vols. Atlantic Highlands, N.J.: Humanities Press, 1981.

Tagliacozzo, Giorgio, Michael Mooney, and Donald Phillip Verene, eds. *Vico and Contemporary Thought.* Atlantic Highlands, N.J.: Humanities Press, 1979.

Tagliacozzo, Giorgio, and Donald Philip Verene, eds. *Giambattista Vico's Science of Humanity.* Baltimore: The Johns Hopkins University Press, 1976.

Tagliacozzo, Giorgio, and Hayden V. White, eds. *Giambattista Vico: An International Symposium.* Baltimore: The Johns Hopkins University Press, 1969.

Vaughn, Frederick. *The Political Philosophy of Giambattista Vico: An Introduction to La Scienza Nuova.* The Hague: Martinus Nijhoff, 1972.

Verene, Donald Phillip. *Vico's Science of Imagination.* Ithaca: Cornell University Press, 1981.

———. "On Translating Vico: The Penguin Classics Edition of the *New Science.*" *New Vico Studies* 17 (1999): 85–107.

White, Hayden. "The Tropics of History: The Deep Structure of the 'New Science.'" In *Giambattista Vico's Science of Humanity,* edited by Giorgio Tagliacozzo and Donald Phillip Verene, pp. 65–85. Baltimore: The Johns Hopkins University Press, 1976.

Other Works Cited

Aristotle. *Ethica Nicomachea.* Edited by W. D. Ross. Oxford: Clarendon Press, 1925.

———. *Politica.* Edited by W. D. Ross. Oxford: Clarendon Press, 1957.

Augustine. *Confessions.* Edited by M. Skutella and L. Verheijen. Corpus Christianorum Series Latina, vol. 27. Turnhout: Brepols, 1981.

———. *The City of God.* Translated by Henry Bettenson. London: Penguin Books, 1972.

Bacon, Francis. *The Works of Francis Bacon,* edited by James Spedding, Robert L. Ellis, and Douglas D. Heath. London: Longman, 1857–74.

Berkowitz, Peter. *Nietzsche: The Ethics of an Immoralist.* Cambridge, Mass.: Harvard University Press, 1995.

Cicero. *De inventione.* Edited by H. M. Hubbell. Cambridge, Mass.: Harvard University Press, 1949.

———. *De legibus.* Edited by C. W. Keyes. New York: G. P. Putnam's Sons, 1928.

———. *De oratore.* Edited by E. W. Sutton and H. Rackham. Cambridge, Mass.: Harvard University Press, 1942.

Collingwood, R. G.. *Autobiography.* Oxford: Oxford University Press, 1939.

———. *The Idea of History.* Oxford: Clarendon Press, 1946.

———. *Principles of Art.* New York: Oxford University Press, 1938.

Descartes, René. *Discours de la méthode.* In vol. 6 of *Oeuvres de Descartes,* edited by Charles Adam and Paul Tannery. Paris: Cerf, 1897–1913.

———. *The Philosophical Works of Descartes,* edited by John Cottingham, Robert Stoothoff, and Dugald Murdoch (Cambridge: Cambridge University Press, 1985).

Fortin, Ernest. "Augustine's *City of God* and the Modern Historical Consciousness." *Review of Politics* 41 (1979): 323–43.

Foot, Philippa. *Virtues and Vices.* Berkeley: University of California Press, 1978.

Foucault, Michel. *The Archaeology of Knowledge.* Translated by A. M. Sheridan Smith. New York: Pantheon Books, 1972.

———. "Nietzsche, la généalogie, l'histoire." In *Dits et écrits,* edited by Daniel Defert and François Ewald, vol. 2 (1970–75), pp. 136–156. Paris: NRF/Gallimard, 1994. Translated by Donald F. Bouchard and Sherry Simon, and reprinted in *The Foucault Reader,* edited by Paul Rabinow. New York: Pantheon Books, 1984.

Gadamer, Hans-Georg. *Truth and Method.* 2d ed. Translated by Joel Weinsheimer and Donald G. Marshall. New York: Continuum, 1989.

Galilei, Galileo. *The Assayer.* In *Discoveries and Opinions of Galileo,* edited and translated by Stillman Drakie. New York: Anchor Books, 1957.

Grotius, Hugo. *De iure belli ac pacis.* Edited by Francis W. Kelsey et al. Washington, D. C.: Carnegie Institution of Washington, 1913–27. Reprint, Buffalo, N. Y.: Hein, 1995.

Hacking, Ian. *The Social Construction of What?* Cambridge, Mass.: Harvard University Press, 1999.

Heller, Erich. *The Disinherited Mind.* San Diego: Harcourt Brace Jovanovich, 1975.

Hobbes, Thomas. *Leviathan*. Vol. 3 in *The English Works of Thomas Hobbes*, edited by William Molesworth. London: Longman, Brown, Green and Longmans, 1845.

Jordan, Mark D. *On the Alleged Aristotelianism of Thomas Aquinas*. Toronto: PIMS, 1990.

Lachterman, David. *The Ethics of Geometry: A Genealogy of Modernity*. New York: Routledge, 1989.

Leibniz, Gottfried. *Discourse on Metaphysics*. Translated by George Montgomery. La Salle, Ill.: Open Court, 1902.

———. *New Essays on Human Understanding*. Ed. P. Remnant and J. Bennett. Cambridge: Cambridge University Press, 1996.

MacIntyre, Alasdair. *After Virtue: A Study in Moral Theory*. 2d ed. Notre Dame: University of Notre Dame Press, 1984.

———. *First Principles, Final Ends and Contemporary Philosophical Issues*. Milwaukee: Marquette University Press, 1990.

———. "Imaginative Universals and Historical Falsification." *New Vico Studies* 7 (1989): 21–30.

———. *Three Rival Versions of Moral Enquiry*. Notre Dame: University of Notre Dame Press, 1990.

Marion, Jean-Luc. *Cartesian Questions*. Chicago and London: University of Chicago Press, 1999.

———. *On Descartes' Metaphysical Prism*. Chicago and London: University of Chicago Press, 1999.

Milbank, John. *Theology and Social Theory*. Oxford: Basil Blackwell, 1990.

Nietzsche, Friedrich. *Daybreak*. Translated by R. J. Hollingdale. Cambridge: Cambridge University Press, 1982.

———. *On the Genealogy of Morals*. Translated by Walter Kaufmann and R. J. Hollingdale. Vintage Books: New York, 1967.

———. *Sämtliche Werke: Kritische Stuidenausgabe*. 2d ed. Edited by Giorgio Colli and Mazzino Montinari. Vols. 1, 3, and 5. Munich: DTV; Berlin and New York: de Gruyter, 1988.

———. *Unmodern Observations*. Edited by William Arrowsmith. New Haven, Conn.: Yale University Press, 1990.

"Only a God Can Save Us: *Der Spiegel's* Interview with Martin Heidegger." Translated by Maria P. Alter and John D. Caputo. *Philosophy Today* 20 (1976): 267–84.

Pascal, Blaise. *Pensées*. Translated by A. J. Krailsheimer. Rev. ed. London and New York: Penguin, 1995.

Plato. *Republic*. Translated by Allan Bloom, *The Republic of Plato*. 2d ed. New York: Basic Books, 1991.

Quintilian, *Institutio Oratoria*. Edited by H. E. Butler. New York: G. P. Putnam's Sons, 1921.

Sidgwick, Henry. *Outlines of the History of Ethics for English Readers*. 5th ed. London: Macmillan & Co., 1902. Reprint, Indianapolis and Cambridge, Mass.: Hackett, 1988.

Spinoza. *Ethics and Selected Letters*. Edited by Seymour Feldman and translated by Samuel Shirley. Indianapolis and Cambridge, Mass.: Hackett, 1982.

Strauss, Leo. *Natural Right and History*. Chicago: University of Chicago Press, 1950, 7th Impression, 1971.

Tuck, Richard. *Natural Rights Theories: Their Origin and Development*. Cambridge: Cambridge University Press, 1979.

Williams, Bernard. *Ethics and the Limits of Philosophy*. Cambridge, Mass.: Harvard University Press, 1985.

———.*Making Sense of Humanity and Other Philosophical Papers, 1982–1993*. Cambridge: Cambridge University Press, 1995.

———. "Replies." In *World, Mind, and Ethics: Essays on the Ethical Philosophy of Bernard Williams,* edited by J. E. J. Altham and Ross Harrison. Cambridge: Cambridge University Press, 1995.